Every Woman Deserves
An Adventure

YVONNE ROBERTS

Every Woman Deserves An Adventure

M

MACMILLAN

LONDON

First published 1994 by Macmillan London

a division of Pan Macmillan Publishers Limited
Cavaye Place London SW10 9PG
and Basingstoke

Associated companies throughout the world

ISBN 0 333 61408 9 (hardback)
ISBN 0 333 63128 5 (trade paperback)

Copyright © Yvonne Roberts 1994

1 3 5 7 9 8 6 4 2

A CIP catalogue record for this book is available from
the British Library

This is a work of fiction. All the characters and events portrayed
in this book are fictitious, and any resemblance to real people or
events is purely coincidental.

Typeset by CentraCet Limited, Cambridge
Printed and bound in Great Britain by
Mackays of Chatham plc, Chatham, Kent

For Stephen and Zoe

By the time you swear you're his, shivering and sighing,
And he vows his passion is infinite, undying
Lady, make a note of this: one of you is lying
DOROTHY PARKER

Erotica is one of the basic means of self-knowledge
as indispensable as poetry.

ANAÏS NIN

I would say that the majority of women (happily
for society) are not much troubled with sexual
feeling of any kind.

DR WILLIAM ACTON, 1857

Acknowledgements

I would like to thank my agent, Jacqueline Korn, who for seven years constantly encouraged me to try writing fiction and never once expressed impatience. Her continuing support and astuteness has proved invaluable.

My thanks too to Suzanne Baboneau, my editor, whose initial enthusiasm and perceptive editing has been a wonderful bonus. I am grateful to my friends, some of whose experiences have helped to mould the themes in this book.

In particular I'd like to thank for their support, Jeananne Crowley, Trish Evans, Josephine Green, Maeve Haran, Nigel Horne, Nicola Jeal, Eva Kolouchova, Frankie McGowan, Angela Neustatter, William Nighy, Chris Oxley, Diana Quick, Gail Somers, Carole Stone, Jeremy Seabrook, Frances Stathers and Ann Treneman.

Lastly, my thanks to my partner, Stephen Scott, who has the most poachable ideas, and my daughter, Zoe. Their company and good humour made the period when I was in purdah, writing the novel, a pleasure.

Chapter One

In the middle of the week that my husband is supposed to be away in a remote cottage in Scotland, writing without the interruption of telephone, radio or television, I visit a pub in Berkshire with my friend Mo and see his left hand gripped round the thigh of a woman occupying a windowseat. His right hand is almost as busy. In broad daylight, he conveys the illusion that he and she are one fleshy little plait. I have never seen the woman in my life before. I decide against saying hello.

Instead, I put one half of lager, one gin and tonic and two ploughman's lunches in front of a rather startled solitary bald-headed drinker and flee into the women's loo. I'm turned inside out with distress but I also feel rather odd. It's like an out-of-body experience. It's not happening to me. I'm looking down on myself in one of those 1940s B movies. I'm dressed in an oyster-coloured satin nightie with my hair moulded into concrete waves, and I'm sobbing into my satin pillow, 'Oh, Norman, how could you, you rotter?'

I don't know why 'Norman'. My husband is called Tom. On the other hand, where Tom is concerned, my instant reaction is usually denial. He does something and I deny it. So I gratefully drop into a familiar routine: it isn't Tom in the pub. He wouldn't do that. He's in Scotland. I've made a mistake. It's my fault. It's always my fault.

I leave the loo and have another look. It is definitely Tom. Tom is rubbing noses. The wally factor intrudes briefly on my

1

grief. What a prat! A grown man of forty-seven (well, almost grown, he's five feet eight but very energetic) rubbing noses with a . . . with a what?

She looks threateningly ordinary. If she's so ordinary, it must be love. Oh, Christ. The light which streams in from the window behind gives her light brown hair a halo effect. 'Split ends,' I say to myself savagely. She has a spot on her left cheek large enough for me to see at a distance of 40 feet and she's wearing quite a nice suit, quite a nice *crushed* suit, since my husband's left hand has travelled up and round her thigh so frequently that the skirt is now in ruts deeper than you'll see in a well-ploughed field.

I retreat back into the loo. Anger and outrage yo-yo with humiliation. I'll denounce him. I'll rush out and yell, 'This is our pub. This is where we always come. How could you – a married man, with twin daughters – how could you do this?'

Or perhaps I'll try a smoother line. 'Hello,' I'll say to Her. 'I don't believe we've been introduced. I'm Kay Woods, Tom's wife.' Briefly, I'm dizzy with power. Then, fear follows bravado. What if Tom leaves me? Christ, what if he loves her? He must love her! Does he love her?

How *could* he, the bastard?

I shoot out of the loo and back into the lounge. Tom and the woman have gone. Empty seats. Five minutes later Mo, in search of her yet-to-arrive gin, finds me sitting by the bemused, bald-headed drinker, weeping loudly.

'Where the hell have you been?' she says, looking at the solitary drinker accusingly. Then, she notices the tears. All the years of workshops and transactional analysis and knowing where everyone else is coming from, except herself, march to the fore. 'You're upset,' she says perceptively.

I don't need prompting. 'I'm a woman who's passed her sell-by date,' I say. I feel the tears well up. 'I'm wrinkled, grey, boring.' The bald-headed man nods in sympathy. I cry harder.

I've never done this in public before and, strangely, I'm finding it quite enjoyable.

'My husband is a shit. A huge shit. He's screwing somebody else. He's a worthless, two-timing, self-obsessed egomaniac. But nobody else is going to have him. He's mine.'

'He looks a bit of a creep to me,' the man next to me says conversationally. 'I can tell 'em. My wife ran off with one. Best thing that ever happened to me. Could I have your pickled onion?'

He spears the onion off the ploughman's lunch and ignores Mo, who is beginning to view him as a rival to her role as counsellor-in-chief. She slides in between him and me.

'Tom's in Scotland, he's writing. He's too busy to mess about,' she says in the tone of a nursery-school teacher tackling the alphabet with a dyslexic three-year-old.

'He's busy all right, busy fucking some woman . . .' I interrupt, catching a glimpse of myself in the mirror above the man's bald head. I look satisfyingly distraught. Then the waves of worry and fear and guilt and sheer bloody anger lap over me again.

'Well, I'd better be off,' the man says. 'Look after yourself.'

Three hours later I sit in Tom's study. I've agreed that later I will go out with Mo and some of her friends for supper. In the car, on the way home, she'd gone overboard on the crisis-intervention technique she'd learnt at the workshop before last.

'You're not going to do anything silly, I hope?' she'd asked, licking her lips. The accent a bit too much on the 'I hope'.

'Silly, maybe,' I replied, 'To myself, no.'

Now, I'm not so sure. Tom, in theory, isn't on the phone, so I can't ring him both to hear his guilt and give him the opportunity to persuade me that it was a mirage. Perhaps I should be like those women who know their partners screw around but pretend otherwise? Perhaps I should be more *soignée*? More subtle? On the other hand, why the bloody hell should I?

Someone has vacuumed my insides out. Even in grief, for a lapsed Weight-watcher, empty insides are an interesting thought. Perhaps this is the brand new F-Plan diet, based entirely on who fucks whom.

Husband screws stranger, partner loses three pounds. Husband screws best friend, partner loses five pounds. Husband screws man next door, anorexia nervosa sets in.

Mo says I'm having these irrelevant thoughts because I'm in shock. I feed Letty. Letty is a large uncoordinated mongrel and she belongs to Kate and Claire. Twins run in my family, so after the girls were born, twenty years ago, the choice in terms of family enlargement appeared to be double or quits. So we quit. The girls are at university in Newcastle, but at present they are in New Orleans, on a year's exchange scheme.

I discover we have no wine in the house. Eventually, in one of the cupboards, among two dozen opened boxes of breakfast cereal, tins of Mexican food that always get bought but are rarely eaten, and what looks like technicoloured muesli for the bottom of the goldfish tank, I find a reject from a night of entertaining: a warm bottle of Spanish white.

It's four-thirty in the afternoon but what the hell? Even a crisis has its perks. I pour a tumbler and go upstairs to weep.

Tom's study is an altar to his ego. Yesterday I might have been better disposed and described it as a modest record of his professional success. Awards on one wall, photographs on the other three. The photographs also spill down the stairs into our bedroom and creep over one of the walls in the hall. They show Tom as a medical student, Tom as a consultant, Tom at a book signing,

Tom on telly, Tom looking earnest, Tom in a dinner-jacket holding a bronze ovary on a stand, Tom at a conference, Tom as a father. Even on the few occasions when other members of the family intrude into the picture, Tom is the hero of every frame.

Tom's photographs are interspersed with Tom's framed book jackets. *Who Loves You, Baby? The Issue of Children's Rights*; *Birth Without Blues*; *You, Me and Baby Makes Three* and half a dozen more. It's amazing how many ways you can revisit a fallopian tube.

At home, in Llanwyn, West Wales, Tom is known as Tommy the Tubes. He is the first in the family to move from blue collar to white jacket. I met him twenty-two years ago. I was a journalist, he was making his name as a gynaecologist. On the second occasion we met, he told me, in a totally non-professional capacity, that I had the longest vagina he had ever encountered. Then, I took it as a compliment. Now, I'd probably regard it as a criticism.

The number of times I've sat at supper in our house listening to debates about the best method of childbirth. These have usually been waged between Tom, 'mothers must have their say but ultimately doctor knows best', and Raoul, a gay Chilean surgeon who used to be a Caesarian junkie and is now an expert on inverted nipples and the importance of breast-feeding; Tuk, a large chunk of masculine Finn who flogs the Scandinavian birthing stool; Saul, a 'child-free' Californian expert in the mobile epidural and Hywel, a gynaecologist who believes that the best mother in delivery is a comatose one. Not so much new men as pneumatic.

'You're the most manipulative man I've ever met,' Mo had yelled at Tom at the end of one of these evenings. As it goes, it's probably one of the nicer comments she's made about him; her dislike is so intense, I occasionally wonder if she fancies him.

'You're overwrought,' Tom had replied. 'It's your biological clock. I quite understand.'

No one can patronize quite as well as Tom can. He is the grit in the oyster that is morning television for women. Every Thursday, at nine-thirty a.m., he offers advice to 3.2 million viewers. 'The man who can make you feel good about being a woman.' Thank you very much, Dr Tom.

Initially, I used to think that Tom's capacity for deflecting criticism was quite charming. More recently, when I've read that he is happily married, I wonder if he realizes that his wife isn't? Not deep down. I wonder if he knows that, at times, resentment flourishes where desire should be – and that I love him least when we are in bed? That sometimes we make love and, to me, it's like two robots clanking in the dark. Tom comes, turns over, sleeps. I stay awake and rust.

I finish the tumbler of wine and begin to do what I have never done before: I pull Tom's study apart.

Within half an hour I find what I'm looking for. Hidden between the pages of the French translation of Tom's *Birth Marks – You and Your Delivery*, is a lemon-coloured envelope. Inside is an unsigned letter. The handwriting has so many curlicues and whirls, it looks as if a spider on speed has paddled in ink and danced a jig across the page. As I read, a voice comes to mind that I can't quite place.

The gist of the anonymous four paragraphs is that Tom is shit-hot. Shit-hot in bed, shit-hot out of bed. Generally just shit-hot.

'No matter what anybody else thinks, you are the most sensitive and caring and considerate man I have ever met.' *Anybody else?*

Speaking as the '*anybody else*', I would say, just wait until you spend ten straight days with him, sweetheart.

'You're generous with your time—' Of course he's bloody generous with his time. He has always been generous with on-the-side bonking time. It's when he's into the it's-just-a-routine-two-screws-a-week-married-time that hump becomes grump.

'You have such funny little ways. When you're gone, a piece of me goes too . . .'

As I read, shaking and shivering, yet unable to stop, the voice becomes much more easy to identify. It's my own. This could be me writing in the first months after I'd met Tom – besotted, flattering, randy – deaf, dumb and blind to everything except his blue eyes, pink bum and navy Y-fronts.

I remained in pretty much the same state for the next few years. Then, looking back, I realized that in the eighties, a turning point had occurred. Tom developed a brief passion for a Japanese acupuncturist whom he'd met when they were both working on a forty-seven-year-old expecting her first baby.

I didn't know about the affair and I wouldn't have known about it but Tom opted to tell me. If you are unaware that your partner is even contemplating infidelity, never mind engaging in it, then you tend to look upon his out-of-the-norm behaviour (in Tom's case, suddenly using aftershave by Gianfranco Ferré and attending a trichologist) as, well, out-of-the-norm behaviour. Only once the trust has gone, only *then* do you realize that anything out of the norm is another way of saying, *I am cheating*.

'I've decided it's much better for you if you know,' he announced one Sunday morning, as we drove out of London late for lunch with friends in Kent.

We were late because Tom is always late. 'I've had an affair. It lasted for twenty-seven days and it's now over.'

'Every day of the twenty-seven days?'

'Not every day. Exactly.'

'What do you mean, "Exactly"?'

'Christ, Kay, does it matter? I've told you because I think honesty is the best policy. I've confessed for *your* sake.'

He went on: 'You were away. And the twins were away. And I was on my own . . . It's done, it's over. It didn't mean anything. It was entirely physical. And it wouldn't have happened if you hadn't been in Sheffield . . . Look,' he said, vocally changing down a gear to the voice he uses on his radio call-in programme when

7

he's about to tell a retired civil servant that it's really OK to wander around Milton Keynes in nappies and rubber knickers.

'Look, I understand that you're upset. I'm even flattered. It means you care. But it's over, it's done. Our relationship may even benefit as a result. I have to say it's certainly helped me to value you far more.'

'Well, I'd better drop a note of thanks to the Japanese acupuncturist,' I replied acidly but with my mouth so dry I could barely articulate the words.

'This is serious,' Tom said. 'Why do you always have to treat everything so bloody flippantly?'

'Turn off at the next exit.'

'What?'

'Turn off at the next exit.'

'That can't be right.'

We spent the next twenty-five minutes trying to get back on route. Tom is genetically incapable of sticking to directions.

'Are you sorry?' I eventually asked.

'No, I've been this way before and I'm sure it wasn't the right turn-off.'

'No, are you sorry about the affair?'

Tom has this habit of pausing as if in serious reflection, which some people find enormously flattering. After running one hand through his hair and scratching the side of his nose, both stock-in-trade, he eventually replied.

'Sorry? Yes, of course, I'm sorry. I mean I don't have to tell you that, do I? Isn't it obvious? I mean I wouldn't have told you if I wasn't sorry, would I?

'I'm sorry, but because I believe that honesty is the best policy, I can't say that I wish I hadn't . . .' He searched for the right words which avoided all possibility of blame.

'I can't say that I wish it hadn't . . . *developed*. But if it's upset

8

you then yes, of course, I'm sorry. I'm sorry and it will never happen again.'

What he forgot to add is, '. . . and it will never happen again with a Japanese acupuncturist whom I happen to meet sticking pins into a forty-seven-year-old primigravida.'

By the time we arrived at the lunch, fifty-five minutes after everybody else, Tom clearly believed that the business had been wrapped up. Nothing like a good confession for improving the appetite.

I was seated next to one of those women who look so fragile, so incredibly well-turned-out, lip-gloss gleaming like a tin tray in the sun, that whatever I said and did, made me feel like a cerebrally challenged, physically dysfunctional giant. I also behaved like one. I knocked over my wine, spilled the salt, dropped the napkin-ring.

The woman said her name was Melissa, she was married, without children and she ran her own recruitment agency. She wore a lime-green jacket, black slacks and patent pumps. Her face was fortyish, but the slightly crinkled cleavage hinted at another ten years or so. She had a dinky nose, significant cheek-bones, long, delicate fingers and she smelt of jasmine. Her hair was silvery-blonde, dyed – but so well that you suspected if she had to flee the house in an emergency in the middle of the night, it would still look 'natural' as opposed to resembling a basket full of fag-ends.

Melissa watched Tom all through the prawn mousse. And, for that matter, all through the chicken breasts, the treacle pudding and the cheese, too. This was not unusual. It's not that Tom is conventionally handsome but he does have a range of poses which speak volumes. He's very into body language, the Esperanto of every television performer.

Pose Number 241 says, 'Don't be fooled by my unassuming

but totally engaging manner. I'm a tiger in bed.' For me, for the last couple of years – bar a couple of exceptions – Pose Number 241 has proved not to be true.

'It must be wonderfully interesting to have a husband who is a gynaecologist,' said Melissa with just a hint of innuendo, cutting ever-such-a-little portion of Brie. 'He looks the type who knows *exactly* what he's doing, if you know what I mean.'

'Well,' I said, smiling back, 'I guess even cartographers have been known to lose their way.'

'All right?' Tom asked as we drove home in the late afternoon. Once upon a time, he would have put his hand on my knee – or higher. I smiled at him but in my head I plotted murder and mayhem. Why is it that memories of past marital injuries can never dissolve? Time may heal all things but not the wounds inflicted in marriage. In my case, from time to time, these memories turn into demons who climb on each other's shoulders and build a tower of resentment the size of King Kong; never acknowledged or discussed.

I recall, for instance, when the twins were three, Tom had gone off for a fortnight's filming and left me with flu, a full-time job, no central heating, a child-minder confined to bed with alcohol poisoning and carless since some sixteen-year-old had decided to 'borrow' the family transport from outside the front door.

On his return, Tom spent the first twenty-four hours telling me how hard he'd worked, how wrecked he felt, how nobody could understand how taxing filming is, how he and the crew had had to endure the hell of four-star hotels, how his shirts always looked so much better pressed when he was away and no, he couldn't bath the dog or fix the vacuum cleaner because he was 'mentally drained'. And how the hell had I managed to spend so much bloody money while he was away?

The next evening when he got back from work, he found a sheet hanging over the front door. On it, written in spray paint, were the words, *Welcome to the Holiday Inn*.

'I suppose you think that's bloody funny?' Tom had said.

'Certainly not,' I replied. 'I just want you to feel at home.'

'All right?' Tom repeated in the car. And what did I do? Did I say, 'No, I'm bloody not? Stop the car, I'm leaving you'? Did I grab his testicles and squeeze hard? Did I say, 'You're a self-centred, uncaring bastard and just so you know how it feels, I'm going to take on as a lover the next eighteen-year-old dispatch rider I see?'

No, I did not. What did I do? I smiled back. Can you believe it? *I smiled back.*

It was some time soon after that I began to feel a sort of irritation, almost a humming deep down inside me. Usually it began at times of mind-blowing mundanity, or when Tom had occupied centre stage for an excessively long time, even by his standards.

Now, as soon as I have the lemon-coloured letter in my hand, the humming turns into an almighty roar. It dies away again, almost immediately. I am obsessed by a single question: how long has this affair been going on? I look at the postmark on the envelope. August: eight months ago. *Eight months.*

Eight sodding months. Eight months ago, Tom had come back two days early from our holiday. *Bastard.*

Half an hour later, I'm in the car and on my way to a meeting with destiny. Or, more precisely, to a meeting with my husband's lover.

Chapter Two

The exterior of Medicatis Incorporated bears a strong resemblance to a 1950s Odeon cinema; flash, splash and polish. A fountain plays in the portico, the rest is marble and mirrors. What lets down the lushness is that it's sited in the seediest part of King's Cross. This is possibly because the res. has potential des. if and when the planned redevelopment of the area takes place. Until then, the building looks as unobtrusive as a gold tooth in an old crone's mouth.

I stand opposite and I am not alone. Two women with an interesting taste in clothes have taken up position about ten yards from me. I have a good idea why they are here, but I'm not sure what *my* reasons are.

On a warm April evening, I am wearing Tom's large khaki mac, a beige skirt and jumper and flat shoes. I must look like a cross between a plain-clothes detective and a female flasher. The older woman, about fifty or so, wears fake leather trousers, black high-heeled boots and a red T-shirt scattered with little beads which pop up randomly like a plague of whiteheads.

The younger woman has invested in contrasts: a very short skirt and a very long cotton skinny-rib jumper. Every so often, when she lifts her arm to pat her hair into place or draw on a cigarette, the jumper lifts to reveal two inches of black Lycra.

I become absorbed. Why does the jumper ride up – but never

the skirt? If the skirt does ride up, will it end up, like an elastic band, looped round her neck?

'What's your fuckin' problem, then?' The voice has fangs.

'Sorry?'

'What's your problem, you've been fuckin' starin' at me and my friend for the last fuckin' five minutes.'

It's the older woman. Years of twenty-four-hours-a-day, seven-days-a-week reapplication of make-up has caused the mascara and eyebrow pencil and eye-shadow to seep into each other. Two panda eyes push themselves into my face.

I notice that she has earrings the size of squash balls. She's lucky her ear lobes don't sweep the street.

'I didn't realize I was staring. I'm sorry. I'm looking for someone. In there.' I nod towards Medicatis. The older woman grunts.

The lemon-coloured letter might have been unsigned, but on the envelope the franking-machine had left its clue. *Medicatis, the Professionals in Private Health Care.*

It is possible that Crumpled Suit is still rollicking with my husband. But Tom is faithful to his priorities. He has four chapters of his latest book still to write and he is much too disciplined and self-interested to get his leg over on a full-time basis during his week of 'solitude'.

If I'm in luck, she might be back at work. She might even leave work at a normal sort of time. If I recognize her face, I could find out her name. And then? Christ knows what. Of course, there is also the possibility that Tom is a serial adulterer. The Lemon-Letter Writer might not be Ms Crumpled Suit.

'Cunts. They're all cunts,' the younger woman says, a touch inaccurately but I sympathize with the drift.

'What do you mean?' I ask politely.

'It's a fella, innit?' she says.

13

I'm startled to find that tears are welling up. If anyone is kind to me now, I'll never be able to pick myself up off the floor again. Fortunately, the two women prove to be tarts without hearts.

A couple of men walk by and look mildly interested. I surprise myself and stare back. Panda Eyes bridles.

'What's your game, then?'

I explain that I don't have one. I'm waiting until six or whatever time Medicatis closes up shop for the night to see if I can spot 'a friend of a friend'. The two women walk off.

At six-fifteen p.m., Crumpled Suit is the seventh to leave the building. She turns left and begins to walk towards the station. I take two steps in the same direction. I want to stop her and tell her twenty-five things she never knew about Tom; how he can neglect and criticize. How he made love to me two nights ago and what he says in bed. I want to hurt her badly. I want to tell her twenty-five reasons why Tom makes me happy – except that I can't even think of one.

I want to say something that gets under her skin and triggers the look of uncertainty in her eyes about whatever future she believes she may have with my husband. Then I feel a hand on my arm. It's Panda Eyes.

'I'll tell you now,' she says. 'She won't believe a fuckin' word.'

At home, Letty looks fed up. I walk her round the park and I have that strange disembodied feeling again. I smile at other dog-walkers, stop to chat just as if absolutely nothing has happened. 'How are you?' 'Very well, thank you.'

No message on the answering-machine from Tom. I keep rereading the love-letter. This time, I tell myself, it won't hurt as much as the last time. Of course it does.

By the time the taxi arrives at nine-thirty to take me to Mo's, the letter is already back in its hiding-place. By now, I know the bloody thing off by heart.

Madame Fifi's is a club which Mo likes. I don't know why. She comes frequently with friends, especially Michael, a teacher and Simon, an unemployed antiques restorer. They are gay and live together without much passion, sedated by an overdose of routine.

Michael always sits with his back to the tiny stage, Simon always sits on Michael's left. Both always drink draught Guinness. I've visited Fifi's a few times with them but without much enthusiasm. Tonight Mo is relentlessly determined to 'take my mind off things'.

We are seated at a table in a room which makes a left-luggage locker appear cavernous. All around are statuesque 'women' with very deep voices, very large Adam's apples and beautiful faces. The music pounds; the fug of smoke makes me gag and the only realistic activity – since conversation is impossible – is to watch and wonder. My wondering is not about 101 ways to hide male genitalia but about Tom.

'When Olivia gets here, we'll have one more drink then move on for something to eat,' Mo mouths over the din and then asks, 'Are you all right?' I nod. Life is littered with daft questions.

The music shifts into a moodier, quieter gear. 'Hello, sir.' A young Asian 'woman' with hips not much wider than a mouth-organ and a glistening black beehive smiles at Michael. Michael smiles back, 'How are you doing, Dan?'

Dan moves on. 'He's in the sixth form at school,' Michael says. 'Very bright.'

I ask, 'Is he going on to university?' I don't remotely care but it's a night for these kinds of conversations.

Michael goes into a monologue about UCCA and Oxbridge and the academic brilliance of some inner-city pupils in spite of the class system and I'm glad that a pseudo-Shirley Bassey manages to drown most of it out. Another couple arrive and finally, very late, Olivia Heimmel-Brown appears. She is not what I expected.

Olivia has just moved into the very large flat above Mo's very small one. Mo is a solicitor and handled some work for Olivia and the two have become friends. I've never met Olivia before and all I know is that she owns Bonne Bouche, a knick-knack shop selling expensive kitsch but her main money – and there's a lot of it – comes from exports.

According to Mo, an Arab or an expat phones from Dar es Salaam, says he wants six spindly chairs, gold-coloured and about 200 years old and Olivia's team of detectives roll into action to find the goods; mail-order antiques.

'Olivia is *nouveau riche*,' Mo had already told me. 'Her money's only been rolling in for the last couple of years and she likes to enjoy it.'

I'd expected rhinestone jumpers, snakeskin boots and earrings like hub-caps, the kind of outfits seen on women entering health clubs in parts of Berkshire, Buckinghamshire and Basildon. Olivia is dressed more like a guest at Balmoral.

Tweedy skirt, cashmere jumper, pearl earrings, flat loafers. She is in her late fifties, she wears a trace of make-up, she is comfortably round, she has beautifully cut, pure white hair, and, surprisingly, she wears an intensely heavy perfume that I don't recognize.

'Love your brooch,' she says, once the introductions have been made, no doubt cued by Mo. I make jewellery out of bits of domestic tat – bottle-tops, bits of Brillo pads, steel brushes – and miniature china and utensils from doll's houses. It started as a joke but now I can make a decent income from it – when I'm motivated enough to produce.

I call the company Kitchen Sync since it speaks volumes about the customers' lack of taste, my total absence of talent and the main source of materials.

Olivia has a deep, melodious voice. 'Mo's told me about the jewellery. Why don't you come and see me?' She hands me her card. 'Perhaps we can do business?'

Mo looks very pleased with herself. As the cabaret begins, the rest of our conversation is drowned.

I sink back into self-pity. In the interval, the noise is still stupendous but as Mike, Mo and Simon are involved in a discussion about time-share in Portugal, I feel obliged to make conversation with Olivia.

'I don't suppose you get much free time,' I say.

'I make time,' Olivia replies, lighting up a cigarette. She has exquisitely manicured nails.

'More to life than slog. When my husband left, I vowed I'd work flat out and then I'd hand over most of the graft to someone else and sit back and enjoy the loot.'

'So what do you do with all this spare time?' I ask, almost on automatic pilot.

'I fuck,' Olivia replies equably.

'I'm sorry?' I say, but I'm not at all sorry, just flabbergasted. Olivia looks more likely to be embalmed than penetrated.

'I fuck,' Olivia repeats. 'You know, fuck as in sexual inter-course? It's very good for the health. And marvellous for dealing with stress, don't you think?'

We move on from Fifi's to a Soho restaurant where every dish comes in a puddle of virgin olive oil and the waiters have developed squints, so determined are they to avoid eye contact with customers.

The coffee has been rush-released halfway through pudding in an effort to make us leave the table within forty-five minutes of arriving, but we hold firm.

'Another cup, please,' Olivia says. The waiter gazes straight past her.

She takes out a felt-tip pen and writes, 'Four coffees, two brandies please,' in large letters on her napkin. She stands up and holds it high like a matador in front of the waiter's face as he passes again. His way blocked, he has no option.

'Thank you,' she says pleasantly and smiles.

Olivia, of course, hasn't always been the Arnold Schwarzenegger of café society. Ten years ago, she tells me, she had a husband, Ed, a former jazz musician with a fetish for making business deals and making love, the latter not necessarily to his wife. They had two children, Amy, then seven and Josh, nine. Olivia had only ever worked part time, doing the books for her husband in whatever failed enterprise he was currently engaged.

'He was a prick,' she says. 'He had an affair three months after we married with a woman in the flat downstairs. He had an affair when I was seven months pregnant. He also always began an affair in January because he said he found the month so depressing.

'He drank, he gambled. He could be charming. I would probably have stayed with him for life. I really believed that wives weren't meant to be happy. They are meant to be contentedly miserable. That's part of the status, part of the security. I was also extremely grateful. I was grateful for the good times when Ed would briefly treat me as well as his latest conquest just to keep me sweet. "Life could be worse," I'd tell myself. And, of course, it usually did get a damn sight worse.'

'What about sex?' I ask, made bolder by Olivia's own approach.

'Sex, darling? I refused to come for seven years and three months on principle. It hurt his pride but I had to have some way of getting back at him. Ed said he saw me as his greatest challenge – and then suddenly he disappeared,' Olivia laughs.

'He ran off with Greta, the au pair, to California. The house was repossessed. The joint account was empty and he left sixty-four thousand two hundred and thirty-three pounds in debts. I haven't seen him since but he writes to the kids. He asks them to visit but he never quite gets round to fixing a date – and they've given up waiting.'

'What happened after he left?'

'I made loads of money. And I grew up. And I decided that I would never be as grateful for so little, ever again.'

'Tell Kay about Des,' Mo instructs.

'Des is small but perfectly formed,' Olivia obliges. 'I keep him on a stud-farm in Hertfordshire so he can train my horses. He's an ex-jockey and very, very good in bed.

'Once the novelty wore off, I got tired of all the ritual of rutting. I thought I'd go for something more regular but Des, poor dear, hasn't quite got the hang of the arrangement. He always feels obliged to say, "I love you, Olivia". And I tell him, he really doesn't have to bother. This is a transaction of the flesh.'

'What about companionship?' I say feebly.

'Companionship? Are you bloody joking?' Olivia hoots. 'Have you ever been to the theatre with a jockey? You can't hear a bloody word because of the noise of his stomach rumbling. Have you ever been out to dinner with one of those men? They eat so little, it takes about twenty minutes flat.

'Oh God, it's nothing to do with companionship. Des doesn't have to talk, lie, make promises, earn money, make a commitment or be nice to my family, friends or kids, he just has to hop in and out of bed when I say so. He used to stay in London during the week but it got on my nerves so much, I banished him to the farm.'

'Is it fair? On him?' I ask.

'Fair? Of course it's bloody fair. He can act like millions of men might love to do. He can hump without hypocrisy. Except, poor love, as I say, he does find it difficult at times. He finds the lack of ties, the lack of all the gumph about relationships and commitment and all that stuff a bit unnerving. Funny, isn't it?

'He's been married twice, he's forty-eight and now he says it's time to settle down. "Well, Des," I say, "find yourself a decent woman and be on your way."'

'Wouldn't you miss him?' I ask.

'Let me tell you a secret,' Olivia replies. 'I used to say to myself, "If Ed leaves, I'll die. I'll lie down and die." I was a fairly normal, stable human being. I cared for my children but I thought I had such a passion for that man, nobody and nothing could replace him. I'd got myself into a catch-22.

'He behaved like a shit and I showed how much he meant to me by putting up with it. And when he went, I had a terrible twelve weeks, followed by a pretty rotten couple of years. Then, I slowly recovered. I survived. How about you?'

The question catches me unawares.

'Well,' I say, 'I suppose I'm lucky. I've been married quite a while and it's really never been better. I mean, well, we've had hiccups. Who doesn't? But it's still interesting. At least, I think it's interesting. Bed, I mean. Not repetitive. Well, not much . . .

'Anyway, I've always thought monogamy is better. You know where you stand. Or lie. Besides, I don't think I've ever really had any offers. I mean, nobody's actually asked me. Not that I would of course, if it was offered. Although I did a couple of times when Tom and I had been married a few years. Even then, the guilt got in the way, if you know what I mean . . . But anyway, we're really fine at the moment, so that doesn't even come into it . . .'

I sense I'm talking faster and faster. Olivia is watchful. Mo is silent.

'If I were you,' Olivia says firmly, 'I'd forget all that crap. Put your money on a good jockey.'

I wake at four-thirty a.m. as if life is normal. The bedroom is as it has always been: yellow walls; photos of the girls; a large plant with more brown leaves than green which has defied death for two years. Next to it is a pile of Tom's medical magazines with horrific scab-encrusted pictures (much more absorbing than toys for the girls when they were young), and a CD player bought by Tom for me as a birthday present with a stack of his jazz CDs by the side. Everything as it has always been – and then, of course, I remember.

This rambling old house which has almost always appeared a friendly comforting place, now has all the attractions of a retirement home in Gosport.

Mo had given me a lift home last night and offered to stay. I persuaded her to leave by promising to go with her tonight to a new workshop. On what she hasn't said, but since she's into a phase of being kind to yourself, it's probably 'One Hundred Ways to Massage Your Own Ego'.

Mo and I met six years ago at a water-aerobics class. I'd taken it up because I'd become bored of swimming on my own; Mo had taken it up because, basically, she takes everything up.

I'd lasted three weeks, she'd lasted two but somehow, in spite of the differences in our lives – or perhaps because of them – we seemed to fit together well.

Mo sees life as a Foreign Legion of the emotions. If the number of self-improvement courses and the acquisition of books on how to change your life were stepping-stones to beatification, she would be Our Lady of all those who love difficult men/hate their mother/have lost the key to self-esteem.

Mo is thirty-four and, apart from a brief marriage at twenty-one and an even briefer spell of cohabitation, she has remained inexplicably (at least to her) single. Her choice of men, it has to be said, has not so far proved great.

'If I walked into a room blindfold and there were thirty eligible men in there, I'd choose the only bastard,' she always says cheerfully.

Mo is happy in her job. She speaks at conferences around the world, she has a large wardrobe of understated suits, she invests a lot of dosh in making herself look as natural as possible (eighty-five-pound haircut; Japanese minimalist make-up etc.), and 'taking care' of herself, physically and mentally: flotation tanks, aroma-therapy, massage, yoga, flamenco classes, rebirthing. She dives into each new enthusiasm with gusto.

Of course, Mo would give all this up instantly – for luuurve. Or so she says. She wants a partner and babies or, at a push, babies and then a partner. The interesting fact about Mo is that in the five years or so I've known her, whenever any man has shown a keen interest, she panics. The wooer is put through a process akin to the Spanish Inquisition. His socks are the wrong colour. Why does he call his mother all the time? Why didn't he bring wine to supper – is he tight? Have you seen the way he slurps his soup? Oh God, he wears boxer shorts. And zap, the man is down and out.

On the other hand, when a man appears cool, Mo moves in for the kill almost before the introductions.

'OK, what do you think?' she asked a thirty-six-year-old management consultant the second time they went out together. The man had his own house, own car, one former partner, no children and he wasn't HIV-positive.

'Is it cohabitation, marriage, do you want children, or what?' Mo believes in being blunt.

'Look, I'm running out of time. I took a policy decision when I turned thirty, no more messing around. I put my cards on the table, you put your cards on the table and we can proceed from there. Or not.'

'Isn't it a bit, well, early . . .?' The poor man had reportedly suggested.

When Mo is on the hunt, she has the sensitivity of an eighteen-year-old who's swallowed twelve pints of lager. 'You do know about babies?' she asked him.

'Babies take nine months. Unless we're really lucky, we're talking two years from the moment we take the decision. And I am thirty-four years old already. You know what I mean?'

He did – and fled. But, one day, I'm sure the approach will work.

I turn on the radio, listen to the five o'clock news, make tea, give Letty a biscuit. Even in our darkest hours, there is a chink of light. I've eaten nothing for twenty-four hours. My hip-bones have appeared for the first time in years. And what's more, *I don't feel hungry*. In a negative situation, as Mo would say, this is a positive.

By six a.m., I've found four more lemon-coloured letters, again none of them signed. One is in a set of handkerchiefs Tom's mother sent him for Christmas and he has yet to use. Another is in his squash bag; two more are filed away under Car Insurance. Tom, it appears, has spent three separate weeks with Crumpled Suit.

'I'm so glad you're saving yourself for me,' Crumpled Suit writes, 'I couldn't bear the thought of you making love to anybody else. What we have is so special . . .'

Yes! One – nil to me. On the day the letter was posted, Tom and I had eaten out with friends. Back home, and surprised to find ourselves still awake at two o'clock in the morning, we'd passed the time by making love.

Tom may be lying, but at least he's lying to both of us.

At eight-thirty, the phone rings. My heart lunges up and gives my throat a wallop. 'Hello.'

'Hello, darling,' Tom says.

'You low-down, lying, duplicitous, skiving, two-timing bastard,' I say. But it's in my head, no words come out.

'Are you there, Kay?' Tom asks.

'Of course I'm bloody here, but are you where you say you are?' Again the words go unspoken.

'Kay, are you there?'

I hear more coins going into the box.

'Yes, I'm here. Have you finished your work? I thought you were going to phone last night?'

'Are you sure you're all right? You don't sound quite yourself. Have you missed me?' he asks as he always does. And as he always does, he moves on before he receives an answer.

'I'm in Glasgow. I'm going to have lunch with Chris Frayn and then I'll catch a plane. I'll be home early evening.'

'Good,' I say.

'Oh, there might be just one snag. Chris Frayn's got an American publisher over here and he thought it might be a good idea if we met. He's going to try and fix it up for tonight, I'll give you a ring and let you know what's happening.'

Inspired, I say: 'Why don't I come up?' A squeak comes down the phone. 'What? Don't be daft.' Tom sounds as if he's having an asthma attack except he's never had asthma in his life.

I press on, enjoying the game. 'If I come up we can stay at The Albany. Is that where you are? I can take a couple of days off and come over the weekend.'

Get out of that, you bastard.

'Look, I wouldn't if I were you,' Tom says. 'Let me get the work out of the way and then we can go off together, perhaps next weekend? No, damn. Not next weekend, I've got to go on the book tour on Saturday – but how about the following Sunday, lunch out in the country?'

Thanks a bunch.

I put down the phone and seethe. I should have confronted him, found out the truth. Told him to sod off. I could get on a plane now, but who knows where Tom is? Sure as shit, it isn't Glasgow. As I walk round the park with Letty, I recall that halfway through one week when Tom was 'away' writing in the country, he'd come back to us just for the evening, to have supper with Canadian friends passing through London.

I'd tried to persuade him to stay the night and drive back early in the morning. No, he insisted, he was 'too far behind' in his writing. So the tail-lights disappeared at two-thirty a.m. and then I'd discovered he'd left his briefcase behind. I phoned the letting agent the next day and asked her to pass on the message to Tom that his wife had called to say he'd left his briefcase at home.

'His wife, you say?' She'd sounded doubtful. 'But I thought . . .' I barely took any notice; infidelity is what happens to other couples. 'Yes, I'm Tom Evans' wife, Kay Woods.'

Tom had been on the phone within the hour. 'Don't think of coming down,' he'd said. 'Whatever you do, don't come down. It's far too much trouble.'

Trouble? You can say that again. I march Letty round the circumference of the adventure playground for the fifth time.

Trouble. Why am *I* never in trouble? When was the last time I disappeared for a week? Until the twins were eight or nine, I travelled around a lot as a writer for American glossies; Middle East, Africa, Europe. Eventually, the partings grew too painful, Tom became more successful as a pundit, so I reduced my writing to a column a month – what Tom supportively calls my Premenstrual Tirade. Then the jewellery began to sell and somewhere along the way, I discovered I'd converted into a homebody. And while homebodies occasionally murder their partners, on the whole they don't make trouble.

Now, while I spend my time sticking miniature knives and

forks on to bits of papier mâché and glass, the girls are white-water rafting in Wyoming and Tom is screwing himself silly in South Mimms, or wherever.

I have only myself to blame.

Sex, for me, has almost always been wrapped up in love and courtship and marriage and monogamy and loyalty. I've always been faintly disturbed by the few friends we have who profess to have an 'open' relationship. But now that Tom has renegotiated his side of the contract . . .

On the way home from the park, I take several important decisions but they boil down to one. Do unto others or, more precisely, to Tom, what he would do unto me. Indoors, on the answering-machine, is one message. It's from Tom.

'Kay, I forgot to say, I love you.'

Tom may be deficient in a number of areas but he certainly knows how to cast a hook. Damn him.

Chapter Three

Mo arrives fifteen minutes early, at six p.m., to take me to the workshop. She's dressed in jeans and a white shirt, with large hoop earrings. I am in my Dull: dull hair, dull complexion, dull clothes. Thinner but dull.

'Any news?' she says, referring to Tom. I lie and shake my head. 'When he turns up, give him hell and turf him out. Change the locks. Tell him to put in for a transfer. Sod off. Plenty more where he came from.'

'Really?'

'Well, if not plenty . . .'

'He's not that bad,' I say. 'Perhaps he's got an explanation. Perhaps it's my fault, I've been neglecting him a bit lately.'

Mo raises her eyes to the ceiling. 'Here we go again . . .'

She wraps her hands around a glass of wine. Her fingers are long and slim. On each finger she has a thin gold band, the combined effect is of two very fragile knuckledusters.

'What's this workshop about?' I ask. 'If it's a rerun on "Being positive about impotence", I'm off. I couldn't feel positive about a free holiday in the Bahamas at the present time, never mind a limp dick.'

Mo laughs. 'No, no, it's nothing like that. Well, not exactly. It's hard to explain. Anyway, you might find it quite useful. In the long run, I mean . . .'

I mention that she looks a touch flushed. 'Cling film,' she says.

27

'Pardon?'

'Cling film. It's supposed to cause weight loss, delay ageing. I *know* I've lost weight because I got so tangled up wrapping the fucking stuff around myself, it took four hours to fight my arms free. I had visions of being found asphyxiated, a victim of a highly hygienic suicide attempt.'

I put a bottle of Chablis in the fridge, a casserole in the oven, just in case Tom comes home, dog food in Letty's bowl and take a look at myself in the hall mirror.

I could be Onassis's mother: black slacks; black tunic top; black bags under the eyes. I'd chosen to wear one of my more ferocious brooches – bits of iron wool gilded over so that to the uninitiated, I appear to have a miniature hedgehog with an overdose of testosterone on my left shoulder.

'You look fabulous,' Mo says loyally as she passes on her way out of the front door. She's so supportive, I overlook the credibility gap.

The workshop is in a community centre on a council estate in north London. The aroma of stewed mincemeat and fags still lingers in the air from the OAP Luncheon Club. The parquet floor is witness to a polish famine. In a smaller room to the left of the main hall, half a dozen women are already seated with clipboards on their knees. On the blackboard is written in large letters, 'Erotica is one of the basic means of self-knowledge' Anaïs Nin. Beneath that is written, 'Be bold in the face of experience'. My heart sinks.

I take a step back, and tread on Mo.

'You promised me it wasn't going to be one of these,' I whisper. I can't see any mirrors or speculums but Mo's fascination for discovering what's round every corner of her interior is not to be overestimated.

'Don't be silly,' she says blithely. 'It's nothing like that. Give it a go. It'll take your mind off things. It might even come in handy.' And for reasons best known to herself, she finds this exceptionally funny.

Five minutes later, calmer, she informs me that the workshop is for those who want to have an orgasm or improve on one. I am trapped.

At seven p.m., a woman in her early thirties who has been sitting quietly at the back of the room walks to the front. She is attractive in an untouched-by-any-additives way; no make-up, good complexion, short, shiny, bobbed hair, an androgynous figure. If she didn't look quite so sterilized, she would be sexy. She wears a wedding ring, navy slacks and a fairly expensive-looking matching designer T-shirt. She could almost be French but when she opens her mouth, she speaks with a slight Yorkshire accent.

'Thank you for being here. My name is Anna. I admire your courage in taking part in this workshop.' I shift on my seat, alarmed. 'Before we go round the room and introduce ourselves, I want to begin with some basics,' Anna says.

'An awful lot of women fail to come. Once upon a time, they were called frigid.'

She writes 'Frigidity' on the board. Everyone else writes the word down, so I do too. *Point One: Frigidity.*

'Now, of course, we know better,' Anna says. 'Frigidity is a temporary state. And what can correct it?'

For a minute I think she has directed the question at me, and I quietly panic.

'Technique,' Anna says with a flourish, scribbling on the board. So we dutifully copy, *Point Two: Technique.*

'But what is far more important than technique is an attitude of mind. So first and foremost, we begin with what's inside our heads.'

I begin to write down *Point Three: Heads*, when I realize that nobody else has her pen in her hand any longer.

Anna continues. 'We are supposed to live in more liberated times and it's true many more women have highly satisfactory sex lives. But others, as we all know, are still conditioned to associate sex with negative ideas. They may, for instance, have been with only one partner for a number of years and they are hesitant to say what they want in bed.

'Other women may find the whole business too messy and time-consuming, and the rewards too small to bother. Some can't enjoy themselves in bed because they don't like to be seen to be losing control.'

As Anna talks on, I notice that Mo, sitting next to me, is writing furiously. I glance at what she's written.

Dear Sir,
    I am sorry to say that your giant-size rubber bands have failed to move even an inch from my buttocks, despite intensive effort on my part. I would appreciate, therefore, the refund of my £15.99 . . . I have enclosed the bands . . .

'Fifteen ninety-nine?' I whisper to Mo. She shrugs. 'Well, they were *miracle* rubber bands. But if I don't post this tonight, I'll be outside the trial-and-return period . . .'

We both look up to see Anna frowning at us.

'As I was saying,' she continues, 'women are also supposed to have a different attitude to sex than men. Men are said to view it more as recreational, women as procreational. I don't buy that.

'Women can have just as much fun. They can be just as turned on by stranger sex. They can fantasize. Over the next few weeks, I will give you exercises and small projects which will enhance your sense of self and hopefully quite rapidly change your appetite for sex.

'Women have an erotica which is all their own. Our small group will become explorers of these – how shall I phrase it? – these wilder shores . . .'

Not one of us moves. I have a terrible urge to giggle. My ability to explore is minimal. I have such a bad sense of direction, I have to call out the RAC every time I try and insert the cap. I can see a small prickle of perspiration on Anna's top lip. Perhaps this turns her on? She speaks again.

'What do we female explorers require most of all, if we are to succeed in our goal?' Silence. I knew this was speculum territory.

'Vibrators?' says a voice at the back. Anna frowns. Two or three of us are finding it hard to restrain the laughter.

'A map?' Mo suggests.

Anna's voice rises to a surprisingly loud crescendo in someone so low-key. 'We need trust, TRUST, TRUST, TRUST!'

Anna turns to the board and writes, 'I like myself. I like my body. When I give myself permission to ask for what I want, I am a truly sensual human being.'

I write down, *Point Three: I like myself.* Five seconds later, I add a question mark.

Anna continues: 'Now, in this group presumably some of you will have never had an orgasm. But is there anybody here who reaches a climax more often than not?'

The woman in front of me appears to raise her arm, so I raise mine too. Too late, I realize she's raised it to flick her hair back over her shoulder. I wish the hand hovering above my head did not belong to me. Mo's look tells me I have committed a *faux pas*: we women are no longer all in this together.

'When you say climax,' I struggle desperately to reclaim my position in the hierarchy of deprivation. 'What I mean is . . . not a climax exactly but a bit of a shift. More like a change of gear really. It's all relative, isn't it?

'And, of course, my husband and I have been together for quite a while, so I wouldn't say it happens a lot. Sometimes, in fact, it doesn't happen at all . . . if you know what I mean.'

Well, of course they bloody do, I tell myself. Otherwise they wouldn't be here.

I'm surprised that I'm still talking but there seems no constructive point at which to stop.

'And tell me,' Anna asks, her voice suddenly deeper. 'How often have you flown?'

'Flown?' My mind is suddenly filled with the image of a winged Tom and Ms Crumpled Suit, bouncing on a large cloud of cotton wool, locked in carnal combat.

'Yes. How often has your body flown, have you been lifted out of yourself, have you reeled and danced with your senses confused and every nerve in your body playing a delicious tune? How often have you lost control definitively, absolutely? How often have you heard your voice lifted in mad laughter as you climax?'

This question is long, but easy to answer.

'Never,' I say dutifully. 'Absolutely never.'

This is more tactful than true. Anna is pleased.

'Well,' she replies, 'you will. I promise you, you will.' She punches the air. 'We all will, *together!*'

'Oh, I'm not too sure about doing it together . . .' says a woman in front of me with a round face. 'Not *together* together.'

Anna looks at her scathingly. 'I am an academic by training,' she says as if this explains everything. 'In this workshop, O is for orgasm, not orgy.'

Anna sprints on. 'Now I'll tell you something about me,' she says, 'then I'd like to go round the room and have you introduce yourselves and explain a little bit about why you're here. But say no more than you want to. *You* are in control.'

In my limited experience, any time I've been told I'm in control, I'm not.

Anna tells us she is thirty-six. She comes from Hull. She works for a company which specializes in 'human resources' and, until two years ago, she had never had an orgasm.

'I was as stable as the next person. I didn't think sex was disgusting. I'm not particularly inhibited. I'd had a number of male partners. I had been living with Dominic for two years, and I'm still with him, but I'd never had an orgasm.'

I find myself writing *Point Four: Anna's never had an orgasm*. And adding, *Do I care?*

'What did I do about it?' Anna demands. 'I decided that I would learn and revise and test myself just as for an exam. And do you know what happened?'

Nobody wants to spoil her pitch.

'I CAME! I SAW! I CONQUERED! But I haven't yet flown.'

We shuffle about a bit on our seats not quite sure of the appropriate way to respond. Should we express regret? Or offer congratulations?

'Now,' Anna says, 'Let's find out about you.' Six of us instantly shrink by several inches.

'Would you like to begin?' Anna points at the woman with the round face. She looks as if she's in her mid-thirties. She wears a serviceable brown check suit and a cream blouse. Her shoes are scruffy, her hair is cut in a pudding-basin style which serves to make her moon-face even rounder. She has rosy cheeks and minimal make-up. The impression she conveys is not so much that she lacks funds but that she has far more absorbing interests than her appearance. She reminds me of the Wing Attack in our school netball team, thirty years ago.

She tells us her name is Elizabeth Stephens and she's usually called Liz. 'I'm a civil servant, in the high-flying stream as a matter of fact. What I want to know is how do you keep passion alive in a long-term relationship?

'Philip and I have been married for twelve years and we're jolly good friends. Not much of a cross word, plenty of interests in common – we're in a Scrabble league, choral singing, lots of hillwalking, you know the kind of thing.

'Well, I've been perfectly happy but clearly, poor old Phil is a bit on his uppers. A couple of weeks ago, he said, "Lizzie," – he always calls me Lizzie when trouble's up – "Lizzie, how would you describe our relationship?" "How would I describe it, dear?" I said, baffled I must admit. "What a silly question." I mean wouldn't you think it a bit of a duff question?

'"I'll tell you how I would describe it," Philip says. "I'd call it a brother-and-sister relationship. And Lizzie, I don't want a brother-and-sister relationship. I want to have sex. Sometimes. Even infrequently will do, but I do want to have sex." And then of course he went on and on. Where was the passion? How do you keep passion alive after a decade? Do I fancy him? Is it because he isn't good enough in bed? On and on.

'In the end, I told him the truth. I said, "Look, Philip. One of your great attractions is that in so many fields you are an enthusiastic amateur. You're perfectly fine in bed, it's just that as far as being a lover goes, at the moment I'm resting. You know, like actresses rest between parts.

'I told him that frankly, I'm a bit bored by the whole rigmarole. I'm not a prude – far from it – I have orgasms.'

Here Liz pauses and looks at me as if to say, 'Well, at least that's one thing we have in common', before she continues.

'But I find the whole business vastly overrated. I've got other interests I'm far more passionate about, squash for instance. You get hot and sweaty, but at least you know it's over in forty minutes and there's a winner and a loser. Sex is so much more, what's the word?. . . Indeterminate.'

Liz pauses for breath. 'Now you might say, "What's the problem?" I'm happy, and Phil will just have to adjust. But the trouble is, while I don't feel particularly randy with Philip, I do fancy other people.

'A friend at work showed me the ad for the workshop as a joke. But I thought about it and decided well, I learnt car maintenance at evening class, maybe I need the same approach to this. I've never been inhibited or anything. Matter of fact, I'm a bit the opposite. And as I say, I fancy lots of other people like mad. But not Phil.'

Liz stops and beams at us. We all smile back. If this was Britain in the forties, one of us would salute and say, 'Glad to have you on the team, Stephens.'

'Thank you for sharing your thoughts, Liz,' Anna says instead and points to the woman on the right of Liz.

She is twenty-four, white face, jet-black spiky hair. She wears a short black dress over long johns. She has one tattoo, silver rings and Doc Marten boots and she looks good. She says her name is Estelle, usually shortened to Tilly. She is a psychiatric nurse from Middlesbrough but now lives in Hackney with her younger sister.

'I know what I look like but it's not how I am,' she says all in a rush. 'I hate sex. I think it's a disgusting, filthy business. I read all this crap in the women's magazines and it's like life is one big orgy, so what I want to know is why am I the odd one out?

'I feel as if everybody in the fucking world is happily at it except me. I sit on the tube going to work and I look at the people opposite and one by one I go through them: "Did you do it last night? Did you?" I say to myself.

'I should be uninhibited. Me mam and dad have always been really open with us. Me mam even suggested I go on the pill when I was sixteen, but I don't know, it's like I'm in a time warp.

'When I read stuff from the fifties, like when women would only undress in the dark and that, I say, "That's me. Ah'm like that."

'But how come? I've never had a bad experience in me life wi' a fella. I've never been raped. I've never been beaten up. I've got no excuses for being the way ah am. I don't know how to say it, it seems so bloody ridiculous, but I'm—' . . . We all wait for the word.

'—Shy. I suppose I'm shy. But you're not supposed to be, are you? Everyone assumes I do – like it, I mean. And I pretend I do. But if you want to know the truth, I reckon I'm the only twenty-four-year-old virgin in the whole of the sodding British Isles.'

At the revelation that she is a virgin, Tilly looks around with murder in her eyes. 'And if any of yous tells a soul, I'll fucking kill you.'

Mo instinctively puts an arm around her. 'We all have to start somewhere,' Mo says banally in her best counselling voice. Anna is delighted.

'You are exactly the kind of challenge we like,' she says. 'Isn't she, Group?' 'We' are less certain.

'If I were you, Tilly,' Liz offers, 'I'd stay a virgin. If you don't like it, don't do it.' Murmurs of agreement creep around the room. Anna moves in briskly.

'I'm sure we can work with you, Tilly. You have no idea what an exciting world awaits you,' she says. 'Yes?' Anna is looking at me.

'My name is Kay.' So far, so good. I can't say, I'm at this workshop on how to have an orgasm because I was tricked into coming, no pun intended.

'I'm rather surprised to find myself here,' I say opting for as close to the truth as I can get.

'I like that openness,' Anna encourages me. 'We can work with that.'

I continue: 'Sex, at times, is more like a set of instructions for a piece of IKEA furniture that my husband and I have put together a dozen times before. It just about works, it's a bit shaky at times but my husband often seems pleased that he's managed to do it at all.'

'I know exactly how you feel,' Anna interjects. 'You look as if you want to rediscover the unknown, pep up what turns you on. Venture into risk-taking, be ready, willing and able . . .'

I resent someone else knowing *exactly* how I feel, when I haven't a clue.

'I also have a thing about quickies,' I ramble on, surprised to find myself telling a room full of strangers.

'My husband is all in favour of them. But to me, a quickie is like the Pot Noodle of copulation; gone in a flash and nothing memorable, if you know what I mean . . . And I hate how sometimes I'm expected to deliver when, as far as I'm concerned, the key is barely in the ignition. But then it's not Tom's fault really. Tom's my husband, by the way.

'Tom often has to get up very early. For me, if it's a toss-up between foreplay and forty winks, the snooze wins every time. But that's not because I'm frigid, it's because I'm so damn tired. Tom would rather squeeze one in, keep his average up.' I pause. 'That's about it, really. Is that OK?'

'A rich vein to explore,' Anna says crisply. 'Next!'

Dionne Wallace is around my age, black and immaculately turned out. The scheme of terracotta and turquoise includes earrings, scarf, shoes and handbag. She tells us she sells insurance and she has just severed links with husband number three. 'As someone once said, I'm a very good housekeeper,' she chuckles. 'Every time I have a divorce, I get to keep the house.'

'I have two sons who are both married and I am happy. But why I'm here is because I'm curious. I have orgasms. I don't have any real complaints but neither would I choose making love as my most favourite way to pass the time. So, I figure, if this is something I'm missing out on, then honey, now's the time to fix it.'

Anna smiles and swiftly moves on to Mo.

Mo has revealed all to so many, so often, that she is able to turn her life-story into a tale of brevity which would do the *Reader's Digest* proud: *War and Peace* in four pages, read aloud in three minutes. Her personal goal, she explains to us with the enthusiasm which makes her so endearing to me, is: to do it *right*. To improve. 'To know that I can orgasm to order.'

'My order.'

The last woman in our group is in her late twenties, long hair, long legs, jeans, waistcoat. 'If she has trouble,' Mo whispers, 'the rest of us really are in deep shit.'

Alex Ellis says she is a model and an addict.

'I'm addicted to sex. As soon as I see a man, I'm thinking, "What's he like to fuck? How quickly can I get him into bed?" I don't feel a man likes me unless I can persuade him to screw me.'

'They need *persuading?*' Dionne chuckles. Alex continues undeterred.

'Once I've had a man, I lose interest. But I'm not like that really. I don't want to use people but it happens over and over again.'

'Gosh,' Liz says, 'Do you really think that's a problem? It sounds marvellous. I suppose you could say you're a sort of sex-machine. How often do you do it?' Anna frowns disapprovingly at Liz's cross-questioning.

'Once a day, sometimes more, sometimes less.'

'What about AIDS?' Mo asks.

'Sometimes a condom, sometimes not. Sometimes the situation is so unexpected and sudden, there's no opportunity,' Alex replies matter-of-factly.

'Oh, I say . . .' Liz is lost for words.

'What I've got is quantity,' Alex explains in a slightly breathy voice. 'What I want is quality.'

'Look, Alex,' says Liz enthusiastically, 'I wonder if I could introduce you to my husband, Phil? He'd give an arm and a leg to be used – even for half an hour.'

Introductions over, we are instructed that we will now write our own short pieces of erotica. Half a dozen women make noises which register alarm, fear, embarrassment, anything but enthusiasm. Anna presses on.

'I want you to describe a brief scene which turns you on. Don't worry about what anybody else thinks, don't worry that it's not like any of the stuff you may have already read. It might be about something completely ordinary, all that matters is that it turns you on.'

For twenty-five minutes, I stare down at a blank piece of paper. I am liberated only by Anna announcing our homework.

We are to complete our stories so we can read them in next week's group; a conclusive reason for never coming back. And we are to make a chart.

'Thirty-one days, each marked with a square. If you make love on any one day, mark it with a spot. If you have an orgasm, circle the spot.'

Anna then places an alarming diagram on the board. She tells us it's the pubococcygeal, or PC. Mo's expression tells me she knew that already.

'If you've ever done pelvic-floor exercises, you'll have some idea of what I'm about to say. If you build up the strength of the PC, if you learn to control its contraction and relaxation, then you will improve your orgasm hugely.

'Next time you go to the loo, see if you can stop the flow mid-pee. The muscle you use to stop the flow is the PC muscle. I want you to contract and relax it twenty times, three or four times a day. I want you to hold the contraction for a little longer each time. You can do it anywhere, at the bus-stop, at home, at work. Nobody's going to know except you.

'Next week, seventeen ways to masturbate. Good-night, thank you . . . and don't forget to exercise those PC muscles . . .' Anna sings out as we leave.

'Don't you think it's all a bit odd?' I ask Mo in the car, driving home. 'I mean, isn't sex supposed to be instinctive, spontaneous, fun? Perhaps we shouldn't worry about doing it "right", or doing it at all. Perhaps all we need to do is find somebody who shares our personal level of incompetence or who shares the same degree of disinterest and just get on with it. Or not, as the case may be.'

'Sometimes I wonder about you,' Mo replies. 'You're so bloody naïve. Sex doesn't just *happen*. Even today, young girls are being brought up to see sex as something you fight against, not something you do for enjoyment. Boys are born to love it, girls are reared to resist it. "Don't lead him on", "Don't look as if you want it", "Don't get into a situation where he might try it on".

'Then, suddenly, when it's considered OK to be At It, we're supposed to slip out of all that previous conditioning and take to it like a duck to water.

'It's not bloody men who have a hundred thousand endless articles written for them about how to give good head, how to be a sensitive lover, how to make your partner feel good. But boy, could some of them do with it.

'Half the men I've been to bed with went down on me like a Labrador lapping up its first ice-cream while the other half announced – usually mid-session – that, "Actually, I've always felt a bit queasy about anything down there.'" Mo imitates the voice of a mummy's boy.

'Anyway, I'm not talking problems here,' Mo says. 'I'm talking *challenges*. My challenge is what's in my head that stops me having nights of incredible, inexhaustible passion.

'I want to feel as if I've got a Catherine wheel in each ear, and my body is so hot I leave a brand mark on the sheets. I want to come seven times in an evening. I want to draw a stranger into the back of a cab and screw him until he's dizzy.'

'In that case, instead of going to a workshop, you'd be better off at a taxi rank,' I suggest practically. 'You'd be swamped with volunteers.'

Mo is scornful, 'It's not just about doing it. It's about feeling it's *all right* to do it. Erotic pleasure. Good functional fucking. Do you know what I mean? Have you ever in your life had any of that? Have you ever *let* yourself have any of that?'

I take my time to reply. 'I think I have . . . I'm not sure really . . . How do you judge if it's good fucking or bad fucking if, relatively speaking, you haven't done a lot of fucking in the first place?' I ask.

Mo clicks on the radio. 'If you don't mind me saying so, Kay, even if it was the first and only fuck in your life, if it was *that* good, you'd know.'

Put down but not put off, I persist. 'If you ask me,' I say more assertively than I feel, 'Sex has become the religion of the twenty-first century. Have faith in it, become one of the Chosen Few who do it well and it will deliver you to your solitary heaven. But somehow along the way, what's got left out is who you do it with and why, and in what circumstance. All that has to matter too, doesn't it?'

Mo shakes her head in mock despair at my unreconstructed romanticism and turns the radio up loud. An old Tamla Motown song fills the car.

'OK,' she shouts, 'It's PC time. Now: one, two, three, SQUEEZE . . .'

Chapter Four

At nine the next morning, I am back outside Medicatis Inc. At nine-fifteen, Ms Crumpled Suit appears, one of a group of four who go up the stairs and enter the reception area together. I follow. In the lobby, a security man is checking passes.

'Morning, Mr Whitcombe, morning, Mr Lansing, morning, Mandy, morning, Brenda.'

I reach the desk. Which is she, Mandy or Brenda? She doesn't look like a Mandy. On the other hand, if pushed, I couldn't describe her as your average Brenda either.

Her hair is the same frizz, clearly an accident of nature; she wears a deeply unsuitable red lipstick and too much plastic, chunky jewellery. Otherwise, even I'm forced to admit, she's pleasant-looking but certainly not glamorous. And her body is too square for the belted suit she has chosen to wear. She might also be slightly bandy. But then I'm bound to have a jaundiced view, aren't I? And as far as Tom is concerned, looks don't come into it. Brenda's most attractive feature will be her passion for him.

The security man is intent on proving himself up to the job. 'Madam?' he asks me.

Out of the corner of my eye, I see the group has been swallowed by the lift.

'Brenda . . . I um . . .' I point vaguely at the lift.

'Brenda Styles?' he says helpfully. 'The lady who's just gone in the lift? You've got an appointment?'

He picks up the phone, anxious to complete his office ritual. 'Who shall I say is calling?'

I glance out of the door and put my hand to my mouth in mock horror. 'Oh, my God. I've left my car on a double yellow line, and there's a traffic warden. I'll be back in a tick.'

Driving to Tom's offices in Camden, I am pleased with myself. At least now I have A Name.

Tom's television production company is in a converted factory. The team is small and includes Pam. Pam is *Photoplay* glamorous and hugely enjoys sending herself up, and everybody else. Her hair is bright red and backcombed to a peak not seen since the Ronettes' 'Be My Baby'; her waist is invariably imprisoned in a giant waspy belt and her heels and her nails have to be seen to be believed. If it's not fifties, you won't find it anywhere near Pam.

Pam is a doctor and a television producer. While people believe that she's the latter, they refuse to take her seriously as the former. She couldn't give a toss.

'Where's your lazy bastard of a husband?' she says cheerily. Pam was born in Adelaide. 'He's been out of this office for nearly three weeks now. The cunt was supposed to be here two days ago.' She pours me black coffee and puts her feet up on the desk.

'He left a message on the machine last night,' I tell her. 'He wanted to know where I was because I hadn't told him I'd be out. And then he said he wouldn't be home because he had a business meeting in Glasgow. And finally, he said that you and me and him are meeting people for dinner tonight who are interested in a co-production. Is that right?'

'So where were you last night then, hon?' Pam says, smiling. 'Anywhere stimulating?'

'A workshop on how to have an orgasm without really trying. Except we were. Trying, I mean. Mentally, we were all trying very hard.'

Pam doesn't stop laughing for a very long time.

'Jeez, what are you doing at a place like that? Can you imagine what Tom, *el ego stupendo*, would say if it got out that the partner of the world's expert on what goes on below the knicker-line is having a crash course on what goes on below the knicker-line? What a treat.'

'I don't give a damn what Tom thinks,' I respond in what I believe is a light tone.

'Quite right too, doll.' Pam pours more coffee while I pick up Tom's post.

'Tom asked me if I'd bring his mail home if I was passing by,' I explain.

Pam has her back to me. As she roots in a filing-cabinet, she says casually over her shoulder, 'She's only written a couple this week. I don't know anything about her, honey, but Tom's a dog.'

At the Palms pool, mid-morning, I'm the only swimmer except for a school group. As I swim up and down my lane, I watch two male teachers shout and cajole and badger the children out of the pool. One teacher looks as if he's been folded away in somebody's bottom drawer for a couple of years. He's ignored by the boys. The other looks more of a jack-the-lad and is constantly in demand, 'Sir, watch this!' 'Sir, Darren thumped me 'ead.' 'Sir, sir . . .'

I swim up and down, up and down, as I have done three times a week for years, thin, fat, pregnant, fatter, now at least four pounds lighter. I wave at the lifeguard, a Greek Cypriot who has lived in Britain for two decades as he tells me three times a week.

He always says, 'How are you?' I always reply, 'Fine.' This time, when he asks, 'How are you?' I shall say, 'Pretty bloody awful. My husband has had one affair and he's now into his second and I think he's going to leave. Worse, half of me wants him to leave.

'The other half of me is a craven, cowardly, pathetic, besotted enraged wife who wants to barbecue his bladder, persecute him relentlessly, prove to his mistress that he's the biggest shit that ever walked the earth, then keep him to myself, happily miserable for the rest of my life.'

'How are you?' says the Greek Cypriot lifeguard as I come out of the pool. I pause.

'I'm fine, thank you.'

In the changing-room, P.P. has just arrived. P.P., as in Pink Plastic, is my nickname for an unknown woman who wears an extraordinary pink plastic mock-leather swimsuit and a matching hat. The combination makes her look like a shiny frankfurter dipping in and out of the water. Today, I am surprised. This is the first time I've seen her fully dressed.

P.P. is a fashion victor. I suddenly feel not forty-four but seventy-four. My hair is a mess, my clothes are a drudge.

P.P. has shoulder-length, richly hennaed hair in a page-boy style, tortoiseshell glasses with frames which wing up at the end. She is wearing an all-in-one black leather catsuit, biker boots and carries a handbag big enough to hold a modest coffin. 'Hi,' she says. That's as much as we've said passing in the pool for the last four or five months. 'Hi,' I reply.

I am wrapped in a large, very old towel on which, I suddenly realize as I pass the mirrors to the lockers, are immortalized the words *Choclax . . . The laxative that keeps the world on the go.*

It was probably given to Tom as part of some promotion or

other. P.P.'s underwear is black satin, the kind you buy in the first throes of romance when, if you're lucky, both of you are so driven by lust such details are overlooked anyway.

'Water cold?' P.P. asks. As she speaks, she stands in front of the mirror stark naked. Her body is lightly tanned, all over. Very gently, very carefully she removes her beautiful head of hair. It rests like a glistening maroon puddle on the shelf.

Decoiffed, P.P. reveals a white-blonde crew cut. 'It's quite cold but OK once you get going,' I reply. And I can't help but notice that P.P.'s pubic hair isn't there. Instead, she has a clean-shaven fanny and a small tattoo.

'It's supposed to be a nightingale,' she says. I trip over the end of the Choclax towel and land with a thump on the bench.

'Oh, I didn't mean, I'm sure it must be, but I wasn't or rather I didn't mean to —'

'It's OK. I wouldn't have it there if I didn't expect to be looked at, would I?' She has a mellifluous voice.

'Didn't it hurt?' I ask.

'Only a bit. The shaving is a damn sight riskier.' P.P. is dusting herself with talcum powder and sliding the pink plastic suit over her bum.

'Do you know why it's supposed to be a nightingale?' she asks.

I pull on leggings and a jumper and shake my head.

'A few hundred years ago, if somebody said they'd been listening to the nightingales, it was another way of saying they'd been fucking — gloriously and with great abandon.'

P.P. smiles. 'Why don't you try it on?' she says, pointing to the wig.

'I couldn't.'

'Why not?'

'Isn't it a bit like using somebody else's toothbrush?'

'Go on,' P.P. says. 'It can't do you any harm. Bend down,' she adds.

'Pardon?'

'Bend down, it's easier to put it on.'

I bend down and she twists my hair up in a knot and fits the wig on my head. A woman comes into the changing-room wearing a large sweatshirt. On it are written the words *Over-55 Ducks and Drakes Palms Swimming Team*. She watches us slightly warily. Are we Ducks, Drakes or dykes?

'Christ,' I say. I look odd. Like something out of Camp On Cleopatra, but at least I don't look *boring*.

'It's all right, that is,' says the woman in the sweatshirt, to P.P. 'Gives her bit of a lift, dunnit? Takes the yellow out of her complexion, like.'

'You should come up and see my wigs sometime,' P.P. says and smiles. This is clearly a game she enjoys. And, whether I like or not, I sense that I am already a player.

After a swim, I drive to Olivia's shop, Bonne Bouche in Pimlico. It is patronized by ageing, very thin, very tall, very unsmiling men and women in black jeans, cowboy boots and dark glasses; rock 'n' roll relics. Also in evidence are a number of voluble Arabic women and a couple of upper-class British matrons trailed by tiny dogs who look like hirsute commas.

Olivia Heimmel-Brown has eclectic 'taste'. On display are stuffed gold lamé cats decorated with diamanté; a transparent life-size tiger with a jumble of neon lights where its internal organs might be; dinner plates like banana leaves; round cushions that resemble giants' eyeballs and wonderfully exotic wall-hangings that appear to have their origins in the Mexican festival of the Day of the Dead.

In the centre of the shop, a life-size papier mâché cleaner wields a mop, a fag hanging out of her mouth, hair in curlers. In several corners there are also some less-than-comfortable-looking 'chairs' shaped in the image of John Wayne's face. Bonne Bouche, of course, does not have a counter. It has a glass-topped table supported by wrought-iron serpents, behind which sit two of the palest women I have ever seen.

Their clothes are rag-and-bone meets Camelot. On a tape, Edith Piaf sings *La Mer*. I suddenly feel like crying. I see no sign of Olivia. It is three p.m., the time we agreed to meet and I am carrying samples of Kitchen Sync in a doctor's bag.

'Excuse me,' I say. The two assistants move from comatose to crass. They both ignore me. 'Excuse me.'

The taller one looks over my left shoulder. 'Yes?' she says. Jewellery is displayed on little velvet cushions in glass cases on the table in front of her. 'Could I look at the jewellery please?'

'Which jewellery?'

This, I do not need. 'That jewellery.'

'All of it? There's quite a lot and most people know what they want.'

The taller one looks at the shorter one and raises her eyes to heaven as if to say She's Another One of Those.

'How much is that piece, please?'

'It depends,' the tall one says, clearly determined not to become saleswoman of the year.

'On what?' I play the game.

'On whether you want it in gold, silver, platinum or plastic.'

'All four.'

'All four?'

'Yes, I'd like to see it in four versions with four prices and then, who knows?' I add, 'I might change my mind completely and not buy at all.' I smile sweetly.

The tall woman's face has developed rigor mortis. She bangs the jewellery down in front of me. 'Sixty-seven pounds.'

'For plastic?'

'For plastic,' she says firmly.

I am delighted. If Olivia agrees to buy even a modest amount of Kitchen Sync then I can keep myself in the style of misery to which I am becoming accustomed; wigs, wine and workshops. 'Haven't you seen our mission statement?' the tall one says. 'If you're a regular customer, you'd know. It's on all our bags.'

She produces a navy blue carrier. Written in gold is the name of the shop and then in what I assume is Olivia's handwriting, the words *Inspiration is our aspiration*.

'Kay?' says a voice from a door disguised as a Roman column at the rear of the shop. 'How nice to see you. Come and have a glass of champagne. I hope Rebecca has been looking after you?'

I smile at Rebecca. 'Well,' I say. 'She certainly has a way with her.'

Upstairs, Olivia has a vast study-cum-sitting-room. It reminds me of a restaurant I once visited in Marrakesh, designed on behalf of tourists to resemble the inside of a Berber tent. She has rich carpets on the walls and floors; copper and brass; a couple of camel-saddle seats; no chairs, only fat cushions in bright colours like giant lozenges; a large walnut desk and a fridge also apparently made of walnut and built like a seaman's chest. Four brass telephones sit on a miniature trolley.

A pile of papers, photographs and catalogues lie in a circle in the middle of one carpet indicating where Olivia had sat before my arrival. She resumes her position, her shoes by her side. She wears what even the most generous would term a sensible skirt and blouse. The overall impression is that the head of the Townswomen's Guild has decided to make a flying visit to Lawrence of Arabia.

'Champagne?' Olivia says, as I stand on the edge of the carpet.

'Are you going to have one?' I reply. One day, I might learn to say, 'No, thank you.' Or, even better, 'Yes, please.'

'Going to? Of course I'm going to,' Olivia roars. 'I always do. I have a couple of glasses every lunch-time. It's my reward.'

'For what?'

'For doing well in the morning.'

'What if you haven't?'

'Then I look upon it as a consolation prize. Take a seat. So what have you got for me?'

As I lay out my bits and pieces on the carpet, she opens the fridge and digs out a bottle.

'I like that,' she says as she lights up a cigarette and gestures to one of my brooches with a burnt-out-match. 'What's it made of?'

'Beer-bottle tops and a nutmeg-grater.'

'Fascinating,' she says. 'I'll take five.'

'Five? You mean mass-produce?' I reply idiotically.

'If you mean more than one, then yes, darling, mass-produce.'

She picks up a pair of earrings and pretends to examine them in great detail, then she suddenly asks, 'So, how's it going? Mo told me a bit about your . . . situation. I hope you don't mind?'

I shake my head and say no. If I had minded about Mo's generosity in sharing my experiences among acquaintances, my friendship with her wouldn't have lasted a fortnight.

Olivia looks at me sharply then speaks again. 'You won't believe what I'm going to tell you, but one day you'll know I was right.

'A couple of years from now – perhaps sooner – you'll thank God that this other woman appeared on the scene.'

'I don't think so,' I say wryly.

Olivia watches me as she lights her cigarette. 'Well, let me tell you this. All the time I was with Ed I thought it was me who had the problem. It was only when the au pair spirited him away, that I began to understand what he was really worth. The same thing will happen to you, believe me.'

'I'm not sure,' I reply. I'm too polite to articulate the truth, that I think she's completely off her trolley if she thinks even six months from now Tom and I will be anything other than cemented together. OK, Brenda may have left her great flat footprint in the wet concrete, but that will be her only mark.

'Tom is inclined to be slightly insecure,' I concede cautiously. 'But then again, he did have a very difficult childhood. His father left the family when he was eleven and his mother—'

'Sweetheart,' Olivia interrupts, pouring us both a second glass, 'Every one of these bastards has a set of excuses. And as long as you accept the excuses, they'll keep right on behaving like bastards.'

'Well, Tom has been supportive at times. For instance, when I've had to work . . . with the children.'

Fact: on the occasions I'd been overextended by work, when the girls were younger, Tom had instantly transformed himself into A Martyr. A Martyr who, he constantly told me, had developed a 'special closeness' with 'his' daughters, simply because he'd picked them up from school three days in a row.

Before Brenda I'd always found a hundred and one reasons to excuse this behaviour. Now, I'm less concerned with the reasons and more preoccupied with just one question: *why have I put up with it?*

'Shall I tell you the prices?' I ask Olivia.

'I like this,' she says in reply. It's a thick mock gold bar, about three inches wide, with legs so it resembles a table. Doll's house china cups and plates hang from it on links.

'How much?'

'Twenty pounds?' It comes out as more of a question than a statement. That probably gives me about ninety-five pence profit; dumb cluck.

'Even at a hundred per cent mark-up, they'd never buy it,' Olivia says smiling. I feel mortified and disappointed. Then, as she goes on, I cheer up.

'Much too cheap, my dear. I sell tat, so I have to be careful. If I price it too low, my customers decide it's vulgar. If I price it nice and high, they think it's an investment, a tribute to their individual taste.

'I don't suppose you could stick a few diamonds on a couple, here and there?' she adds. I shake my head.

'Pity, they'd go down well in Bahrain. Look, I'll tell you what. I'll give you forty-five pounds for the small pieces, a hundred for the bigger pieces.'

'I couldn't possibly—' I begin to say, then I stop myself. Of course I could. Whether the two buzzards in black downstairs will be capable of selling any of the finished products God alone knows. But that, as they say in the trade, is not my business.

'Now, how did it go last night?' Olivia asks. I look blank. 'The workshop,' she prompts. 'Mo told me you were going. She tried to persuade me to go too. Not on your bloody life, I told her. I don't believe in all that before-and-after stuff.

'Listen, when Ed left I had no money, but I did have a thousand pounds in a post-office account which was supposed to be for the children. I spent it. I had my hair cut, my nails done, I lost two stone in weight. I bought a wardrobe full of the most ridiculous clothes and I went out.'

'What happened?'

'Sod all.' Olivia smiles. 'I felt uncomfortable and I acted it. I was permanently starving and ratty and the only men I attracted were salesmen and retired professional footballers. God knows why.'

'So what did you do?'

'I decided that I'd reverse history. I'd go back to the "Before" I'd been before I'd become the "After". And that's how I discovered something very important. It's all in the head. Did you know that?'

Suddenly, downstairs, a series of bells go off, followed by a loud scream and the sound of breaking glass.

'Shoplifter,' Olivia says casually. 'Veronique lives for the moment.'

'Veronique?'

'The short one with the winning manner,' Olivia says drily. 'Customers like our assistants to treat them like dirt. Sado-masochism sells. We get a couple of shoplifters every day. We never prosecute. Why should we? It adds enormously to the buzz of the place.' She shrugs and pours the last of the champagne.

'When you said, "It's all in the head",' I ask her, 'what do you mean, exactly?'

'Once I realized that I could enjoy sex on my terms, in my way, I really began to have a good time. It's a scent. You give it off. And once you do, believe me, it's like seeing the world clearly for the first time.

'Sex *is* power, my love,' Olivia says, draining her glass. 'And too many women see sex in terms of giving. As something mystical. As something tied to love and the universe. I don't any more. I see it as taking, too. Once you get to that stage, you're as powerful as the next fella.'

'It sounds awfully dehumanized,' I say.

'Dehumanized? Certainly not. It's simply stripping away all the hypocrisy from sex. Enjoy men for their bodies. If you involve their minds, that's a different game altogether.

'You think I'm pulling your leg, don't you?' Olivia says. 'Try it out. Bums, wrists, ear lobes, anything but those horrible bloody pony-tails. Find the bit that turns you on and start looking. Compare a bit, imagine you can have whatever you fancy. Imagine it dressed and undressed.'

I hear myself laughing. The laughter temporarily sops up all the uncertainties and fears and anxieties and rage and disappointment of the last couple of days.

Later, as I'm leaving, Olivia asks: 'Why don't you come to the farm for the weekend? You can meet Des the delightful jockey and a couple of other friends.'

I hesitate. 'I'm sure Tom will be too busy.'

'Let's hope he is,' Olivia says firmly. 'He's not invited.'

Back home, I take the three lemon-coloured envelopes collected from Tom's office out of my handbag and steam them open, one by one. Three times I pull out a single sheet of unsigned notepaper and three times my heart does a high jump over my rib cage.

Brenda is nothing if not repetitive. She is also quite creative. On one sheet is drawn a very high heel.

My darling Toots I read, *I want to hold you, comfort you –* Comfort him about what? Me? Bloody cheek – *I want to lick you and love you and tell you over and over again how much you mean to me and how soon we'll be together again. This time, for always.*

What does *that* mean? 'For always'? A suicide pact? Hardly, if Tom's involved. He's much too self-centred. Divorce? What I do know is that if I give away what's in the letters, Tom's dexterity is such that the issue will no longer be his infidelity but my invasion of his privacy. So how *do* I tackle it? Do I pretend ignorance but step up domestic service to a competitive level?

Do I say, 'By the way, darling,' as I hand him a glass of chilled white wine and a small plate of canapés I've knocked together before giving him his welcome-home massage, 'By the way, I know just how tough life is out there and I quite understand if you need extra comfort now and then . . .'

But I don't bloody understand at all.

At six, half an hour after Tom's promised time of arrival, the phone rings. 'Hello. Kay, is that you?' Tom says. 'Sorry, darling, I've been held up a bit. Is it OK if I meet you at the restaurant? Kay, are you there?'

I am here but the roar has crept up and over my entire body. It fills the telephone, it embraces the microwave, it engulfs Letty and it sweeps me away on a bright red throbbing haze. Finally, I speak.

'Sod off,' I say clearly and succinctly, and bang the phone down.

I dial again.

'Hello, Olivia? About the weekend. I will come if that's OK. No, not this weekend. Next weekend. Is that OK?'

Then, I sit down and make a chart. I draw thirty-one squares. In the area marked for this week, Sunday to Thursday, there are five empty little boxes. I pin the chart up on the fridge door.

'I like myself. I have great value,' I say loudly but without any conviction. I go upstairs and see if, at forty-four, I can learn to stop my pee mid-flow. It's not much, but everybody has to start somewhere.

Arrivisti, Tom's favourite restaurant, is packed. It always is – and it's hard to know why. A décor which involves hideous contraptions like rejects from a torture chamber on the bare brick walls, tables packed closer together than at a furniture auction, minute portions even further dwarfed by being deposited on primary-coloured plates the size of Boadicea's shield plus a lot of pidgin English from waiters born not far from Birkenhead. If the food was good, all that might be acceptable, but it isn't. Every dish comes lukewarm – even the 'home-made' ice-cream. The greater the loss of heat, the higher the price.

I see Tom before he sees me. And I suddenly feel distinctly shaky; as I did when we first met. He is rubbing his chin often.

This is a bad sign. This means he's on stage; whether we like it or not, he will entertain us all evening.

Next to Tom is Pam dressed in a black silk suit with a waisted jacket, gloves and a little hat last seen on Doris Day. She looks terrific.

I am wearing a white shirt, a black-and-white check jacket and black trousers. Kate and Claire put the combination together for me for a wedding last Christmas. They said I'd become too reserved, clothes-wise, and needed 'shaking up'. Now I'm well and truly shaken up, it seems the appropriate outfit to wear.

Pam and Tom are talking to another couple, in their thirties. The woman has wrists thinner than chicken's legs. She wears several layers of beige silk and a pair of cream tennis shoes. It's a style which should be in your glossy magazines very soon. She also has blonde streaked hair and a stunning smile which she uses often.

Her husband has grey flecked hair and a tie that if it isn't a one-off, it should be. As I come closer, I can hear his voice rise above the crowd. He's a straight-from-the-East-End-money-hasn't-changed-me-you-can-have-a-laugh-with-me-but-don't-forget-I'm-boss kind of bloke. Even if he says so himself. His scalp indicates that eczema might be a problem.

Tom spots me and puts out a hand. 'Hello, Kay.' He draws me in as he kisses me on the cheek; an ice-pack is warmer. He gives me a little squeeze. Pam hugs me. 'Hi, hon.'

'Kay, meet Carl, he's head of KBTV, one of the biggest cable stations. And this is Zoe, his wife,' Tom says.

'Partner,' Zoe states firmly. 'I'm a cohabitee – by choice, I might add.'

'I bet you're child-free, too,' Pam slides the knife in with relish.

'How did you guess?' Zoe says, oblivious to Pam's jibe.

The second couple arrive. He is tall, bearded, slim but with a startling pot-belly as if he's swallowed a football. He is also barely awake. She is small, intense, hair thinning. She wears a fuchsia suit which looks two sizes too big and she wrings her hands constantly, her head thrusting backward and forward like a sparrow. She is clearly a woman accustomed to being thought clever.

'Sandy, good to see you,' Tom says. 'And Creola.' Tom explains that Sandy runs a production company partly here, partly in LA, and Creola is a barrister.

'And what do you do?' is Creola's first question to me at the table as we choose from a menu scripted in illegible handwriting.

'Well, not a lot really.' I wonder if Creola has ever heard of the PC muscle? I wonder if she knows that she could be exercising at this very moment in time, without a soul knowing? I wonder if Creola has orgasms?

Actually, I don't wonder at all. I know. Creola looks like the kind of person who will schedule three orgasms a week into an already very full schedule.

'Oh, come on,' Creola says in the jolly voice she probably reserves for her Romanian au pair. 'I'm sure you do something jolly interesting.' Condescension is clearly going to be the dish of the day.

I make a bet with myself that if I ask Creola what time she gets up each morning, she's bound to say, 'Five-thirty, I'm afraid.'

'I suppose with all the court work, you have to get up quite early?' I ask.

Creola rises to the occasion: 'Well, four children and all that . . .'

'Four? Oh, my God, how could you?' Zoe shrieks.

Creola wrongly assumes this is a compliment. She smirks and continues, 'Well, with four children, I'm afraid it's five-thirty, Monday to Friday. I have to otherwise I wouldn't get the book done.'

I couldn't care less if she's rewriting the Book of Job, but I do my duty. 'The book?'

'Yes. I write thrillers. This is my third. I have a female heroine who's a health and safety inspector in Birmingham.'

'Brilliant,' breathes Pam. 'Sisters are sewering it for themselves.' I'm the only one who laughs.

'Now about you,' Creola persists. This woman is extremely irritating.

'She makes jewellery,' Pam offers. 'Out of junk.'

'Oh, I see . . .'

'And she writes a bit,' Pam adds.

'Oh, a novelist,' Creola says, perking up. 'A fellow scribbler.'

'No,' I reply, 'I write a monthly column in a magazine.'

I don't say that *Tangiers* is a magazine for 25,000 geriatric hippies too disorganized to cancel their subscriptions, first taken out in the sixties. Creola is not impressed.

'Oh, you're a *hack*,' she says dismissively.

'But now you've got a mixed portfolio,' Zoe offers helpfully.

'Yes, I suppose I have.'

A mixed portfolio sounds so much better than pin-money. In the pause that follows, I suddenly notice the waiter, or, more precisely, his bum. He is on my left and placing a plate in front of Zoe. His bum is compact and his face, when I eventually get a glimpse, is quite neat too. It's speckled with freckles and garnished with a red moustache. It occurs to me that I have never seen a man with a ginger willy.

'Penny for your thoughts,' says Creola in her isn't-life-spiffing voice.

Tom's conversation at the other end of the table intrudes. '. . . Of course, man is a hunter, a warrior. He is naturally promiscuous. He can spread his seed and—'

Next to Tom, Sandy appears to be in a deep sleep.

'He works seven days a week,' Creola whispers. 'When they were small, the children used to call him Ring-Ring instead of daddy, because they never saw him, they only heard his voice on the telephone. Isn't that a hoot!'

Tom's voice invades again, '. . . fidelity is, of course, the ideal but it comes much easier to the woman. When a man commits adultery, it is often nothing more than a simple matter of the flesh. When a woman—'

'What a load of old cock,' says Zoe flatly. 'Women have got the pill, some of us have got money so we don't need you for security or a roof over our heads any more, thank you very much, and a lot of us don't give a damn what the next-door neighbour thinks. The taboos are out the window, pal. We'll screw who we like.'

'But what's *the point*?' Sandy has come to life. 'I've had my share of one-night stands. In the early years of course . . . and never have I experienced a more lonely, soul-destroying form of occupation.'

'It's ego, isn't it?' says Pam. 'And insecurity and a need to confirm that you're constantly attractive and virile and—'

'. . . And it's bloody good fun,' Creola looks startled to hear her own voice.

'An adulterer in our midst!' Tom says jokingly. I have to admire his nerve.

Creola looks mildly discomfited. 'What I meant,' she flounders and then drops back into legal conciseness, 'is that hypothetically, it must be great fun. If you can stop yourself thinking of the consequences and the guilt and how the children are getting on. And so on and so forth.' She looks at Sandy but he has sunk back into a semi-slumber.

I decide to make my contribution. 'Tom doesn't bother himself so much with consequences, do you, darling? He doesn't have to, because he operates on the belief that since what he does is always for the benefit of others, everybody else *has* to be better off.'

I'm surprised at the bitterness in my voice, but helped by four glasses of wine, I continue.

'Personally, I think we're only just waking up to the fact of how much women have got going for them – sexually, I mean.

We have multiple orgasms, our libido gets better as we get older. What holds us back is a mental chastity belt.'

Carl chips in. 'What's wrong with that? It's your morality, innit? The touch of your rights and wrongs. You can't just do what you want, can yer? I mean you've got to have some kind of code, don't yer?'

'Too right,' Tom agrees. My husband is such a creep. Tom goes on, 'A woman who sleeps with someone stands far more chance of involving her soul. Women are more caring, less able to cut off from their emotions. They know that about themselves . . .'

The waiter offers the menu for desserts.

'What you're trying to say is, I'm all right, Jack,' offers Zoe.

'Not me,' Tom smiles. 'Kay and I have a solid basis of operation, don't we, darling?'

The fucker. Literally and metaphorically.

I smile at the waiter and the roar which has taken me over wraps him up too. It's not such a bad sensation, when it's shared. I hear that I am speaking, but it's as if my voice doesn't belong to me.

'Well, I have to say, Tom, it was made much less solid when you had the affair with the Japanese acupuncturist.'

Silence follows. 'Yes . . . well . . . I don't think we need to go into that,' Tom mutters.

'Oh, come on! Hold nothing back,' Pam says enthusiastically. 'We're grown-ups here . . . Tell all.'

So I do.

In a light-hearted way, I tell them about the Japanese acupuncturist. And the time just flies by.

'How could you do that to me?'

Tom is driving the car with the accuracy of a rogue ball in a pinball machine.

'How could you do it? I've never been so humiliated, so embarrassed in all my life.'

'You, embarrassed? You, humiliated? All that crap about "solid basis of operation". Everyone could see that's a joke when you could barely bring yourself to say hello to me. I'm your fucking wife, not your aide-de-sodding-camp. "Basis of operation", my fanny.'

'You are so bloody difficult, Kay. Tonight was about *us*. It was about business, making money that *we* can enjoy. Do you think I *like* being away from home, working my butt off?'

This is vintage Tom; personal pleasure repackaged as sacrifice.

'You've no bloody idea, have you?' he is saying. 'No bloody idea at all. You're the most demanding woman I've ever met. All I ever get from you is criticism.' He caricatures my voice with a skill that's impressive. 'We never see you . . . why don't you stop treating this house like a hotel . . . you said you'd be home two hours ago . . . why didn't you phone when you said you would . . .'

Since we've been through this script many times before, I am, of course, ready with my reply.

'That makes me demanding? In my book, that makes me *normal*!' I scream. 'I've got every bloody right to make those so-called demands. If you did what you promised, you wouldn't have sodding demands made on you! DEMANDS WOULD NOT BE MADE!' I am shouting. I lob a grenade.

'YOU HAVE BEEN SCREWING AROUND AGAIN,' I shout.

'I beg your pardon?' Tom speaks with such wounded pride, I am almost thrown. He has that effect on me; he can shake the most solid of my convictions by the force of his own certainty.

'You've been sleeping with someone! You didn't go . . . oh, stop the car.'

'Look, I don't know what you're—' Tom begins and then he says, 'Oh, Christ . . .'

A police car has loomed up behind. Tom pulls over, the officer walks towards us briskly and bends down to talk to Tom.

'Everything all right, sir?'

Tom is preening. He expects to be recognized. Fat chance, not unless the policeman happens to be a huge fan of relentlessly detailed descriptions of candida and cystitis broadcast on morning television. Someone only has to say to Tom, 'Haven't I seen you somewhere before?' and his day is made. The officer fails to oblige.

'Speeding a bit, weren't you, sir?'

'I am so sorry, officer.'

Tom has had two glasses of wine and sprayed half a gallon of Alpine mouth freshener down his throat. The officer must imagine he's on a Swiss mountainside.

'You seemed to be going a bit fast, sir. There is a forty-mile-an-hour limit in this area, sir.'

Tom grovels and the policeman eventually lets him off. We resume driving. Neither of us speaks. My accusation hangs in the air.

Once home, Tom says he's going to take Letty for a walk around the block. I watch from our bedroom window as he walks to the end of the road. He crosses the square and slips into the phone box. A private call.

I look up Brenda Styles' number in the telephone directory, copy down her address and dial her number. It is engaged.

Later, in bed, I make no sound as I cry. Next to me, Tom gently snores and twitches. He is wearing boxer shorts in a hideous pattern which I have never seen before.

This exhibition of bad taste alone is enough to make me want to weep. But that's not the cause of the tears. I cry for myself and for Tom and for what's to become of us.

Chapter Five

'Take a little fresh mint, preferably from your own garden, two tablespoons of cottage cheese, a couple of good *pomodori*, smidgen of garlic – in the garlic press, puull-lease! – none of this dried-in-a-bottle stuff – and serve with pitta bread and Welsh butter. A side-sauce of pesto and *perfetto*! A light meal for the junior gourmet.'

Martin West, founder of *Adam's Apple*, the quarterly magazine 'for the man who puts gender on the agenda', stands at the breakfast-bar in his kitchen and makes supper for his children. Martin is thirty-eight and one of the new male tribe who are colonizing the women's pages of the daily newspapers. He is resident cookery writer for a national newspaper and for a glossy monthly.

In his column, Martin shares his joy when he discovers that if you mash cooked fish with leftover potato, goodness, you get FISH CAKES! The poor love can barely wait to rush into print.

Martin shares child care. A term which I've come to realize, in the case of him and his partner, Charlotte, means they share carnage. The offspring are allowed to rampage pretty much as they please, since 'boundaries are too authoritarian' and Martin has technically sacked himself from his role as father because he wants 'no truck with any patriarchy'.

The two have produced Carlos, five, Otis, three and fourteen-month-old Tristan.

In addition, there is Tabitha, eleven, the offspring of one of Charlotte's earlier liaisons.

'Look,' says Martin to me, as Otis pours tomato sauce on Tristan's head, much to the latter's delight. 'Interaction. Isn't that beautiful?'

In conversation, I am wary of Martin. He can slide me into a forty-five minute discussion on the ethical versus practical considerations of cloth and biodegradable nappies before I am even aware that there's been a change in topic.

As God is my witness, I have seen women many years past the menopause feel obliged to offer their views on such a subject simply because they have no wish to discourage Martin's enthusiasm. I am not nearly so fussy.

Martin is highly sensitive, or so he says. Each and every day, he is personally compelled to apologize for man's inhumanity to women. Or, more specifically, his own inhumanity. This evening is no exception.

'I was walking into the library with Carlos and there she was, Kay,' he tells me as he pours us both a glass of wine. 'I couldn't help myself. She had the most beautiful pair of breasts I have ever seen. They moved under the cloth, they were full and ripe. She was how I imagine wet-nurses must have looked.'

'Were there stains?' I ask.

'What?'

'Were there stains? You know, milk-stains? Perhaps she's breast-feeding?'

'Christ, Kay, sometimes you are so *basic*. I am speaking poetically here. Metaphorically she looked like a wet-nurse. Do you know what I mean?'

He doesn't wait for an answer. 'And, of course, I hated myself,' he says.

'How could I be so bloody sexist? How could I be so basic? So primitive? I mean, you wouldn't look at a man's arse or his cock or something like that, would you?'

I nod my head affirmatively but Martin doesn't notice. 'I have to say, Kay, that I felt quite proud that I did look at her in that way. And then I felt terrible that I felt proud because that's even worse than being sexist in the first place . . . Oh, Christ.'

This kind of behaviour, of course, requires a lot of introspection on Martin's part and a degree of boredom for any female who happens to be drawn into his 365-days-a-year confessional. That I can just about endure. What drives me crazy is Martin's insistence that women are somehow spiritually superior.

'You are so much *nicer* than men,' he always says. And, 'I wish I could be like you females, the rhythm of the month, the moon, that sort of thing. You're intuitively in touch with your feelings.'

While some men might hunger after a Lancia or a week's fly-fishing in Scotland, Martin is more likely to put PMT and labour contractions at the top of his most wanted list.

My view is that there is nothing wrong with Martin that a sex change wouldn't put right. He's not effeminate or gay but he is, at this point in his life, so aspirationally female it has reached the level of obsession. Martin prefers to call himself a Twenty-first Century Man; a man of the millennium.

He has flashes of humour but not enough to survive having his leg pulled by others in this delicate area. I once suggested, tongue-in-cheek, that he was post-masculinist. 'Are you taking the piss?' he demanded crossly.

Yet, in spite of it all, there is something about Martin that I really like. Tom says that's odd.

'Charlotte'll be here at eight,' Martin says. 'Where's your old man?'

'He's working. Where else? He said we should start without him if he's late.'

Otis – so called because he was allegedly conceived in a lift – has curled himself up in a ball on the kitchen floor and is asleep. Tristan is attempting to net the goldfish with a soap-powder dispenser. Carlos is 'killing' aliens with a squash racquet since no guns are allowed in the house.

'Something simple tonight,' Martin says. 'How about beef and *foie gras carpaccio* with truffle oil, chicken breast with juniper berries, and chocolate and strawberry roulade?'

I smile weakly.

A couple of hours later, Martin is behind a Berlin Wall of cookery books while Tom and I, Charlotte and Mike and Angela Robinson are sitting in the garden drinking Pimm's.

'God, you *have* lost a lot of weight,' Charlotte had said to me when she arrived. She almost always manages to make a compliment sound like an accusation. She had waved briefly to her children and swept upstairs. She descended fifteen minutes later looking majestic.

Charlotte is tall and solidly built. She has blonde-streaked hair and in the evening goes in for a lot of magenta and electric blue – to startlingly good effect. We met at university and for reasons best known to herself, Charlotte has determinedly stayed in touch. Once she decides you will be her friend, you will be her friend. She is seven years older than Martin and, initially, adamantly refused to have any children with him. Now, her fertility has become her future.

In the sixties, her career as a journalist began while she was still a student. She interviewed pop stars and usually got them into bed before the piece was published. In the seventies, she sent dispatches from various Sheraton and Hilton hotels around the world, mostly tear-jerking stuff about the down-trodden. In the early eighties, she became a feminist columnist of sorts.

She provided a diet of weak puns and uninformed opinion, sporadically making references to how nasty men might be (which is how she met Martin who agreed with her whole-heartedly) but much more often having a dig at her own gender. Charlotte also gave good television.

Then, in 1990, somewhere on the way to Studio Three at Century Television in Birmingham late one Friday night, Charlotte saw the light.

Charlotte (then with a three-month-old baby), suddenly realized that society was going to hell and back because women had *drifted away from their natural place*. Mothers had *denied their natural instincts*. Charlotte became a born-again traditional woman.

Not one to keep such things to herself, she wrote a 4,000 word article for the *Sunday Telegraph* reneging on all her previous experience, punishing herself for her earlier promiscuity, castigating Quality Time, rubbishing feminism, sympathizing with all the thousands of children neglected by their working mothers, praising the powerful man and launching a crusade: the Mission for Undervalued Motherhood, MUM. Slogan: If You're in the Home, You're in Their Heart.

'If women want children then they've got to accept that they forfeit their careers. Who wants all those hormones dripping over the market-place?' she crowed.

The call for all women to return to the home, exercise their maternal instinct to the full, acknowledge man as the head of the household and reject any shame that 'others' might wish to impose on them for holding such views, resulted in thousands of women signing up for the cause.

Charlotte has found herself, yet again, in a new decade with a new role. She is now almost continuously away at conferences, or on television and radio, hyping her books, appearing in public debates. The fact that until recently she appeared to be continually pregnant has been no disadvantage.

At the same time, her followers have been far too enthused to draw the obvious conclusion: MUM flourishes so successfully and has such a fully committed leader for one reason alone. The West household certainly has a mother at home but it isn't Charlotte – it's Martin; happy to be chief cook and nappy-washer while his wife proselytizes.

I suspect Charlotte finds Carlos, Tabitha, Tristan and Otis a touch tedious. But, to her public, she is MC – Maternally Correct – because no nanny, no au pair, no child-minder has ever crossed the threshold. One result is that at ten p.m. this evening, the children have happily fallen asleep in odd corners of the house, the kitchen is chaos and Martin is still enthusiastically slaving over a hot stove. While, in the garden, Charlotte works hard on me because I refuse to have any sense of guilt whatsoever for the crime of always having had a job.

'Can you honestly, hand on heart, say the twins have never suffered?' she trumpets.

'I can honestly hand on heart say they would have suffered a helluva lot more if I'd been a full-time mother.'

'Nonsense!' she declares. Charlotte is rarely confronted with her own somewhat patchy maternal record, and I'm not about to start now; one battle front at a time has always been my motto.

Tom, who arrived late, has barely spoken to me except to announce that he is away next week for two days, delivering a speech at a conference in Newcastle.

Charlotte turns to Angela Robinson, who runs the South London sector of MUM.

'It's terribly exciting,' she says, 'you know Tom has agreed to appear in the talks we're giving around the country as well as the discussion at the end of the telly programme? Haven't you, sweetie?' Tom nods.

'How's it going?' he asks.

'The series is almost finished,' Charlotte froths. 'We've just got to record the commentary then we're up and running.'

'What's all this about then?' Mike Robinson asks, sounding not remotely interested.

'Oh, God, Michael, don't you ever listen?' Angela says in the tone she reserves only for her husband.

Mike Robinson is in his mid-thirties, an employee of Hebrides plc, the international conglomerate which provides friendly Bettabuy supermarkets (without packers or loos or crèches) in your neighbourhood.

Angela says (frequently) that her husband is a high-flyer. She also prefers him to refer to Hebrides plc rather than Bettabuy. The latter she regards as naff. Mike and Angela used to be our neighbours before Angela, ever upwardly mobile, moved to a larger house and a greater burden of negative equity. Mike and I still occasionally have a drink or a cup of coffee. Angela I avoid. She once told me that I was 'a plateau person'.

'You're going nowhere, Kay.'

Angela has chosen to stay at home and care for one son and two daughters, but she's the most (vicariously) ambitious woman I have ever met, constantly planning Mike's next career move. I am allergic to ambition.

'Christ, Tom, you haven't signed up with Mums' Army, have you?' Mike asks.

'No, nothing like that. Charlotte and I decided we could be mutually useful. My book *Father Forward* is coming out in paperback, and so is Charlotte's book, *Does Mother Know Best?*. So I've made a small contribution to Charlotte's series, and she's in my documentary and we're going on a quick jaunt round the country. Nothing too elaborate.

'It's worked quite well actually,' Tom continues, smugness oozing out of him like ectoplasm.

I feel nauseous. Charlotte turns to Tom: 'That little researcher you recommended proved a gem, Tom. A real goer – full of beans. What's her name . . . Barbara . . . Betty?'

'I've forgotten,' Tom says smoothly. 'I've got her name somewhere in the office.'

'Brenda! That's it. Brenda Styles,' Charlotte shrieks. 'She says she knows you quite well . . .'

Tom doesn't miss a beat. 'Really?' he says.

Then Martin, Otis asleep in his arms, shouts from the French windows, 'It's ready. A feast awaits you,' he adds. Modesty in the kitchen is not Martin's strong point.

As we move inside, Tom suddenly smiles at me; such an open, friendly, *honest* face.

In the car on the way home, I resolve to say nothing, not to speak, to stay calm. It lasts until I cross our threshold. 'Tom,' I say. 'I have to talk to you.'

'Not now. I'm dead beat.'

'It's got to be now. I can't stand all these lies.' Tom groans. 'You're having an affair. I know you are. I can tell.' Why don't I just tell him I've read his mail? Am I *scared* of this man?

Tom runs his fingers through his hair, rubs his eyes. 'Of course I'm not bloody well having an affair. You know where I am every minute of the day.'

'What about Scotland?'

'What about it?'

'I called the letting agent. You left after four days.' This is a lie, I never called but it works.

'Well, I did. That's true. But I told you why. I had a couple of meetings in Glasgow.'

'No, you didn't. You lied. You're a liar. You're always lying.'

This is a bad move on my part. Tom claims injury time. 'I'm not putting up with this,' he shouts back. 'Who the hell are you to stand in bloody judgement?'

He stamps upstairs and I hear the key turn in the lock of his study. I sit at the kitchen table and wait five minutes. On time, Tom comes back down the stairs.

'OK,' he says. 'I lied. I'm sorry. I haven't had an affair but I have been out a couple of times with a woman I met on a plane. She lives in Moscow, she's no threat. It was stupid. Nothing. I don't even like her particularly. She's barely here. I shan't see her again. I'm sorry. What else can I say?'

Dispassionately I watch him. This is happening to somebody else, not me. I feel no pain. But I do know. *I don't want him to leave.* I want us to go back to what we were.

'When you say Russian, do you mean Russian?' I press him. 'Are you sure you don't mean Latvian or Belorussian or . . . You know, everything is different now.'

'For God's sake, Kay, she lives in Moscow. She's Russian,' he adds emphatically.

I stand up and as I walk out of the kitchen, I pass the unmarked chart on the fridge door. I turn to Tom.

'Brenda Styles,' I say, 'is a bloody funny name for a Russian, don't you think?'

The next morning, I swim early. P.P. has left a message for me with the attendant.

If you feel like a cup of coffee, call in. I live around the corner. Best wishes, Rosemary Witherspoon.

By the end of my swim I've decided that a cup of coffee is exactly what I need.

Twenty Trinity Street is a long, lean building in a genteel square. It looks as if it might once have been a warehouse. A small brass plaque says *Venus Inc.* A young man in white opens the door and I walk straight into a vast room; white walls, white floor, a tube of neon light like a squiggle of toothpaste written across the white ceiling.

Along one of the walls are large framed black and white photographs. They are of the same medium-built man. His face is obscured by a black net like a macabre wedding veil; he wears a suspender belt, stockings, high heels and nothing else. In some photographs his penis is erect.

On the other wall are framed covers of *Venus* magazine. Each cover shows a famous work of art with no hint of what's within.

The man notices my interest. 'They put it together upstairs,' he says, nodding at the magazines.

'Who's the editor?'

'Rosemary. The person you've come to see.'

In the centre of the room is a giant rotating copy of the Venus de Milo, gently spotlit. Across one shoulder and held in the crook of her neck is balanced what appears to be a large log.

'What's that?' I ask the young man.

'What is it?' This apparently confirms for him my status as a vintage wimp.

As I walk slightly closer, I understand his bewilderment. 'It' is a giant vibrator made of the same fake marble as the statue.

'A joke?' I suggest feebly.

'Certainly not,' says the young man primly. 'Sex is our business and we take it very seriously indeed.'

Engraved at the foot of the statue are the words *Venus Incorporated. In the business of being 'armless.*

'Stairs or lift?' the young man asks. 'Venus believes in good health. Healthy life, healthy profits.'

'Lift,' I say. And we ascend in a glass elevator. We pass the second floor where a gang of people work in an open-space office. We stop at the third. Suddenly, for no clear reason, I am nervous.

'Rosemary's in the AER,' the young man says.

'AER?'

He sighs. 'Audio Erotica Room. Cyborgasms, you know.'

I don't, but I'm not about to reveal any more of my ignorance.

He presses a button and a panel of white wall slides open to reveal pitch black.

'In there,' the man says. 'You go in there.'

'I do?' He nods his head encouragingly.

As I step into the gloom, the panel slides back. It is warm. My eyes adjust to the dark. I hear a rustle and suddenly a voice, Rosemary's voice whispers so close to my ear that I jump.

'Lie down.'

It is Rosemary's voice but there is no Rosemary.

A couch covered in black satin silently slides out of a wall. 'Enjoy,' says another voice. All this for a cup of coffee? I ask myself.

Very gingerly, I lie down on the couch about as relaxed as someone who's just been told she's going to be lobotomized without the benefit of an anaesthetic. Suddenly, all around me, everywhere, I hear voices softly moaning; breath rising and falling, sometimes quicker, sometimes more slowly. The sounds have a strange hypnotic rhythm.

The room is empty. Yet the sounds fill the place. I begin to feel less tense. Then it occurs to me someone may have one of those infrared cameras. Someone might be *spying on me*. 'Relax,' says Rosemary's voice. 'What you are about to hear and feel is highly explicit audio-sensual erotica. Welcome, Kay, welcome to the world of cybersex . . .'

The room darkens again, it is ink-black. The couch seems to be moving under me. My heart stops. A hand has appeared. Two hands. *No shame, only pleasure in erotronics*, says a man's voice in my right ear. But still there is no one.

Am I frightened? No. Do I want to leave? Absolutely not. This is a ghost train for the libido and much more preferable to a mid-morning cup of coffee.

The hands glide to my feet and remove my shoes. I feel naked. Each hand begins to massage a foot. The hands wear gloves and they feel almost human but they are not. Above me, it sounds as if a couple are moving slowly, leisurely but resolutely to a climax.

'Oh, yes, I like that, I like that . . .'

'Let me take you, let me have you,' says the man's voice. 'Take it all . . .'

As a first-time voyeur – audeur? – I am enjoying every minute. Something like silk strokes my arms, my legs. 'Sit up,' says a male voice. I am safe, relaxed, almost sleepy.

My jacket and shirt are removed by three more sets of 'hands'. I am naked from the waist up but because it is dark, I feel safe; the whispers and sighs make no words that are recognizable but the message is unmistakably sensual.

Yessss, a man's voice hisses gently in my ear.

A hand is stroking my inner thigh. Is this when I make my excuses and leave? As if reading my mind, a matronly voice speaks softly.

'You can leave at any time. You can stop at any time. You are not being filmed or observed. You are in total control. You have a button on your left side which once pressed returns you to reality . . .

'If you wish to stay and you desire some particular service, you only have to speak and the hands will do as you dictate.'

I stay resolutely silent and my hand hovers above the button. Is this any way for a grown woman to behave? What would Tom say? Worse: what if I like it? What if I become an audio-erotic freak? But at least this isn't adultery. What . . .? What the hell—

A young male voice laughs to my right. As if on cue, the whispers and sighs and the sounds of wind and rain and the sea breaking on rocks, mingle and fill the room. The room is blacker still, I can no longer see the hands but I can feel six of them in play; their touch is soft but measured like no human stroke can ever be.

One hand gently kneads my inner thigh, one is making circular patterns on my chest, two are rubbing my temples and one is massaging my foot. And where is the sixth?

It has gently travelled down from my stomach and is inside my pants. The touch is light and not at all insistent. It is precisely because it has no desire propelling it, no possibility of danger, no price attached, that I relax in a way that I haven't for a very long time.

The hand gently inserts two fingers inside my labia, and with small, steady movements, coaxes not just the clitoris but the area around it.

'More,' I hear myself say. 'More . . .' I have never asked for more in my life.

Instead, first, I have the sensation that I am falling in slow motion through layers and layers of cotton wool. Then, it's as if Chinese crackers have been set off in every chink and corner of my body.

I come for what feels like minutes but is only seconds. I come with a sense of total relaxation – and still the other five hands stroke and soothe. And then they're gone.

There is silence.

Very slowly, the room becomes lighter and lighter. Muzak takes over. I stand up, dress, the couch slides into the wall. Ridiculously, the Max Bygraves song repeats itself in my brain. *You need hands* . . . Tom's right. I am flippant.

Gradually, on three sides of me, the 'walls' slide back to reveal a large room. Windows look out over Covent Garden; the décor is cream with plants everywhere and there are four bronze statues. In one corner is a massive desk. On its left is a table which, at first, looks as if it is covered in a job lot from an artificial-limbs factory. None are hands I recognize.

Rosemary, in granny specs, dressed like Jackie Onassis circa 1960, with a short black wig and a beautifully cut pale blue sheath-dress, stands in the middle of the room with a cup in her hand.

'Coffee?' she asks.

Chapter Six

The editorial floor of Venus Inc. holds a number of earnest young men and women, identically dressed in black, who show all the joy of a team of undertakers who've just been told that the secret of eternal life is now known.

Rosemary comes to a stop in front of an illuminated table on which several dozen slides are spread. 'Have a look,' she instructs. She hands me an eyeglass.

Gingerly, I inspect a variety of naked men. They remind me of the occasion when I took the twins, aged four, to the Reptile House at London Zoo. The visit coincided with teatime. The twins stared fascinated as the boa constrictor swallowed whole, several creatures which bore a striking resemblance to our family guinea-pigs.

The snake's body acquired several bulges which, much to the girls' delight, glided intact down its trunk; slow, mobile muscles. I've never looked at a man with weightlifters' proportions in quite the same way since. I constantly expect his pectorals to begin inching earthwards.

In the slides before me, each man strikes a pose which is singularly unnatural, veins protruding from over-exercised limbs like gorged worms. These models also appear to have been castrated since cocks and balls are either concealed by legs or arms or hands or are shadowed out completely. The only erection in sight is the scaffolding across which some of them are draped, in some cases, a touch too coyly for my taste.

Female cheesecake has changed with the times. Today's waifs are but a shadow of the form of Jane Russell and Betty Grable and Sophia Loren. But male beefcake is stuck immutably in the fifties; Charles Atlas still rules.

'So, what do you think? What do you honestly think?' Rosemary persists. I decide to be honest.

'Dead boring. None of this lot look human. They look so self-obsessed, they probably think the G-spot is the name of the best gym in town.'

'What about him, then?' Rosemary asks. She shows me three black and white photographs of a man in his late thirties. He has an average face, a square, thickset body and beautiful eyes. The third photograph indicates that his bum isn't bad either; compact, firm without looking like a couple of boulders from the Grand Canyon.

In the first photograph, the man is curled in a foetal position, asleep. In the second, he is sitting naked at a breakfast-bar eating cereal and laughing. The third shows him back to camera, his penis only just visible between slightly open legs.

'He's more like it, I suppose,' I say.

'Why do you like him and not the others?' Rosemary persists.

'I suppose it's because he looks . . . Well, he looks normal,' I offer feebly. 'He looks . . . he looks like a human being with a history. He looks as if he might be interested in somebody run-of-the-mill like me or you.'

I pause as several strands of Rosemary's wig brush my cheek. 'Well, perhaps not *you* exactly . . .'

'*That's* what's missing,' Rosemary suddenly shouts. 'That's why the magazine doesn't work. Get me real people! I want real people! Klaus!' she yells.

78

'Klaus, fetch in some ordinary men. Ordinary, *straight* men,' she adds as Klaus sashays past.

'Coffee? Turkish, Greek, filter, cona or cappuccino?' Peter, Rosemary's male secretary is so neat you feel that his shirt-tails are probably tucked into his boxer shorts like the corners of a hospital bed.

'Herb tea? Camomile, peppermint, fennel?' he intones. His sense of humour went with his umbilical cord.

'Mineral water – Badoit, Perrier, San Pellegrino? Liqueur? Grand Marnier, Courvoisier, Amare—?'

'You wouldn't have any Alka-Seltzer, would you, please?' I ask.

His mouth tightens a little. Rosemary and I have had lunch in her office – a vegetarian concoction produced by a very jolly young woman with apparently a deep affection for red chilli, since it appeared in every course.

I ate sparingly, memories of Brenda ruining every mouthful, but still the spice has caused acute indigestion. Rosemary ate even less but she consumed so many cigarettes that as I sat opposite her, my mouth afire and her body wreathed in smoke, I had the strongest conviction I'd ended up in hell. The roar was no more. I was lunching with the Devil.

Now, as I listen, I begin to think that if not the Devil, then Rosemary just might turn out to be my Avenging Angel.

'I want you,' she begins.

Startled, I spill my Alka-Seltzer. Then she continues, 'I want you on board this magazine.'

She stands up, presses a button on her desk and the room goes dark. I look at the robotic limbs on the table and think, Oh, God not again. Thankfully, they remain still. Instead, a screen descends.

Click! The screen is filled with previous covers of *Venus*, followed by a quick flip through some of the photo spreads and features.

It is not a pretty sight. I've never bought *Venus* or any magazine like it and now I know why. *Venus* seems to be a man's idea of what women *ought* to fancy in a soft-porn format. Anything John has in *Penthouse*, Janet must have the equivalent in her female version. But in erotica, perhaps men and women are equal in their appetite, but different in what satisfies it. *Venus*, in my opinion, has no humour, no style.

Women like to put a person to the pudenda. They like their sex less disembodied. Or so I've read. I examine one of *Venus*'s better photo-captions under an impossibly chiselled 'gypsy' wearing one gold earring and nothing else.

'*Mario is a big man*,' the caption reads. '*He lives in the wilds of Spain. He plays guitar and rides bareback. His dream is to make love to the woman of his dreams under the Spanish stars.*'

Just visible on his left buttock is a small heart-shaped tattoo which, when I borrow Rosemary's eyeglass, bears the name, 'Tracy'. Perhaps 'Mario' entrapped a wandering spirit from a Benidorm package holiday, on the Spanish plains?

Rosemary registers my interest and shrugs. 'All right, he comes from Bromley. But women like escapism. They don't want to know he's called Steve and is a part-time fireman. Do they?' she asks, suddenly uncertain. 'I'll be frank,' she adds without waiting for an answer. 'As you might guess, *Venus* has a problem.' Rosemary taps her nails on the desk in a rhythm of irritation.

'We have a circulation of two hundred and fifty thousand.'

'Isn't that pretty good?' I ask.

'It would be if the readers were women, but God knows how many are gay male, and that makes it very difficult for us to attract the right sort of advertisers. What we're after is the SAFCITT reader.'

'SAFCITT?' I repeat.

'SAFCITT stands for Sexually Aware Female Consumer In Their Thirties – and beyond, of course,' she adds hastily. 'We want to attract the woman who is interested in sex as a fantasy or as a realized activity in her life and – and this is the difference from ten to fifteen years ago – who is prepared to spend money on that interest. We know there is huge potential in the market and, so far, only the male pocket has been picked, so to speak.

'Now, of course I care deeply about a woman's right to express herself fully and I think sexuality is an important area of expansion.' Rosemary sounds like a preacher who has given one sermon too many.

'So, in the name of—'

'Emancipation? Equality? Erotica?' provides Peter the ever-ready secretary.

'Profits?' I suggest tentatively.

Rosemary is fleetingly undecided how to react. Then she smiles, inserts another cigarette into her holder and takes her time before she speaks.

'Look, let's get this straight,' she says equably. 'Of course I'm interested in money. But I'm talking conviction here. I'm talking a crusade. I'm talking sexual politics. I'm talking about leading women out of the wilderness of their own inhibitions and into the deep, dark, unending and totally pleasurable tunnel of their own lust.

'That's the message of *Venus*. That's its role. I am a sex-positive Feminist,' Rosemary announces, hands on hips, wig swinging. 'I am a Spinster with a capital S and proud of that position in society. It is not a role I wish to relinquish.

'I don't want any favours. I want no concessions. I believe that sexual intercourse is good for the ego, the body, the mind. It releases energy, it kick-starts creativity.'

Rosemary suddenly strides over to the sofa where I am struggling to restrain the burps induced by the Alka-Seltzer. Her face close to mine, she says,

'But do you know what buggers it all up?'

I'm desperate to answer because out of the corner of my eye, I see that Peter's mouth is opening, a list at point of delivery.

'Guilt?' I suggest quickly.

'OHB,' Rosemary says.

'OHB?'

'Other Human Beings,' Rosemary explains.

'Other Human Beings. I like sex, I can't stand the chat, the lies, the post-coital fag, the awful realization when you're in his bathroom that the man you have just shared a bed with has skid-marks on his underpants. I hate the fake intimacy. What I believe in is an honest exchange. I don't want love, so leave love out of it.'

'You don't want love?' I say. 'Actually, it can be quite pleasant.'

'If and when I seek love, I'll look for it,' Rosemary says dismissively. 'For now, I prefer sex. And what better than to be able to do it when you want, with only yourself involved? *Venus* is at hand to help you in the enterprise. *That* is my crusade.'

If Rosemary is interested in mass masturbation, it's hardly a new idea.

'Come with me,' she commands.

A man has appeared by her side with what initially looks like a giant-size Duracell battery on his head. A great deal of electrical equipment runs from the 'battery' to the large glove he wears on his right hand. He is as expressionless as the members of the *Venus* staff I've already met.

'Another one of your live wires?' I ask Rosemary's disappearing back.

The basement of Venus Inc. is vast, lit with a soft green light and divided into cavernous rooms, each with its own frieze of computers. In one room, a human body – it's impossible to tell whether it is male or female – reclines in a highly padded armchair. Its head is concealed by a helmet which gives the person the appearance of a hornet. The body is wired to several machines. Every so often, it shakes or lifts.

'Strap in, turn on,' says Rosemary. 'Welcome to cybersex, the wonder of the virtual-reality orgasm. James, would you explain, please.'

'Are you familiar with virtual reality?' James asks. The memory of the morning's encounter makes me blush. In this gloom, I probably just go a deeper shade of green.

'Virtual reality allows the computer to create a "real" world. It's a world that doesn't exist but you experience it as if it does through the use of computer graphics and high tech. Here, we are working on immersive VR. You are completely enclosed in the artificial world, you "see" through these "eyephones", you "feel" through these high-tech gloves.

'It's a three-dimensional experience, so you can instruct the figure or figures to do as you wish, to deal with you as you wish,' James speaks in the kind of voice you might expect to hear from a guide on his 250th tour of the original Kentucky Fried Chicken plant.

'The images are still lacking in detail and flawed but those on the team who have experienced cybersex – albeit in this crude form – say it's highly satisfactory,' he continues.

'It's also safe, physically and mentally. No broken hearts; no sexually transmitted diseases. In sum, once this project is perfected, you or any other individual can tune in and make the earth move, *as and when you choose*.'

James clicks his heels to indicate his spiel is at an end.

'What about companionship, getting to know someone, the chase, that sort of thing . . . Isn't that all part of desire too?' I ask, and trail off. The irrational is clearly out of place here. This is sex reduced to a purely physical reaction.

'If you want to waste time on that sort of stuff, then feel free. I'm backing SAM,' Rosemary says, a shade impatiently.

'SAM?' I ask.

'The Simulator Advanced Model, the VR project you're looking at here. More accurately, it should be called SUE – The Simulator Under Extension. But a lot of the women on the team found it inhibited their performance. They couldn't relax, not when it was called SUE,' Rosemary explains.

'What? You mean they acted as if the computer was a human being? A woman? A *lesbian* robot?' I try not to smile.

'Yes, exactly that,' Rosemary says. 'Funny things, people.'

'We face a difficulty,' Rosemary explains. We are back in her office and, to my surprise, she has several issues of *Tangiers*, the magazine for which I've written for years, on her desk. I try to remember some of the subjects I've covered recently.

It must have been the jelly. The only article I've produced which is even faintly erotic was a supposedly humorous piece on the pleasures of jelly. All the rest have been an odd mix of profiles and interviews and polemical pieces. It must have been the jelly.

'Virtual Reality is going well,' Rosemary continues. 'The plan is to have a centre in every major town by the year 2010. A truly adult leisure centre. The sale of sexual aids is going brilliantly. The videos we import from the States are so-so. But in the magazine we have a problem – and you can help to solve it.'

As Rosemary lectures, I muse on the results should she ask for references from those nearest and dearest to me. Among the many skills at which I am considered cack-handed including driving, nurturing goldfish (fourteen have died so far), playing chess, handling filo pastry, typing, singing, keeping accounts and performing fellatio, it's the last in which I am most deficient.

Within a few months of meeting me, Tom had to spend several days with a bandage round his penis. He told his colleagues in the football team for which he then played that he'd caught his cock in a drawer. But he and I knew differently.

'So, will you do it?' Rosemary asks.

'Do what?'

'Write for us. Become our roving correspondent. Set a different tone for *Venus*. Make sex warm, humorous, real enough to be part of female fantasy – if you know what I mean.

'You can write what you like, go where you please, Scarborough, Santa Fe, Saigon—'

'Sort of *Around the World in Eighty Lays?*'

'Kipling? Conrad? Collins?' says the secretary, back in his stride.

'Jules Verne, Peter,' Rosemary says smiling. 'So how about it?' she repeats the question.

'Look, I'm really sorry,' I begin.

'If you're worried, you can use a pseudonym,' Rosemary interrupts. 'We won't tell a soul, will we, Peter?'

Peter is already on the job. 'Patricia? Louise? Felicia?'

I shudder.

'Try it for three months,' Rosemary persists. Her face is so close to mine, I can almost see myself mirrored in her lip-gloss.

'Or don't go anywhere, if you prefer. Stay at home. Make it up, like real journalists do.'

'It's very kind of you,' I try again.

I am flattered. No one in journalism has ever sought me out before. And Rosemary doesn't even know that I can do the job.

'This is virgin territory,' she says. I start to smile and then remind myself: at Venus Inc., *sex is a serious business*.

'We have to take a risk because we have no precedents. I've read your stuff, you've got four ingredients which make me think it could work. You are passionate.'

'I am?' I say dubiously, certain that she has no evidence of this.

'You have a sense of humour. You are curious and you are sensuous. Oh, and your writing's not bad.'

Rosemary suddenly stands and raises her right hand in a salute not unknown in the Third Reich.

'Above all,' she bellows and Peter beams, 'you are brave! You are brave enough to encourage other women to do as they really wish to do. You can lead by example; stimulate by description; challenge deep-rooted fears with wit—'

Now I know she's lying.

'OK. The bravery bit is bullshit,' Rosemary concedes, resuming her seat. 'But I really do think you could have enormous fun. And convey that to the reader.

'Look on it as a voyage of discovery, Kay. A safe voyage of discovery. You are exempt from guilt. You are only doing your job. Can't do better than that, can I? And I'll pay two grand an article, plus expenses.'

The money helps me to make up my mind.

'I'm really sorry,' I say. 'I've enjoyed being here and thank you very much for having me, but I couldn't possibly take the job. Apart from anything else, I'm happily married and to be honest, I'm probably too conservative and inhibited. And boring.'

The longer I speak, the more interesting the job sounds.

'And as I said, I'm married. Happily. Very happily.'

Rosemary throws her arms around me and gives me a huge kiss on each cheek.

'You are a doll,' she says. 'A real doll. Think about it. Don't rush into a decision. *Venus* has been around a very long time. We're not going to go away overnight. So why don't we talk when I see you tomorrow?'

'Tomorrow?'

'At the pool . . . Oh, and Kay,' I stop at the door. 'Why don't you keep this as a souvenir?'

She walks over and gives me a mechanical hand, concealed in a chamois-leather glove, on a small stand. My first trophy.

'The key to this,' Rosemary says, pointing at the hand, 'Is that it only works because *you* want it to work. Life can be so simple when we want it to be, can't it?'

At home, opening the fridge for a pint of milk, my attention is caught by the workshop chart on the door. Does this morning's robotic experience count? I fill in one of the squares with a circle and a dot. And then I add a question mark.

Tom is away in Newcastle, the fridge is empty, so on automatic pilot I decide to go to the supermarket. Why? Because my mother always programmed me to believe that a household without at least a stock of assorted tins of food and an overloaded fridge is a household *unprepared*.

My mother, one day, will defy all those who say you can't take it with you. Wedged around her in the coffin will be a complete range of canned meats, in case someone decides to call.

Before I leave the house, I phone Medicatis.

'Press and information please,' I say in my most authoritative tone.

'Hello, this is the South London Free Press here,' I improvise, my eye falling on the newspaper, folded on the kitchen table. 'Is your conference in Newcastle, this week?

'Yesterday and today . . . Oh I see. Usual place, is it? Gosforth Park Hotel, you say. Of course it is. Yes, I'd like the number, thank you very much.'

I dial the hotel. 'Hello, could I leave a message for Dr Tom Evans, please? Yes, I'm sure he's staying there.'

Silence as the receptionist searches for the name. When she returns to the phone to tell me he isn't registered, I try another tack.

'Is there a Mr and Mrs Styles registered? There is? Could you leave a message for Mr Styles, please. Could you say his wife, yes, his wife, W-I-F-E, called to say that she's out for the next two days?'

I put the phone down and I hear not so much a roar as a tiny whisper.

Oh, Tom.

Chapter Seven

In Asda, I am suddenly struck. I am suddenly struck by how much variety is on offer when it comes to light-bulbs; shapes, colours, screw or non-screw, basic or luxury packaging. This *has* to be one of the real privileges of being a home-maker and a fully-fledged consumer in the modern western world.

Another perk is the facility with which the process of agonizing over my serious marital dilemma dances to the tune of various ancient advertising jingles inside my head.

At what point did my sex life with Tom go off the boil? And why? *All around the house spring-clean with Flash!* What if Tom wants a divorce? Who'll want me now?

> *The Esso sign means happy motoring,*
> *The Esso sign means happy motoring,*
> *The Esso sign means happy motoring, call at the Esso sign . . .*

Why don't I face up to the fact that my life is a mess and only one person is responsible for it, me? Face up to it and then do *something* about it?

Just one Cornetto . . . Just one Cornetto . . . (Destined to become one of the classic mental ram-raiders of all time.)

To strangle Brenda – or simply to incinerate her alive? *Hands that do dishes can feel soft as your face, soft as your face . . .*

I decide that the only immediate way out of this torment is to concentrate on which light-bulb offers the best value. If Charlotte were here she would no doubt award me MUM's medal of honour for such housewifely diligence. In truth, I'm falling back on a habit acquired in childhood.

I tell myself that if I can get twenty-four light-bulbs in the trolley plus my other shopping and put it through the checkout without breaking a single light, then Tom will appear tonight and everything will be back to normal, except better.

The infant version of this at the age of ten, *circa* 1957 or 1958, was: 'If I can get from the wardrobe and on to the bed in four jumps, then my mum won't find out from Peter and Fiona's mum that I played doctors and nurses with Peter and Fiona.'

Thirty-four years on, it ain't quite so easy. Even if I pass a hundred small tests, I know nothing is going to change the fact that I am in a situation over which I don't have any control. And I lack the courage to seize it.

My tears start to fall. Why are tears always so much larger in public than when you cry alone?

I choose a mix of two dozen light-bulbs and shove them into the trolley. I try to wipe my eyes surreptitiously on my coat-sleeve as I do so. Nobody loves me any more. Plop, plop. *Perhaps nobody ever did.* Plop, plop, plop. Self-pity is something I do best.

'Anything wrong?' Mike Robinson has Henry in the trolley and a week's supply of food.

'Hello, Mike. Wrong? No, nothing at all. Nearly finished?'

'Yep,' Mike says.

Charlotte calls him bland. I disagree. Mike is measured; he has no desire to hold the floor at dinner parties; he waits for others to take an interest in him – and he's funny. He has a self-deprecating sense of humour which, of course, makes every woman rush to offer reassurance.

'Oh no, Mike, I'm *sure* you're terrific with the kids . . .' 'Oh, come on, Mike, I bet your work colleagues don't *really* see you like that!'

What we women don't understand is that when Mike puts himself down, *he is only joking*.

'Well, I've got the loo paper which I forgot the last time and I've got extra-lean minced meat. Mustn't forget the *extra-lean*, you know how little things mean a lot,' Mike says. 'But I'll be damned for the faggots and peas.'

'Why?'

'Angela does not regard them as socially acceptable cuisine. Meatballs, yes. Faggots, no; prosciutto yes, corned beef, no; Bel Paese yes, Dairylea cream cheese, no, no, no.

'Angela also talks the international language of microwave. I don't. It's one of my many failings, I'm afraid . . .'

'Come on, Mike,' I fall into habit. 'You cope with the shopping really well.'

Mike could, of course, shop at Bettabuy. As a senior executive, he'd receive a 25 per cent discount and enjoy home delivery, but Angela says Bettabuy's image is too down-market. Another source of contention is that Angela doesn't just send Mike shopping. She sends him shopping *with a list*.

'She wants me to do my bit but strictly under orders. No deviation, repetition or hesitation – just get what's on the list. Where's the creativity in that?' he says in mock anger.

On the one occasion when Mike opted for free expression and brought home his own choice of goods, Angela took to her bed with a migraine for three days. Who says some women don't wield any power in the home?

'Fancy a cup of tea?' Mike asks. Every Saturday he plays squash (it used to be football but Angela felt that wasn't aspirational enough). Every Tuesday, the Robinsons go to the cinema. Every Friday, they entertain or are entertained by others. This is followed by sex. Sex also occurs on a Wednesday. But Angela is having second thoughts about this, she says.

A couple of months ago, she read some American research on

the Love Lives of the Baby Boomers which, according to her, conclusively proved that we have all been conned. The national average for copulation is not twice a week but once and, in some cases, *even less*.

Rations consequently may well be cut back in the Robinson household. As far as Angela is concerned, sex is not something she does for pleasure with her loved one. It's something, she says, she 'gives him', to a) prevent him going off elsewhere in search of it and b) to keep him docile.

'The key to husbands,' Angela once told me, clearly disapproving of the way I failed to handle mine, 'is to tell them that there is always a choice but to indicate firmly by body language, moods, approval, that there is only one serious option. Yours.'

Angela is in her early thirties but untouched by any modern trends in sexual politics. She comes from a long line of matriarchs who believed that manipulation promises the best rewards. Her daughters will be exactly the same.

I say 'her' daughters because that is how Angela views them. Any contribution Mike has made since their conception is severely downplayed to the point of active exclusion.

'My idea of a nightmare,' Angela says often, 'is for one of the children to wake up in the middle of the night and call for Daddy. I'd die. I'd really die. I mean what are women *for*, what are *mothers* for, if it's not to feel wanted?'

Suggest to Angela that Mike as a father might need to feel wanted too and she smiles grimly.

'Maternal instinct,' she once explained to me. 'He hasn't got it. So it's no contest. He occasionally does put the children to bed, but somehow he just doesn't do it *right*. I find that so infuriating, don't you?'

Angela's addiction to control is the other extreme of my apparent inability to exercise it at all. She views her obsession not as a malfunction in her character but as the essential lifebelt which will get her and her family, including her husband, through the dangerous sea of unpredictability which she believes contemporary life has become.

In practice, this means that the Robinsons do less and less outside the home. They are caged in by Angela's fears. Ask them out for a Sunday-morning walk and the answer is no, because Angela can't then cook the roast lunch, *which they always have*, and she certainly isn't going to stay in on her own.

Ask the family to come away for a weekend and Angela says no, because 'All three of my little ones hate to have their routine broken. It takes weeks to get them settled down.'

So why does Mike accept Angela's strait-jacket apparently without protest? My view is that Angela's ability to plan, her ambitions for him, her hold on the household were probably precisely some of the qualities which attracted him to her in the first place. Now, who knows?

Mike's friends can't understand what he sees in her; Angela's friends can't fathom what she sees in him. But I've always assumed that as a couple they were happy enough, secure in their own little conundrum.

At the cash till, the assistant checks through my two dozen light-bulbs.

'Afraid of the dark, are we, love?' she remarks. I smile politely.

'I buy them to smash up,' I reply conversationally.

'No need for sarcasm,' she bridles.

It's true. I smash the bulbs and use the filaments to construct brooches for Kitchen Sync. At this point, Henry, aged four, opts for a demonstration. He helps himself to two bulbs out of my bag and stamps on each.

'Henry,' chastises Mike, 'you're a little bastard.' Henry smiles delightedly. I'd rather have Mike's direct approach any time. If

Martin were here with Carlos, he would have given the five-year-old a bear-hug and told him, 'It's all right to be angry. It's good to share your pain.'

Not with my bloody light-bulbs it isn't.

'Sorry, Auntie Kay,' Henry smiles.

Perhaps he isn't such a little bastard after all.

'How's it going then?' I ask Mike. We sit in the supermarket cafeteria with two cups of tea the colour of oak. 'Fine, fine. How are you?'

'Nothing to complain about.'

'Tom all right?'

'Fine, fine. Busy, of course. But then he always is.'

Alarmingly, I feel my eyes fill with tears again. This will not do.

'Can I ask you something?' Mike suddenly says. 'When the girls were younger, you know, when they were small, what did Tom used to do . . . about them I mean?' Mike watches as Henry uses a spoon to mix orange squash and a doughnut in a cup.

'How do you mean what did Tom do? He used to take them to the zoo; go on bike-rides, that sort of thing . . . Well, perhaps one bike-ride is a bit more accurate.'

'No, I mean really *do*. Was he around much? Did he know when their first tooth fell out? Did he get them up in the morning, put them to bed, take them to the dentist? Did he go away with them on a holiday by himself?'

'By himself?'

'Yes, by himself, be in charge, take the decisions, tell them it doesn't fucking matter whether they've cleaned their teeth. And yes, they can wear whatever they bloody well like, they don't have to look like the Royals going to bloody church in 1948. And no, the nasty policeman isn't going to come and get them if they're not in bed by six-thirty. And of course they can bloody eat chocolate spread for breakfast.

'Did Tom encourage the girls to break the rules now and then? Or did he discover as I'm slowly beginning to discover that his wife has cloned all his children from an image of herself? I am father to a bunch of sanctimonious, snobbish, conformist pinheads . . . Or at least I will be unless something drastic doesn't happen soon.'

Mike stirs his tea with such fury a miniature tidal wave builds up in the cup.

'Do you know what the three words most used in our household are? Do you know them? Do you know what they are?'

Henry trickles his disgusting cocktail on to the table. 'Clean it up, Daddy,' he demands authoritatively.

'Have a guess at those three words,' Mike says relentlessly, not expecting an answer.

'Well, I'll tell you what they're not. They're not, "I love you." Oh, dear me no. And they're certainly not, "Fuck me rigid".'

An older woman at the next table in a damson-coloured velveteen hat and pale pink tweed suit shudders and lowers her eyes. Serves her right for listening.

'I'll tell you what those three words are.' Mike pauses for effect. 'IT'S NOT ALLOWED. Got that? It's not allowed. That's all I hear all day – or at least, the bits of the day that I'm around – and most of the bloody night. It's not allowed.'

'Fancy a quick pillow fight, kids?' Mike puts on a child's voice. 'Mummy says it's not allowed.'

He rubs his face with both hands and flexes his shoulders as if he's trying to shrug back into his more familiar, easygoing style.

Not only have I never seen Mike so angry, I didn't even realize he was capable of such strength of feeling. He gives the impression of going through life with the volume turned down low.

'Sorry,' Mike briefly puts his hand on my arm. 'Sorry, Kay, I just sometimes look at my life and think, *what has this got to do with me?* Do you ever think that?

'It's all out of my hands and yet like some bloody feudal serf, every minute of my day is accounted for. Every minute of the day I am responsible for someone. But it's responsibility without bloody power. And it will be for ever, as far as I can see.'

For the first time Mike smiles ruefully. 'Ironic, isn't it? High-bloody-flier in the corporate structure but stuck at middle-management level in my private life.

'And every time I try and change the routine, just a little bit, Angela says, "That's not like you, Mike". And the office says, "That's not like you, Mike".

'And I feel like yelling, "This is like me. This is me. I'm not the other Mike Robinson. I'm this one." But I don't. Too bloody scared. That's the irony. Too bloody scared of the consequences.'

The words wrap me in ice. *Too bloody scared of the consequences.* Mike takes a long drink of tea. I say nothing. If this had been Martin, I might have come up with something banal. Mike is different.

Mid-life crisis? Man on the verge of an affair? Man who feels sorry for himself? Man running away from his commitments? So what's new?

The list might be equally predictable when it comes to me. Woman pushed to one side by husband? Woman aware her children have left the nest? Woman mourning the decline in her looks, her prospects, her role as a wife and mother? So what's new?

Well, what's new is that it's Mike and me. Both *too bloody scared of the consequences.*

Over the past eight years or so, we have chatted at length and easily about every imaginable subject. Two subjects we've avoided are his partner and mine. That's what makes my friendship with Mike different from the relationship I have with women friends.

Another difference is that until this afternoon, I've never had any idea what Mike really thinks *about himself*.

Women friends you don't have to ask – they tell you. And, more often than not, it's something negative. Mo says it doesn't happen with men because generally they feel so bloody marvellous about themselves – they don't need anyone else to confirm it.

I think it's more complex. Perhaps Mike hasn't talked about how he feels because nobody's bothered to ask.

Later, in the car park, after Henry has been strapped into his seat, I give Mike a hug.

'Are you OK?' I ask.

'I'm fine,' he says. 'Really, I'm fine. You?'

'Oh, I'm fine too.'

Apart, that is, from being *too bloody scared of the consequences*.

At home, I spy what looks like a very large, mobile bale of cloth circling our front door.

It is Mo, viewed from the rear, dressed in a loose-fitting many-layered garment (she believes that layers lead to miraculous weight loss. God knows why.) She is on her hands and knees whispering obscenities through the letter-box to Letty. The dog is howling in reply.

'Anything wrong?' I ask, as I dump the shopping on the step. 'What on earth are you saying to Letty?'

'I'm telling your dog that she's an evil-smelling pile of crap and she should be shot in the back of the neck.'

'This isn't some kind of canine therapy, is it?' I ask mildly. 'Knock 'em down to build 'em up?'

Mo ignores the remark.

'I stuck my fingers through the letter-box to get the key and that bloody dog nearly bit them off.'

'Quite right too,' I say, letting us both in. As we pass the hall mirror, Mo checks her chest.

'Notice anything different?'

'Five pounds lighter?' I suggest, not bothering to look.

'Not less, MORE!' she shouts enthusiastically. Letty yelps in alarm.

'Christ, that dog's neurotic,' she says which is rich coming from her. She smooths the cloth over her chest. 'I'm bigger.'

'You are?'

'This wonderful man in Hampstead has hypnotized me. I've got two more sessions to go and I swear I'm going to make it to a C-cup.' I am baffled.

'Hypnotherapy can develop your breasts. I've done it. I know. It works,' Mo explains.

Five minutes later, I am still laughing. I can't help it. Mo pours a glass of wine and stares at me morosely.

I suspect that at least some of my hysterical response is due to Tom's continued non-communication – no message on the answering-machine, no note from the office, no nothing. But a lot of it is to do with Mo's mammaries.

'He didn't ask you to take your top off, did he?' I eventually choke out.

'No, he did not. He is a doctor, not a deviant.'

'Dr Gossard, I presume?'

'That is not funny,' Mo says. 'If you took care like I attempt to take care of myself, you'd be in a much better state.

'You need someone who'll encourage you to break out a bit, live your own life, sod Tom. Who does he bloody well think he is? Wales's answer to Michel Legrand?'

'Odent,' I say.

'What?' Mo asks, irritated.

'Odent, you mean Odent not Legrand. Odent is the natural-birth guru, Legrand writes sloppy music.'

'Well, you know what I mean. Everything in this house revolves around Tom-bloody-Evans and it always has done. At what point are you going to take responsibility for *yourself* and let Tom take responsibility for what *he* does?

'He behaves exactly as he likes because he knows you will put up with it.'

'Well, it's not quite like that.'

'Isn't it?' Mo asks. 'OK then, tell Tom now that he should clear off for three months. Tell him he has to decide what he wants from life, you or Brenda, and when he's made up his mind, he can let you know. In the meantime, tell him, you will also be making up your mind about how you wish to proceed.'

'Then what?' I say cautiously as I put away the shopping.

'Then you tell him to bugger off. You're happier alone – at least that way nobody lies to you or cheats you or makes you feel second-best all the time.'

'But, Mo,' I interrupt gently, 'I *won't* be happier on my own. I'm not built for it.'

Mo is unimpressed. 'It's one of those things, kiddo. Until you've tried it, you won't know – and anyway,' she adds, smiling, 'all misery is relative; some is worse than others. At present, I am single and moderately miserable.

'In the past, I have found myself in an intense, passionate relationship and more miserable than I could ever imagine.'

'So which is better?' I ask.

'Without a doubt, being more miserable that I could ever imagine. Divine pain!' She rolls her eyes melodramatically. 'Oh, the ecstasy, oh, the agony of it . . . Anyway, that's not the point. Don't you remember what your mother used to say?'

Mo and I speak as one, 'Don't do as I do, do as I say . . .'

Mo looks at her watch. She has promised to give me a lift to Olivia's shop with a fresh stock of Kitchen Sync since Tom has left his car at the airport and my clapped-out Mini is in the garage.

'If you don't get a move on, you'll be late.'

Mo has also asked to borrow Tom's electronically warmed back-pad since she believes that a recent night with an athletic lawyer may have damaged one of her vertebrae.

'Did you have a good time?' I shout as I struggle to retrieve the back pad from all the other bits of Tom's bought and discarded pieces of electronic equipment (foot-massager, the infrared lamp that turned his face orange etc. etc.) hurled down into the cellar.

'It was so-so,' Mo shouts from the top of the cellar stairs. 'He wore the most hideous hand-painted braces. I didn't see them until he took his jacket off and by then it was too late. I would say the encounter wasn't so much passionate as pre-orgasmic . . .'

'Pre-orgasmic?' I ask, coming back up the stairs. 'What does that mean? You couldn't come?'

'Kay,' Mo says, 'why do you always have to be so *basic*?'

Upstairs in my bedroom, on my own, I look for something to wear. Mo's right. I am basic. Basically bloody awful. Look at these clothes. Unimaginative, uninspired – grey, black, blue, brown, boring. I walk into Claire's room – black and white and nothing else; but somehow Claire's black has more zap in it than my black. I do miss the girls terribly.

In the window, Claire has a hundred and one scarves camou-flaging her old rocking-horse. I pick out a couple in tangerine and cream and deep amber. Famous wives have themselves featured in glossy magazines wearing exotic creations in colours like these, looking years younger and pounds thinner – just to show the world that ever since their husband ran off with another woman, life has improved 100 per cent. *Up yours!* Or rather, up everybody else's except yours, my dear, departed husband.

One day soon, I shall take the entire £789 I have in the Kitchen Sync account and spend the lot on one strikingly coloured outfit. One day.

'You dirty old dog.' Mo is standing in front of the fridge and examining the chart. 'Now when did this happen? Is this or is this not an orgasm I see before me? There's me banging on about the need for change, the need to look after yourself and here you are, quietly, well, quietly banging on! Here's to you,' she takes a sip of wine.

'It's not quite like that—' I begin, but one look at Mo's face tells me I'm not going to get very far.

'Look, did you or did you not engage in activity with someone or something other than yourself?' Mo smiles broadly, and slips into Anna-from-the-orgasm-workshop's nothing-is-so-embarrassing-it-will-throw-me-out northern accent.

'And we're not talking vibrators here, are we, Group?' Mo intones.

'No, we're not,' I reply. 'But it's much too technical for you to understand . . .'

In the car, Mo, who drives with the aggression of a Dobermann pinscher typecast in one too many Hammer horror films, says she wants to give me her total support.

'Confide in me, lean on me. If you've got worries, let me help. It's a bloody awful time for you . . . I mean how old are you, forty-eight?'

'Forty-four.'

'You've got the menopause looming, kids flown the nest, old man out on the root, not sure what your identity is, wardrobe definitely indicating a lack of self-esteem, of COURSE, you're going to feel down. So what's a friend for?'

Call on me, day or night . . .

'Get out of the way, you silly old wanker,' she shouts at a mild-looking elderly man on a bike whom she would have treated with the utmost courtesy if she had met him as a pedestrian in the street.

'I don't feel quite that bad actually—' I begin, but Mo is on a roll.

'Look, depression: I've been there. Believe me, I've been there. And I can tell you now, one day, you'll look back on this and laugh.' She takes a quick look at me.

'Well, perhaps not laugh exactly, but you'll certainly be able to say, Kay Lilly Woods, I am a survivor.'

I am about to tell Mo about Rosemary's job-offer as it might incline her to a touch more optimism on my behalf, but she is off again.

'Bloody foreigners,' she says, cutting up a car with a Jersey number-plate.

'Kay, I want to ask you a straight question and I expect a straight answer.'

Alarmingly, Mo turns to look at me, leaving the road totally unattended for what feels like a long weekend.

'Would you call me co-dependent?' she asks.

'Co-dependent?'

'Yes. I have an uncomfortable feeling that I may be co-dependent. A person at work has been going to a co-dependency group and the more she tells me about it, the more I suspect I'm a prime example.'

As Mo chats on, I mull over whether there is an equivalent word to hypochondria for those who diagnose themselves in need of every kind of therapy available. Therachondria?

'Mo—' I say. She is oblivious. 'Mo . . .'

'. . . On the other hand,' she continues, 'I do think I give too much of myself. I mean I think I give quite a lot. Do you think I give quite a bit? I feel I'm fairly sensitive to other people's needs. In fact, probably too damn sensitive—'

'Mo!' This time I shout.

'Ask anything you want, how can I help?' Mo replies. 'I'm really listening.'

'Mo, you drove past Olivia's shop about five minutes go. I did try to tell you.'

'Jesus,' says Mo, attempting to do a U-turn in a one-way street and almost colliding with an oncoming car. 'Doesn't anyone know how to bloody drive any more?'

Chapter Eight

At a distance, they look like something nasty speared on giant iron skewers. Close up, I can see that age and ill-treatment has remoulded and mangled the artwork and brocade and exquisite sequins and satins of once-splendid hats and head-dresses.

'Antique Chinese,' says Olivia cheerily. 'Americans adore them.' Her voice grows gentle. 'Can you imagine how lovely these must have been when they were first worn? Like butterflies' wings. I get very cross when they're not cared for properly. One bloody stupid woman had her hat in a perspex case in her Jacuzzi. You couldn't see it for steam.'

In the empty and now closed shop, Olivia steers me over to a Victorian mangle. A length of green velvet material is halfway through the roller, its folds gracefully pleated on to the floor. Both mangle and cloth are on a large circle of mirror. Pinned to the cloth are brooches and earrings, illuminated by small spotlights. On discreet black labels in gold ink are the prices and the words, *Exclusively for you by Kay Lilly Woods.*

'Well?' says Olivia again, smiling.

I am rendered speechless, mainly by the amounts she has decided to charge.

'Really nice,' I eventually say. 'But you don't think Kay Lilly Woods . . . Well, I know it's my name but don't you think it makes it sound as if the jewellery's made by Mrs Reagan's astrologer or something?'

'Two words,' Olivia responds firmly. 'And remember them for all time. The two words are: high-profile. You have something to sell, it is unique, you want your name on it and up front because believe me, sweetheart, in a couple of months versions of these will be on sale all over the place. And you won't get a bean. Don't be self-effacing, darling. It doesn't suit.'

As she talks Olivia turns off the lights in the empty shop and shepherds me upstairs to her office. She gestures towards the window seat and sits opposite. Street lights and a giant candle on the table provide the only illumination.

I watch as she takes a cigarette and inhales deeply, sinking back on the cushion, at peace. Olivia genuinely seems to have disentangled what she wants for herself from what everybody else expects. But it's taken her a long time to achieve it. Are there no short cuts in this apprenticeship?

'Drink?' Olivia hands me a glass and we chat about her children and Kate and Claire and eventually, inevitably, the institution of marriage.

'I've come to this conclusion,' Olivia offers. 'A certain type of man is attracted to a strong woman. At some point, he begins to fear that he, the honcho, will become henpecked.

'So he tries to chip away at everything that helps to make the woman strong – her opinions, her energy, her interests. He resents her friends, her job, the children they've had together—'

'Is that what happened to you?' I ask.

'Yes, and it took me too long to realize the real problem. If a strong man chooses a strong woman, they can work it out together. They can make compromises and adjustments, I really do believe that.

'In my case, Ed was a weak man who wanted to *believe* that he was strong. So, his only solution was to make his problems *my* problems. Not, of course, that I didn't have faults. Christ, did I have faults, but I don't believe they happened to be the ones he spent a lot of time pointing out.'

'What's that old saying,' Olivia adds, pouring another glass for each of us. '"Any woman who has a great deal to offer this world is in trouble"'?

'Well, sweetheart, it's only trouble if you let others convince you that it's trouble. I used to say to Ed that there are four stages in a lot of men's lives as they graduate from husband to divorcee. Do you know what they are?'

I shake my head.

'Self-centred, self-righteous, self-catering and self-pity. If you're lucky, you find a man who's reached stage five. And if you do, and he's considerate, you've hit the jackpot.'

'So what's stage five?'

'Self-aware.'

'Would you live with anyone again?' I ask.

'Me? Live with someone? As in a proper partnership?' Olivia appears scandalized. Then she smiles.

'Of *course* I would. I can't imagine anything better – but next time, if there's a next time, I want to bring out the best in somebody else, not the worst. I hope he can achieve the same in me . . . I don't want to feel that huge poisonous boil of resentment, I don't want to pour on him all the contempt I feel for myself because I'm too weak to leave and too demoralized to try and initiate change.' Olivia shudders. 'A nightmare, a living nightmare.'

'You've told me a lot about your marriage but you don't ask much about mine, do you?' I say to her.

'It's none of my business,' she replies promptly. 'Actually, it's not just that. It's because what you'll tell me is what you want to believe. And I don't think that's a healthy activity.'

106

The sharpness of her words catches me unprepared. I look at my reflection in the window-pane. Shadowy, unclear.

A terrible aching sadness rolls over me. When it reaches my throat, it almost scalds. Self-righteous? Self-pity? No male monopoly on those. In fact, I can go one better. Self-bloody-obsessed.

Something has to change.

The hotel is camouflaged as a large, private house. No name-plate, no reception area. A massive hall has several comfortable armchairs, a large open fire. Two or three young women dressed like traditional butlers supervise trays of tea. Olivia has been invited to drinks by a couple whom she first met as clients four years ago and who, she says, have since become friends.

She insists that the hotel is on my way home and I must come. 'Look on it as a selling opportunity.'

She and I, like newly decorated members of *Dad's Army*, are both festooned with Kitchen Sync. She has a brooch which looks about as suitable on her cashmere sweater as baby's vomit on a feather boa. While I wear a trio of miniature Victorian shop scales which, though resprayed, still go up and down. For some reason, people find this irresistible, poking the scales (and therefore me) to make them work. For this reason alone I rarely wear the brooch.

Under normal circumstances too, I wouldn't come uninvited to somebody else's party. But I don't much want to go home. Also, in Olivia's company I find it easier to cherish the illusion that life can and will get better.

We are shown into a small, discreet lift which descends. The door slides open and instead of the gentlemen's-club décor I am expecting, we appear to be on the set of *South Pacific*.

I behold tropical flowers, a couple of parrots, three or four pools of varying sizes, hammocks, grottos and a humidity which is opening up pores with such speed that some of the faces have the texture of Aertex vests.

About twenty people circulate, sit, talk, walk and drink. Especially drink. Multicoloured cocktails and mineral water seemed to be the two choices. The snacks and canapés share one aspect in common: they are all blue. I am about to place a cracker in my mouth on which I believe is crab and mayonnaise when I stop; there is something very disconcerting about blue crabs.

Olivia sees someone she knows. 'Won't be long,' she says. At sixteen, those words used to strike terror into my heart. You'd go to a dance with your best friend, promise on pain of death to stick to some complicated code so you would know whether you both fancied whichever two blokes looked interested. But then, suddenly, she'd break all the rules.

'Won't be long,' she'd say, avoiding your accusing eyes as she galloped off with Mr Tasty, leaving you with the one with a dirt ring on his collar and a dribble.

'I'll only be a tick,' Olivia repeats. I decide to make my way back to the entrance. As I turn, I almost trip over a woman sitting on the side of one of the smaller pools, her feet dangling in the water.

'Excuse me,' she says.

'No, it's my fault, I'm sorry, I didn't see you down there,' I reply.

'I'm hiding.' She smiles. 'I figure if I sit here for half an hour, I can leave having done my duty and without all the hassle of having a hundred conversations with people you hope you will never have the misfortune to meet again.' It's my turn to smile.

'Your plan too?' she says. I nod.

'To be honest, I don't know anyone here. Not even the hosts. I came with a business acquaintance,' I explain.

'I'm here for business as well,' the woman replies.

'Drink, madam?' A young unsmiling man offers me a tray.

'Go on,' the woman says, 'take a seat. Invisibility is so much more rewarding when you can share it with somebody else.'

We each help ourselves to an inflamed-looking cocktail and I sit cross-legged beside her. I am not a cross-legged sort of person, if you know what I mean. I always find it slightly off-putting when a person insists on treating a perfectly good sofa as if it is a flying carpet. I prefer to keep my feet on the ground.

In this instance, short of dangling both shoes in six foot of steaming chlorine, cross-legged is the only option. The woman smiles again.

'Go on,' she urges. 'Take your shoes off . . . What the hell?'

I'm about to say that no, I couldn't possibly and then I decide she's right, what the hell? I pull off my boots and Kate's zebra-decorated socks and roll up my leggings. I take a swig of the cocktail which settles in a stomach devoid of food. It feels as if several of my internal organs have suddenly been detonated.

This does not stop me from taking several more sips. I am suddenly very, very comfortable. The air, originally so cloying, now works like an all-embracing and very welcome electric blanket.

'My name's Jenna,' the woman introduces herself.

'Mine's Kay. What part of the States do you come from?' I make conversation.

'Toronto,' she replies deadpan. Then adds, 'It's OK, I've lived in the States most of my life. We work in New York but we have a small home in Montana. We travel quite a bit, so sadly I don't get to see either much. But I will; another couple of years and then we'll call it a day.'

'We?'

'My husband and business partner, Joe. He's here somewhere. He likes these things much more than I do. We always stay at this hotel because it's low-key and then he usually gets involved in something which hypes the whole thing up.' She shrugs. 'What can you do?' She doesn't sound too displeased.

We fall into amiable silence. Normally, I would have been far more curious; who, what, why? But the booze has acted like an epidural on my brain, numbing most of it. As we sit companionably, I realize that a number of people wander up to say hello to Jenna, exchange a few words and then move on when she says in a gentle but clear form of goodbye, 'I'll see you around.'

'I've got twin girls. They're twenty. Both of them,' I suddenly blurt out. I sincerely hope for everybody's sake that the alcohol is not going to encourage me to become maudlin. Maudlin mothers are death.

'They really are terrific, even if I say so myself. They're in the States now. We have a sort of "God, Mum" relationship. Do you know what I mean? Everything I do, they say, "God, Mum."

'You probably don't have that problem . . . ?' I end vaguely.

Jenna, I reckon, must be mid- to late thirties but at first glance, she appears much younger. She has baby-fine blonde hair caught back in a bun, perfect skin. She wears a tiny diamond stud in each ear and a single diamond on a very long, thin gold chain around her neck. She is dressed in black crêpe flared trousers and a plain matching tunic top which seems to have a great deal of fullness at the back.

She smells of orchids and wears almost no make-up. In short, she's exactly the kind of person you least want to meet when you look and feel like a turd.

'Sure I do,' Jenna says. 'My boys rip me apart. I mean really apart. My six-year-old tells me he's too embarrassed to go out with me because I wear jeans mostly and he wants me to dress up like other boys' mommies at his school.' She laughs.

We discover that we both love the sea, neither of us can cook and we both have middle names we divulge only under duress. (Hers is Muriel.)

Jenna tells me that her father is a career diplomat, she is one of four children, her parents are happily married, but the whole family has constantly moved because of her father's job.

'I always promised that I would have roots, I'd stay in one place. I'd never leave my children. And here I am, we travel several months of the year and sometimes we have to leave the boys behind.'

'That's really strange,' I reply. 'My parents travelled quite a bit and when I was first married I used to travel a great deal too. Now, it's my husband who's away more often than not.

'We always planned that we'd have roots too, real roots . . . Perhaps there's nothing any of us can do about it,' I add, surprised to find myself suddenly sad. 'Perhaps it's in the blood.'

The only element in my blood now is 100 per cent pure alcohol, so I continue to rummage shambolically for coincidences in Jenna's life and mine, where none exist.

'You were born on the fifth of July?' I burble. 'Now isn't that strange? My second cousin had a baby last year and she was born on the fifth of July too. You're both Cancers: that's a very nice sign . . .'

'Are you happily married?' Jenna eventually, inevitably, asks. It's that kind of night.

'Your old man, is he your best friend? Is there much you haven't shared?'

Now, Jenna and I may be working towards instant best-friendship, microwave mates, but we are also talking friendly female competition here.

Besides, I have a vague suspicion that while I am close to being sozzled, Jenna is a person who can hold her drink. By which I mean she has literally held on to her Bombay Bushwacker and drunk very little while I have sipped and sipped.

If Jenna is happily married, then dammit, so will I be. And if she has shared everything with her 'old man', then so have bloody I.

'Yes, my husband is happily married,' I reply solemnly. I have some pride. I can at least draw a distinction between myself and Tom.

For some reason, Jenna finds this very amusing indeed. What's more disturbing is that she thinks I *meant* to be funny.

In the time we've been talking, the numbers in the room have trebled. Damp patches have broken out all over the Armani suits so even the most suave look pitifully piebald. It's time to go. Olivia is nowhere in sight.

'Look,' says Jenna. 'Why don't you stay and have dinner with my husband and me? These things always go on and get out of hand. I was planning on slipping away.'

As I stand up, I am instantly aware that if I don't eat something fairly quickly, I will be compressed between the floor which is coming up rather fast and the ceiling which is descending at only a marginally slower rate. Pragmatism takes over from my usual prevarication.

'I'd love to eat,' I reply, then through a drunken haze, several azure crabs float into view. 'I just hope it's not cordon bleu.'

The food which arrives fifty minutes later, in Suite 1204, is mostly green. This could have had a disastrous effect if my nausea hadn't been lifted by five glasses of water and a bowl of green-pea soup. Suite 1204, it transpires, is a little joke since there are only forty suites in the hotel.

I sit in a room which is dazzlingly white, as are the two vast bedrooms and the adjoining bathroom, glimpsed through open doors. The table is set for three in front of a vast fake open fire. Two female butlers attend Jenna and me. The soup is followed by asparagus quiche and greengage fool. Only when I bend to retrieve my napkin from the floor do I realize that I am still barefoot with my leggings rolled up.

Jenna raises a glass of champagne, 'To—'

The greatest amount of sound since attending an INXS concert with Kate and Claire in the late eighties obliterates whatever she says next.

'It's Joe,' she explains smiling. 'I'll show you.' She turns to the two women. 'We can manage now.' She takes some money from a jumble of clothes heaped on one of the vast sofas and tips each gracefully. 'We'll look after ourselves, thanks.'

We move into the dimly lit bedroom. Along one wall a temporary rock-face appears to have been constructed. Closer inspection reveals it to be a massive sound system. Scattered around the room is a variety of musical instruments. Joe sits on the edge of the bed. He is using a couple of hairbrushes to beat out the rhythm on a dressing-table stool.

Jenna pre-empts my middle-aged question. 'Soundproofing,' she says. 'They're used to people like us.'

Joe is not good-looking. He is the same height as Jenna and both are a good deal shorter than I am. He is tubbyish with jet-black crew cut hair. He wears jeans and a T-shirt and sand-coloured boots. 'Kay, this is Joe Oakford. Joe, Kay . . . Kay is a fellow gypsy.'

Joe's hand when he shakes mine has the alarming consistency of uncooked liver. When he smiles, however, he offers one excellent reason why any number of women might choose to pursue him.

The smile warms his face and reaches his eyes, thus encouraging me to abandon my initial impression that Joe looks like a Turkish Cypriot Cabbage Patch doll.

'Sit down and we'll play you some more. See what you think,' Jenna says. The only uncluttered space is the floor. I sit with my back to the wall.

'Now feel free to say that it's the worst crap you've come across,' Joe instructs and smiles. 'But don't expect us to say goodbye as you leave.'

I realize that I have been exceptionally slow. 'It's *your* music, isn't it? It's terrific . . . lovely . . . really good,' I hunt desperately for the right response. I actually do like it – sort of Edmundo Ross meets Pink Floyd but having been raised on Tamla Motown and rock 'n' roll, old habits die hard.

The music swells and fills the room. It sounds wonderful. But then so would Mantovani if played at this volume and in my present frame of mind. I am intoxicated not only by alcohol but because once again, I am completely and utterly out of my depth. And enjoying every minute.

What is it about middle age – cynicism, caution, an overdose of forward planning, a passion for routine? – which blocks off spontaneous opportunities for fun? This dinner hasn't been booked ahead for weeks; it isn't part of Tom's excessive commitment to brown-nosing; it's a chance encounter leading to who knows where. And that's its pleasure.

At forty-four, I may be old enough to know better, but being old enough to experience worse is so much more *interesting*.

The music changes to a much slower rhythmic beat. Joe takes up a handful of pills from the dressing-table and swallows the lot. I suspect these are not to help him with high blood-pressure.

Jenna offers me a small African drum. 'Try it,' she says.

'I couldn't possibly, I'm hopeless at this kind of thing,' I say, not quite truthfully since I can't recall the last time someone handed me an African drum.

''Course you're not,' Joe interrupts. 'Show her, Jenna.'

Jenna picks up the rhythm and begins to play.

114

Joe offers me a hand. 'May I?' he asks. He proves to be an excellent jiver.

'Have you ever thought of Cuban heels?' I tease as he stretches on tiptoe to spin me round.

'Have you ever thought of having a couple of inches cut off below the knees?' he replies amiably.

'I'm sorry. I didn't mean to be rude,' I apologize.

'I'm a songwriter, honey. If you think that's rude, let me tell you what they say about my lyrics,' Joe smiles.

'Is that what you do for a living?' I ask, breathless.

'You don't know?' Jenna says, gently mocking. 'And I thought you looked so much like *Melody Maker*'s average reader.

'Joe and I write together and I sing and play. Sometimes he plays with me, sometimes not. Sometimes we both play together in another group . . . It pays the rent.'

'What do you call yourselves?' The question seems crude but I'm in one of *the* age-old quandaries of celebrity etiquette. Joe and Jenna are famous but *I don't know who they are*.

'You're very good about not being recognized,' I say, partly in compensation, before they can answer.

The ghost of Tom wags a finger at me; time to go home.

'I've had a terrific time, but it's getting awfully late. I really must go now . . .'

'One drink for the road,' Jenna says. 'A drink to friendship and brief encounters. Shall I take your address? We leave for home tomorrow but I'd love to look you up next time we're in town. Life gets so un-normal, it's nice to have an—'

'Ordinary?' I suggest.

'Yes, a wonderfully *ordinary* evening with a regular sort of person,' Jenna says emphatically. It may sound like an insult, but I think from her perspective, it's meant to be complimentary.

'This is us,' she gives me a handwritten card. 'We have oceans of space, so come and stay any time you're in New York.'

I put the card down on the writing-desk and look for something to write on.

'Drinks here,' Joe shouts from the sitting-room.

While Jenna goes for the drinks, I pick up a Spanish guitar, sit on the side of the bed and pluck a couple of strings.

'Look,' Jenna is suddenly back at my side. 'You don't hold it like that. Let me help.' She kneels on the bed behind me and puts both arms around me, readjusting my hold on the instrument.

'Relax, drop your shoulders, keep the arms loose. Good, you look so calm and yet your body's so tense. Here, take off your jacket. Let me give your neck a massage.'

She slips off my jacket as she speaks and rapidly yet smoothly begins to knead the knots of tension in my back. The pain is excruciating but slowly, pleasure seeps through.

'You have a serious problem,' Jenna clucks. 'Lie face down, take off your shirt and bra and close your eyes.'

Since the instructions are issued in a 'doctor knows best' tone of voice and the cure has already begun to work, I obey.

Jenna sits astride me. She slips a satin scarf around my eyes as a blindfold and the room is filled with the sounds of rain falling on leaves to the tune of a solitary tin flute.

'Do you like this music? I use it to help me to sleep at night . . .' Jenna's voice, naturally soft, is now almost inaudible.

'I want you to visualize a lake of midnight blue. I want the blue to fill every corner of your mind, wrap itself around you.

'You are afloat on a sea of mystery, blue, dark blue, all blue . . . so blue . . .'

Warm oil pours drop by drop on the centre of my back. A small trickle slides down my right side and lays a track to my left breast.

I feel a cupped hand scoop the oil, pass my breast and glide on to my back. It is not Jenna's hand because she is already stroking, gliding, gently pushing and pummelling my back.

116

Oil is poured on the sole of one foot and gently the whole area, instep, ankle, toes are massaged with a stroke which is strong and consistent. The rhythm makes me drowsy. Jenna begins on the second foot, then my calves, hands slide my pants down to my knees.

Oil seeps across my buttocks. 'Go, baby, go.' The voice belongs to Joe. He whispers in a highly annoying fashion like some punter at the sexual Olympics.

I decide to ignore his presence. When I turn over on to my back and lift the blindfold slightly, I can just make out in the near-gloom of the room that this is probably wise. Joe has a penis like an artichoke heart, pubic hair curling around in a protective fashion garnished by two testicles the size of cherry tomatoes.

Jenna restores my blindfold. Her long hair falls loose, accidentally brushing my stomach. She pours more oil on my skin and spreads it gently upward and downward. It trickles into the V-shape that my crossed legs make. Jenna gently uncrosses them, bends them at the knee and the oil flows free.

Oh, the joy! This is the first time in years – holidays apart – that I have had the pleasure of messing up somebody else's sheets. And what sheets. Thick and slippery, warm, satin, the colour of freshly fallen snow.

A tentative tongue begins to lick my nipple. This has never been an activity which has produced much in the way of results for me before. Now, the knowledge that not one tongue but two are at work on my body, melt the 'should or shouldn't I?' into 'why not?'

Jenna licks the inside of my thigh. A flick here, a flick there, nothing predictable. Anticipation works as the strongest form of arousal. She reaches the top of my thigh and – stops.

Nothing. Nothingness. A swirling deep-blue soft satiny nothingness.

I am floating, I am truly rootless. I have no connection with these people, they have no tie to me. We can do and be and act however we choose, safe in the security that we will never meet again. Sexually, I am whom I choose to be, ageless, without history.

Until now, Jenna and I have been silent. Then she says one word, 'More?'

'Oh, yes . . .'

I sense that she is kneeling between my open legs. She skilfully inserts her tongue, fingers gently clearing the way. From time to time, she whispers encouragement.

At first, the small iron padlock of my own reserve prevents loss of control. But she is patient and almost roughly persistent. 'Help me,' she says. 'Help me, honey. Let go. Surrender. Come on, surrender to me.'

Warm waves lift my body. Colours which are strangely transparent, moving and shifting and dazzling like a Victorian kaleidoscope fill my eyes. I am going under, deliciously, deeply under.

Quickly, Jenna turns me on my side, slides so she is lying cupped into my body, behind my back. She puts her arm over my leg and inserts three fingers in the large, warm and open place where her tongue has been. She slides her other arm under my leg and inserts two more fingers. I am in a clamp which moves and fills, fills all, and sets off fresh triggers.

Jenna picks up the pace, almost hurting, pushing hard, aware that I can't escape, that I don't want to escape. Within seconds, my body tenses and I am home. But hardly dry.

I hear a rustle, clothes being removed. Jenna begins to murmur with pleasure. Joe's voice says, 'Take it, baby, take it . . .'

A very small sigh escapes from Jenna, her warm breath against my back. I doze. A little while later or perhaps a very long time later, a door closes. I sense that Joe has gone out of the room. Jenna curls up by my side, stroking my skin.

'Is this something you do for Joe?' I eventually ask, not particularly bothered whether I am user or used.

'No,' Jenna says. 'This is something I do for myself. I like the power of being in bed with another woman. I like to feel her surrender. You can never have that with a man. I like to feel in control of what gives her pleasure.' She pauses.

'If Joe said stop, I'd stop. But I guess he's decided it's no threat. Other men he would object to. But deep down in his macho soul, he firmly believes that no woman can give his woman what he can give her.'

'Call him back.' I announce, competitiveness rampant. 'Tell the man the show has only just begun . . .'

I wind the top sheet round my body and while Jenna waits, not quite sure what is in store, I suddenly tickle her in a way that has always worked on Kate and Claire and Tom.

She shrieks and giggles. We laugh, roll all over the bed, which is the size of a parking-lot. She falls off, shrieks some more and I refuse to let her back on. I defend my patch with a pillow in each hand. Jenna stands on the bedside table and dives into the centre of the bed, sliding on her stomach until she's almost off the other edge.

'Jesus Christ,' says Joe petulantly, as he stands in a dressing-gown, silhouetted in the doorway. 'I thought you guys were having *serious* sex in here.'

He is not pleased that this induces uncontrollable laughter in both of us. I was right. He *does* look like a Cabbage Patch doll.

'Come and sit down,' Jenna encourages him, patting the bed. Joe pads over. 'Lie down,' she orders.

Joe obediently lies down. 'Stroke his head,' Jenna instructs me. I am uneasy. Now this may seem strange, considering what has gone before, but stroking the head of a man who is not my husband, in bed, well, that's a different game altogether.

119

As I hesitate, Jenna pulls on an extra-large T-shirt and sits cross-legged with Joe's head in her lap. She rubs his temples and coos away. In less than a minute, Joe is snoozing like a baby.

'Why don't you sleep here?' Jenna says to me. 'It's much too late to go home. Come,' she says.

I follow her into the second bedroom. It is littered with boxes and carrier bags.

'We have to leave at eight for the airport, so I'll give you a shout when we go. There's no reason for you to be up early.' Jenna kisses my cheek; the boundaries are back in place.

'I think you're terrific,' she says suddenly. 'You are a very beautiful woman. You know that, don't you? It comes from inside.'

The last comment I could have done without.

The door closes behind her and I sit on the edge of the bed, my clothes gathered around me. I feel absurdly pleased with myself. 'She's right,' I say out loud. 'I *am* a beautiful woman. A *very* beautiful woman. And not just on the inside, buster.'

Five minutes later, I modify that view. My hair stands on end, mascara is smudged. Without lipstick and under the neon light, I look as if I require an emergency blood transfusion. A spot that was just a small bump on my chin earlier in the evening has erupted. My optimism is dented but not entirely gone. 'Not bad,' I say to my reflection, 'Not bad at all.'

I do a little skip on the way to the shower. My skin still tingles. Does this make me bisexual? Contemporary at last? But as the soap and hot water wash away the massage oil and the remaining effects of the alcohol, a cold fear begins to take hold.

What do I *do* in the morning?

Do I appear at seven-thirty as if nothing has happened? Or do I say, 'Thank you very much for having me but please on no account contact me ever again?' Or do I act like an over-age groupie and casually say, 'Nice one, Jenna'?

And what happens when they see me in the cold light of day? Come to that, what happens when I see Joe? Artichokes will never be the same again.

Jenna I liked, Joe I hardly exchanged a couple of sentences with, much less fancied. It has been alarmingly easy. If fanciability is no longer a criterion, the whole of the male world lies at my feet. In theory at least.

Isn't this what some men are supposedly keen to do, when they choose? Hitting the sack with a female of any age, shape, state or condition?

I did it because I felt sorry for her. I did it because it was too late to get out of it. I did it because I fancied a bit and I thought she'd do.

I climb out of the shower, wrap myself in a towel and sit down on the lid of the loo. That is exactly Rosemary's argument: depersonalized sex. Copulation without companionship. OK now and then, but as a way of life?

I look at my watch. Four-thirty. Time to leave. I write a quick note: *I had a marvellous time. Thank you. Love?* Certainly not. *Yours sincerely?* Too formal. *All the best?* I sound like a wing commander. *Kay?* Well, at least it's my name.

I dress, tiptoe into the sitting-room and prop the note up on the now cleared table. I feel slightly miserly that I haven't left an address. It's not a very adult way to behave. Still, I haven't been behaving in a very adult way for the last twelve hours, so why start now?

The taxi-driver on the journey home delivers a twenty-minute diatribe about How Britain was Once Great but It All Changed after the Blacks arrived.

'You work?' he suddenly asks. I have an irresistible urge to say,

'Yes. As a matter of fact, I'm a middle-aged groupie. I specialize. *Ménage à trois*, actually.

'Had a *Moi*, her and him only, last night. Very famous. Ever done it? Highly recommend it.'

Instead, I say, 'Can you turn left at the top here, please?'

I smile. For the first time since seeing Tom in the pub with Brenda, I feel I have something to smile about.

Half an hour later, as the early light paints different colours in the park, I walk with an exuberant Letty. We stop in a greasy-spoon café by the railway station. Letty sits outside the door and stares at me accusingly, while I drink a mug of coffee made with milk and eat a fried-egg sandwich.

For the first time in days, I can actually taste the food. I write a letter to the girls, telling them everything and nothing at all. Inadvertently, I sign it with a blob of tomato sauce.

Back home, I add another circle and dot to the chart on the fridge door. I also erase the question mark after the first circle.

In the bathroom, the scales register that I've lost nine pounds. I'm at the weight I was when I first met Tom. Sadness surges back. I turn up the volume on the radio and sing so loudly in the bath that Letty howls in protest.

At eleven a.m., I wake up, go downstairs to make tea and press the play-back button on the answering-machine. A couple of messages for the twins and then a disjointed conversation. Even before my brain has begun to decipher it, my instincts signal, *bad news*.

'. . . look, she's not here. I had to come back to pick up the tapes I need. Yes, of course I love you . . . I will tell her, I promise. Now, I've got to go. I don't want Kay to know I've been back. I don't want to hurt her . . .' the conversation fades out.

The machine whirrs on. A call from the features editor of *Tangiers*. Where's my copy? A call from a friend with whom I occasionally go swimming. Then, Tom's voice again.

'Hello, darling. Newcastle went very well. Be home about seven-thirty. I'll try to pick up some shopping for you on the way back for supper. Love you.'

I hear the roar.

I hear the roar for two reasons. First, because my husband always assumes that all the shopping in the house is 'mine'. Second, because I realize that the hills and valleys of his Welsh accent, almost bulldozed flat by twenty-five years of living in London, become pronounced once again when he talks to his mistress; a boyo on the bonk.

. . . *I don't want to hurt her* . . . Jesus. His master's voice. I remove the cassette and replace it with a fresh tape.

I do so without enthusiasm. Revenge is no substitute for a happy ending.

Chapter Nine

'Come with me,' Martin says as soon as I walk into the hall of the West residence. I pick my way through the flotsam and jetsam which makes their hall such an interesting challenge if you are wearing tights. As, indeed, a few of Martin's male friends occasionally do.

'Kitchen's very clean,' I say conversationally as gleaming tiles catch my eye. This is not the kind of remark I'd make to my women friends, but I know Martin appreciates such observations since it's how he imagines women *do* chat to each other.

'New policy,' he replies. 'The kids can mess up all the other rooms but not that one. It had to be done. A couple of Charlotte's warriors were round last night.

'They started to witter on about how men,' here he adopts a female voice, 'Bless 'em, do try, but they haven't a clue when it comes to the house. Still, definitely points for trying. Must give them that, points for trying.

'I had to tell them that the house is the way it is not because of my incompetence but because of a conscious decision not to encumber the children with the strait-jacket of a house-proud upbringing.'

'I'm sure they must have taken that really well,' I say, stooping to pick up Otis who is fast asleep halfway up the stairs. 'Given that they each probably spend at least twelve hours a day scrubbing the underside of their dining-room chairs and vacuuming up the loose peas in the deep-freeze.'

Martin smiles wanly. 'Anyway, I decided I was not going to be judged unfairly . . .'

'But I thought you welcomed female criticism,' I interrupt. 'I thought you said you saw it as part of the exorcism of two thousand years of male brutality? Isn't that what you read out from *The Effeminist Manifesto*?'

Martin, now on the upstairs landing, ruffles my hair as I follow him up.

'What I like about you, Kay, is that you mock but you don't moralize. It's the bloody moralizers I can't stand.

'Not every bloody woman is a natural, full-time, home-made-apple-pie-mother and I certainly don't think every man is geared to rearing kids or being a red hot corporate shark.'

I am mildly surprised at Martin's vehemence since he has spent several thousand pounds at a variety of weekend encounter-groups allegedly learning how to channel his anger. On the other hand, living with Charlotte must at times fill the channels to overflowing.

'Do you know something?' Martin asks, gently stroking Otis's sleeping head. 'I'm beginning to think Charlotte's lot are enemies of freedom.'

'Really?' I reply. I wonder what took him so long.

He continues: 'They are actually *frightened* of variety. So they're determined to make those who don't conform feel very, very bad indeed.' His voice rises.

'Well I, for one, refuse to feel bad about it. If Charlotte wants to return to being a full-time mother, it will be over my dead body.'

It is now my turn to stroke a brow: Martin's. 'Look,' I say, 'You know Charlotte. She loves to be in front. She'll never be happy staying at home all the time, and why should she? She'll probably come back as a band-leader in the next life.'

125

Martin begins to cheer up.

'How long has this MUMs stuff been going on – eight, nine months?' I ask. 'I bet you've seen Charlotte even less than you usually do. Does she know Tabitha is having cello lessons? Does she know that Carlos is allergic to . . . what is it?'

'Tartrazine.'

'Tartrazine?'

Martin smiles weakly. The front door slams and Tabitha arrives home from school. 'Hi there, Marti,' Tabitha shouts up in a good attempt at an American accent. 'Hi, Kay.'

She disappears into the kitchen and shoots out again, pretending to make death-rattle noises in her throat.

'Christ, what's happening? Look, if we're going to go all clean and tidy round here, if we're going to go all *suburban*,' she vomits out the word, 'I'm leaving right now!'

Tabitha, though eleven years old, frequently acts and talks like an adult since, until Martin arrived, she was treated as one. No moo-cows or choo-choo trains for her. Instead, from the age of roughly nine months, Charlotte would discuss with her baby daughter the difficulty of keeping up with the mortgage; the unreliability of local garages; the irresponsibility of certain men; the benefits of a private pension plan, etc. etc.

As a result, Tabitha prematurely developed the conviction that life is a series of intractable problems and that anyone over thirty-six inches in height is not to be trusted. By the age of six, with too little knowledge of fairy godmothers, good witches, wise wizards and happy-ever-afters and too rich a diet of adult company and television, she had become permanently anxious and highly precocious with a tendency to talk in the tongue of soap operas; drama and high drama.

Martin's arrival changed much of that. He lifted the load, took away from Tabitha the responsibility for Charlotte's worries and

126

injected back a little of the childhood magic that had been missing from her life. Plus, Martin took pains to tell Tabitha something Charlotte assumed her daughter knew.

'You're loved,' Martin still says often to Tabitha.

'No I'm not,' she always replies happily.

I have a lot of time for Martin because of his efforts. Tabitha is now insufferably overconfident, far too bright and usually bloody cheeky – but at least she is no longer a miniature adult but a child again; caring under the bravado. And she's often extremely funny. In short, Tabitha has been rendered almost normal. Step-parenting has its plusses.

Tabitha sits on the bottom step of the stairs and chats to us both. 'Do you know,' she says conversationally, 'There's a girl in the fifth form and she's been to bed with so many boys they call her the Public Ledger.'

'Why?' asks Martin innocently.

'Because she's had so many entries,' Tabitha answers unsmiling and then chortles with delight at the expression on Martin's face.

'It's all right, it's not true. You don't have to worry,' she reassures him. 'Educated girls wait until they're seventeen. I read it in the newspaper. Anyone like a Coke?' Tabitha disappears into the kitchen.

'Does she get her sense of humour from you?' I ask Martin. He looks doleful.

'How can she?' he replies. 'Her father was either a Chilean resistance fighter or a pop singer who once got to number twenty-three in the charts. Charlotte's not quite sure. I wouldn't have thought humour was a strong point with either.'

'Well, perhaps Tabitha has acquired her sense of humour from you by osmosis,' I suggest. 'It can happen in step-families.'

'We're not a step-family,' Martin corrects morosely. 'We're a unit. We called ourselves a unit when I first moved in so that

Tabitha wouldn't feel unduly threatened. But now Carlos has got hold of the idea and seems to think we're all in some sort of Panzer division. He's such a militaristic little bastard.'

'Well, you gave him a good start with his name.'

Martin blushes. For a brief period in 1981 he apparently allowed all his suppressed inclinations out to dance in the battle-grounds of the Falklands War. Carlos is named after Carlos Bay although only Martin's closest friends know this fact. Charlotte says that if they are watching an old war film and the tanks begin to rumble, Martin turns into a lion in bed.

Martin changes the subject. 'Come in here, I want to show you something. I'm very, very excited about it.'

We go into Charlotte's bedroom. I say Charlotte's bedroom because while Martin sleeps here too, it is entirely her domain. It is a frill palace; peach, cream and more peach. Vast fitted wardrobes open up to reveal more compartments than a high-speed train.

'Well, what do you think?' Martin asks as I deposit Otis on the floor.

'About what?'

'About this.' Martin gestures towards the bed. I can see nothing unusual except two large white T-shirts lying side by side.

'Give me a clue.'

'It's the T-shirts,' Martin gesticulates impatiently. 'Look at the T-shirts.'

'I've got it,' I shout enthusiastically. 'One T-shirt you washed in any old powder, for the other you used new, biologically recharged, colour-formulated, very large size, Powerful Persil.'

'God, Kay, this is serious,' Martin says wearily.

'OK. OK, I'm sorry,' I reply. 'I give up. I don't know what I'm supposed to see.'

'The slogans. Read the slogans.'

One T-shirt says in large letters, *I am a male oppressor*. The other reads: *If I don't love myself then who else can love me?*

'These T-shirts are symbolic of how far I've travelled,' Martin explains patiently. 'I bought this one in 1991 and I bought that one,' he gestures to *If I don't love myself etc.*, 'last weekend. Don't you see the significance?'

I shake my head, mystified.

'I'm moving away from the guilt and penance number. I'm beginning to realize *it isn't my fault*. I have to tell myself, "Martin, you're all right."'

'Our men's group is working on asserting how valuable the male contribution has been to society. We're emphasizing the qualities and characteristics that the masculine personality offers which are unique and not to be undervalued—'

I came to see Martin because I am worried about Mike. I'd hoped to enlist his help. This is not the time to ask.

'. . . So men don't have to feel dwarfed and diminished. Look at prostate cancer, look at access to children . . . We need to take control of some of these areas, we need to rival the feminist effort.'

'Martin,' I interrupt, realizing with a glance at my watch that I have sixteen minutes to get to the workshop. 'Sorry, I've got to go, I've—'

'Jeez, Martin,' Tabitha stands at the bedroom door, Coke can in one hand, peanut-butter sandwich in the other, 'I think what you've missed out is that you're already on the winning team. It's tough for men, I know, but that's the way it is.'

Chapter Ten

'He had *what* stitched to his thigh?' I hear Dionne's voice and a squeal of delight from Liz. In the room, tables and chairs have been arranged in a circle in preparation for the workshop. Alex and Liz are seated next to each other, plus a new woman with the kind of badly dyed blonde hair which in my experience usually indicates the owner is a professional hairdresser.

She wears black leggings, brown boots and a pink jumper patterned with brown and black suede squares and tassels. Round her neck are several gold chains. She is probably in her late twenties.

In contrast to the first session, Alex is dressed in a style not dissimilar to an Afghan tribesman: dun and cream-coloured loose-fitting garments. Liz wears the same outfit as she did at the first session. Dionne is magnificent in pale lilac with matching stiletto shoes and earrings.

'God's honour,' Alex says as they wave hello. 'He had an ear stitched to his thigh.' Liz doubles up with laughter.

'What did you say, "Ear, ear"?' she squeaks out.

'It was very disconcerting,' Alex says, straight-faced. 'I thought, if his ear is down there, are any of the other parts where they ought to be?'

'It's a trick,' says Mo, newly arrived. 'He says, "Whisper in my ear". And suddenly you find yourself going down on the prat. How cheap can you get?'

'I felt really sorry for him,' Alex explains. 'He said he'd had an accident at work. They were going to graft his ear back but, in the meantime, his thigh was supposed to be the healthiest place for his ear to wait.'

'And what did you say, Alex?' asks Mo. '"Do you come ear often?"'

In the middle of our groans, Tilly walks in. Instinctively, we turn to watch her as she stands at the door. She says nothing but carefully walks to a seat, sits down and smiles broadly. Seconds elapse.

'Well?' Liz finally says.

'Well, what?' Tilly counters.

'Well, are you all right?' Liz ends lamely.

We are all much more comfortable with each other tonight than at the first session, but certain questions one does not ask. Or, at least, there are certain questions a sensible senior civil servant like Liz does not ask. Mo, of course, has no such restraints.

'You've gone and done it!' She shouts triumphantly. 'You've fucked a fella!'

'To be frank, girls,' says Tilly, adopting an air of mock superiority, 'I'm not sure that I should be here any more. I don't want to attend under false pretences, now do I?'

'You self-satisfied little sod,' Alex says, giving her an affectionate punch on the shoulder. Mo is about to follow through with a barrage of questions when Anna arrives.

The hard work of having a good time begins.

'Have you noticed something interesting about this?' It is twenty minutes into the session. Anna has introduced the new member of the group as Carol. She has come with Liz whose hair she does every Saturday.

Carol is softly spoken and hesitant. She says she is twenty-nine and has two children. She has been married for eight years, her husband is a self-employed painter and decorator and she has never had an orgasm in her life.

'He thinks foreplay is something to do with tennis. I wrote to an agony aunt and she told me that I needed to talk to my partner honestly and openly,' Carol says. 'What do I tell him? I've faked it eight hundred and twenty-seven times? He'd be terribly hurt. He'd take it personally.'

After the introduction, Anna asks us to write down three sentences about ourselves. While the others write, I spend most of the time musing on why I'm here at all.

It's partly because I promised Mo that I'd stay the course. It's partly because I'm intrigued. If the way to a man's heart is through his stomach, the route to my soul might well turn out to be via my pubococcygeal muscle. *My main squeeze, honey.* Lastly I'm here because well, we're sort of a team.

'Kay?' Anna is speaking to me again. 'Kay, I asked if you noticed anything in particular about your three sentences?'

I shake my head. I have written: *I am indecisive. I am careless with other people's feelings. I am not focused enough.*

The latter, I admit, I nicked from Mo who constantly tells me she's not focused enough and then proceeds to pack the equivalent of three lives into every day.

'You seem to have such a negative view of yourself,' Anna says in the soft, I-can-really-control-my-aggression-but-you-can't voice which is beginning to needle me slightly.

'Could you think of three positive things to say? I'm sure you can if you try.'

I shake my head firmly. Anna may know a lot about orgasms but I definitely know more about me.

'No, I'm very sorry.' I am emphatic. 'Positive feelings are off the menu tonight. Couldn't drag one up to save my life,' I give her a huge smile. 'Sorry!'

'We'll see,' Anna says knowingly. 'I want you to hold on to your slips of paper and look at them again just before the end of the evening, please.

'Now,' she continues, 'What is all-pervasive? What colours much of what we do? What inhibits and can be highly destructive?'

Anna looks expectantly at us. No one stirs. I wonder if anyone else feels slightly rebellious.

'Shall I tell you what it is?' Anna asks.

She turns and writes in large letters on the blackboard, SHAME.

'Shame is what stands between too many women and their right to pleasure—'

'Now hold on a minute here, hon,' Dionne interrupts. 'When you say *right* to pleasure, I'm not sure about that.

'I tell you now, with husband number one, I'd lie back so rigid I made a plank look relaxed. And I wait for him to "give" me sex.

'That was my *right*; no effort on my part; no attempt to adjust my mind, get in the groove, you know what I'm saying? Sex was something men did *to* me, not something I did *for myself*. Do you read me?'

'I hear what you're saying, Dionne,' Anna says, 'But what we have to challenge here is *why* you felt that you should contribute so little.'

'I know *why*, woman,' Dionne replies laughing. 'Because I was told by my mamma that anyone who looks like she knows what she's doin' in bed, is a no-good, whorin' slut.

'By the time I got to husband number two, I changed all that. I decided to be *bad*.' Dionne hisses the word out appreciatively. 'And do you know, he didn't mind one bit. On the contrary. We still meet now and then, for old times' sake.' Liz whoops and claps her hands.

'Elizabeth, please,' Anna says, frowning. 'This is not a revivalist meeting.'

'Now, the fact that I had to wait until husband number two to get with the programme, that *was* a shame,' Dionne says. 'A *real* shame.'

'Well, let's pursue this thought,' Anna suggests and begins to write on the blackboard. She writes 'cunt' followed by 'fanny', 'quim', 'muff', 'snatch', 'bearded clam', 'pussy'. I notice that Carol has gone several shades paler.

Anna writes: 'beaver', 'cabbage', 'cherry', 'bird's nest', 'twat'. The list goes on and on. By the time Anna begins on nicknames for male genitalia, it's become a group activity.

'Prick!' yells Liz.

'Balls!' suggests Carol timidly.

'Dick,' I offer, mainly because I'm worrying about Tom so Dick and Harry pop into mind.

'Pork sword,' Dionne contributes.

'Yuk,' replies Tilly.

'Pego,' Anna writes.

'Pego? Isn't that a computer game?' asks Alex.

'Eighteenth century,' Anna replies briskly.

'Oh, well, if we're dipping back in time,' responds Mo in a mock-authoritative tone, 'how about womb-brush, kidney-wiper, beard-splitter, holy pole and—'

She suddenly realizes we are in awe.

'I had a boyfriend once called Hector,' Mo explains airily. 'He had the largest collection of slang words for male genitalia in the world. And before any of you ask, the answer is his was average.'

'Middle leg,' offers Liz and adds as if to prove her own literary credentials, 'James Joyce, *Ulysses*.'

'Middle leg?' Tilly interrupts. 'Middle leg? We can't have *that*.'

'Why not?' Anna asks.

'Well, it sounds like something out of a Habitat catalogue, for Christ's sake. It's not exactly *rude*, is it?' Tilly replies.

'Isn't that the point?' Carol offers quietly. 'Most of the words for women's . . .' she hesitates slightly and draws courage, '. . . private parts are in some way slagging-off or nasty. The men's bits sound a lot better. When you say somebody's got balls, it's a compliment, isn't it?'

'Very good, Carol,' Anna beams. 'That's *exactly* the point.' The rest of us squirm. We too want to be the teacher's pet, however insufferable the teacher may be.

'What we have to tell ourselves is that our vaginas are beautiful!' Anna says, her excitement building. 'They are good, they are positive. If they smell, they smell of the riches of life. They are stunningly attractive works of art.'

I must say that I have never looked on my vagina in this way. In truth, I have never looked on my vagina at all. It's not that I'm ashamed of it – her? – it's just that since it's been there for as long as I can remember, I tend to take it for granted.

If pushed, I'll admit that female elasticity is a miracle of engineering but since it's not the kind of topic that comes up much in conversation, I haven't gone into that idea very deeply either.

If pushed, I'll also confess to being surprised by the vast range and variety of muffs – information acquired from frequent use of swimming-pool changing-rooms.

Mo, in contrast, has great affection for her vaginal area. She has several posters of Georgia O'Keefe paintings in her bedroom – interior decoration in more ways than one.

'Kay!' says Anna, aware that I am drifting again.

'Sorry,' I apologize, not for the first time.

'I want us all to visualize our vaginas as part of a great work of art or a particular flower or a specific colour,' Anna says.

'I don't know that many works of art,' Carol says hesitantly. 'We've mostly got animal prints at home.'

'Then what about thinking of your vagina as a tigress, Carol?' Anna says.

'Well,' says Carol, 'I'd have to talk it over with my better half first.'

'. . . *Priscilla allowed him to take off her satin panties—*' Liz is reading from her notebook in a style of delivery that I normally associate with Enid Blyton.

'Panties?' interrupts Tilly. 'Who the bloody hell wears panties?'

Liz gives her a scathing look and continues to read out from her homework.

'*As he did so, she watched his throbbing, glistening male member rise gloriously in salutation—*'

'Pull-ease,' says Dionne. 'I keep reading this throbbing member stuff. I'm damned if I've ever seen one. Alex, you've seen more members than most. Ever seen one throbbing?'

'Liz, take no heed,' says Anna. Liz continues.

'. . . *Priscilla's cunt called out to be filled—*'

'How come my cunt's never called out for anything?' Mo asks. She affects a soft, girly, American accent.

'Hello? Is that room service? This is the cunt in suite forty-two speaking, have you anything particularly *filling* . . .?'

'You shouldn't use the c-word,' Carol says. 'It's not nice.'

'Point taken,' says Liz brusquely and ploughs on. '*Priscilla felt her womanly juices flow. "Oh, Reggie . . ."*'

Alex screeches.

'Reggie! Reggie! You *cannot* have a hero called Reggie,' she squeals. 'I would refuse to go to bed with any man called Reggie on principle.'

'What principle?' Liz asks.

'The principle that it is impossible for anybody called Reggie to be good in bed,' Alex replies.

Liz glares at her and continues, '*Reggie's tongue licked Priscilla's breast and reached for her nimbus, hungry, searching, desperate—*'

It's Dionne's turn again.

'Nimbus? Nimbus? Honey, nimbus is a *cloud*. Do you hear my meaning? What's a cloud doin' around her breasts?'

'No, it isn't, as a matter of fact,' says Liz fiercely. 'It's a part of the nipple and very erotic. Now *please*...

'... *The crown of his cock plunged past the outer and inner lips of her cunt...*' Carol grimaces.

'... *Priscilla's moist slit cried out for more as Reggie's huge powerful penis drilled away. It spoke to her of lust—*'

'You've heard of the speaking clock,' Mo interrupts again. 'Well, Reggie's got a speaking cock.'

'*Warm, welcome sperm skipped their way into Priscilla's womb. She loved to be taken by him, to be overpowered, to feel that her mound belonged to him as they wrestled with an orgasm which endured as if for all time...*'

Liz closes her eyes dramatically.

'*Ero, eras, erotica...*'

We clap, we stamp, we whistle.

'What did you think? Tell me honestly,' Liz's eyes light on Mo.

Mo stops clapping.

'Honestly?' she says.

'Honestly,' Liz insists.

'I honestly think it is very, very funny but absolutely not a turn-on,' Mo says. Liz appears crestfallen.

Is this criticism fair? We know that when Liz said 'honestly', she didn't mean *honestly*.

'Could you elaborate further on that, please, Mo?' Anna asks.

Liz interrupts. 'It's all right. I confess,' she stands up, a smile on her face. 'I didn't write it. I nicked it. It's all Tanya Clapstick's stuff. You know. She writes dirty books for women. Still, you're right,' Liz sounds faintly bemused. 'When you get down to it, it's not actually very titillating, is it?'

'It's all male soft-porn stuff,' says Tilly. 'It's all about being conquered and taken and overcome. Like sex is some fuckin' great Battle of the Boyne.'

'It is a *bit* odd, I must confess. But then again, women buy the books, old bean,' Liz informs Tilly.

Anna intercedes. 'Perhaps we buy them because we have no erotica, soft porn, call it what you please, that appeals to women's experiences?'

'I read somewhere that Bette Midler once asked her boyfriend to kiss her somewhere dirty,' says Liz, 'So he took her down a sewage works. That kind of thing appeals to my experience.'

Anna ends the laughter by calling us to order. 'Have you written anything, Dionne?'

Dionne, confident, positive Dionne, suddenly becomes unsure.

'It's not much . . . I know it won't appeal to anybody else because it's not dirty *dirty*, if you know what I mean. But it sort of strokes me in the right places.'

She clears her throat and we grow quiet. Her voice is low and rich.

'*I am alone in a lagoon at midnight. The water is warm and clean and I swim naked. From time to time, I stop and stand and let bits of seaweed, soft like velvet, move across my body. I am at peace.*

'*Moonlight throws silver streaks across the water but my face is in darkness. I hear the sound of a swimmer. In the distance I can see small splashes as a figure moves towards me. I am not afraid.*

'*I lie on my back, close my eyes, float and wait . . . I drift away.*

'*The swimmer draws near. I cannot see his face but I know that he is young, experienced and strong. I stand in the water, relaxed, my legs*

138

apart. He dives and I see that he has long, dark hair which flows out behind.

He dives twice and swims twice between my legs. I feel his skin brush my calves. I feel his hair flow around my legs. We have no eye contact.

He swims behind me and lays my head on his chest. He runs his fingers through my hair again and again. I can feel his body supporting mine and it is warm.

Eventually, I give the signal that he knows and he dives again.

I feel his salty tongue between my legs. It goes deep, deep into the blackness which the interior of my body has become.

His hair swirls and moves against my breasts and arms like a million tentacles of pleasure. His tongue dances inside me until I come. Then, silently, he surfaces and swims away.

I will never see him again . . .'

Dionne closes her exercise book and sits down. We are silent. The brief story seems to have pushed each of us out on our own raft of fantasy.

Inevitably, it is Liz who speaks first.

'Gosh!' she says. 'He must have had a simply HUGE—' Anna glares at her.

'. . . Pair of lungs,' Liz finishes meekly.

'Wonderful, Dionne, really wonderful. It hinted at all sorts of imagery and sensations . . . wonderful,' Anna effervesces.

'Now who else has done their homework?'

None of the rest of us have. Then I recall an event which happened to me about fifteen years ago. If I was working for Rosemary now, I might use it for a column. But I'm not, so it will have to do as homework instead.

'I haven't written anything down but could I tell you something based on a true story?' I ask. Anna nods and I begin.

Initially, I am self-conscious then I gradually forget that I have an audience.

'*The house is part of a terraced row in Manchester. A woman comes to visit the occupant. On the first evening, at about seven, she is in her bedroom, unpacking. She happens to glance out of the window and notices a lighted room opposite.*

'*Some instinct makes her switch off the light, sit on the edge of the bed and watch.*

'*Within a couple of minutes, a man appears in the window, his back to her. He is naked. It is impossible to judge whether he is old or young but the body is compact.*

'*The man stands immobile, hands by his side for several minutes. Then, suddenly, the light goes out and he is gone.*'

'Is that it?' Tilly asks and Dionne tells her to shush.

'*The next night at seven, the woman takes up her position on the edge of the bed and waits. Exactly on time, the man appears, his back to her, apparently unaware that he is watched.*'

'He's not . . . you know . . . is he?' Carol interrupts.

'You know *what*?' asks Liz. 'Oh, God, how silly of me. You mean, is he wanking? Good question. Is he, Kay?'

'*The man is absolutely still, his hands are by his side, he does nothing. The woman has the freedom to watch – or not to watch.*

'*The third night, she is ready again. She finds the anticipation erotic. She has spent the day thinking about the man. She fantasizes that he is her slave, that he will do as she wishes. He is her sexual object. She has commanded him to stand like a statue, divorced by service to her from his own desires.*

'*The time reaches seven, then quarter past, then half past. The man fails to appear. She is as desolate as if she has been spurned by a lover. He is more than a sexual object, he has become an equal player in the game.*

'*On the fourth night, she goes to the bedroom a little before seven, she turns off the light, reaches the window – and he is already there.*

'*She knows he is aware of her presence. His legs apart, this time she*

140

sees just a glimpse of his cock between his legs. He stands immobile as before – but this time for almost half an hour.

'When the light goes out in the room opposite, both she and the man know he will not come back.'

'Well, what was all that about, then?' Carol asks, a shade aggressively.

'What do you think it was about?' Anna asks.

'Men's bums?' suggests Liz brightly.

'Power,' offers Dionne, 'It's about power.'

'Good woman!' says Anna, fast becoming the Butlin's Redcoat of the erogenous zone.

'The woman in Kay's story is in control. She is a voyeur but the man is a willing accomplice,' she elaborates, presumably on my behalf.

'What if he'd turned around and given her a quick flash?' asks Mo. 'Then she wouldn't have been in charge at all. She would have been bloody furious. Or at least, *I* would have been bloody furious. I'd have dialled nine-nine-nine quicker than you can say pubococcygeal.'

Anna looks at Mo askance, unsure whether she is taking the mickey. She decides to give her the benefit of the doubt.

'Mo, this is *fantasy*,' Anna says patiently. 'In fantasy, any fantasy, even if you fantasize that you are a victim of gang rape, you are always in control. *You* wield the power.'

'If you're saying sex is about power, then it doesn't hold out much hope for a helluva lot of women, does it?' Mo counters in her cut-the-bullshit voice.

Anna pauses for dramatic effect. 'If you *perceive* yourself to be sexually powerful, on equal terms with a man, then you *will* be powerful.'

'Not in my book, honey,' Dionne whispers.

Anna persists. 'Take Kay. I asked her at the beginning of the session to write three positive sentences about herself. I don't think she'll mind if I say that she found that a little difficult.' Anna gives me a sickly smile. I twitch back.

'Once she can do it easily, that will be the beginning of her acquiring a better sense of her own worth. From a sense of worth comes a sense of power.'

'Have you written anything fresh yet, Kay?' Anna asks.

'Not exactly,' I reply.

I hand over my piece of paper. On it I've drawn a large moon-face with a bright smile, a spot on the face and lots of curly hair. A large arrow sticks out of the scalp.

'Goodness,' Anna says. 'We *are* feeling down about ourselves, aren't we?'

I smile and grit my teeth.

On the contrary, I feel like saying, 'we' are feeling very much better about ourselves, thank you very much.

The drawing does not represent me – as Anna assumes – it is a doodle of Brenda. The drawing also represents a milestone.

I've decided I'm no longer going to blame myself for failing to keep my spouse's undivided attention. From now on, I'm going to blame Brenda.

And yes, I do feel powerful.

At ten, all of us – except Anna – go to the pub. She has given us a sheet of paper with seventeen suggested ways of masturbating, some of which we are supposed to try before we meet again.

'Why seventeen?' asks Liz. 'Why not fifteen, or twenty? I find seventeen's a very untidy number. It's unsettling, don't you think? Besides, Phil is in enough of a state *sans* sex without him discovering I'm filling up all my spare time in solitary pleasure.'

'Why don't you kill two birds with one stone and masturbate in front of him?' suggests Alex casually.

Liz looks as if she's about to have a seizure.

'Good God, what do you think I am? An exhibitionist? I couldn't possibly do that. Some things I just won't even consider, and that's one of them.' Liz pauses then adds defiantly, '*And* I'm not ashamed to say so, so there.'

'How about you, Kay?' Alex asks, half teasing. 'What will you never do?'

I think for a couple of minutes, then I say, 'What I will never again do, for as long as I live, is accept that a half-hearted hump with my husband on a Friday night after a take-away chicken tikka passes for passion, or lust, or love. It's none of those things, it's just making do.'

The others look slightly uneasy. Am I serious? Am I joking? I raise my glass in a toast.

'To risk!' I say.

Slowly, one by one, Liz, Mo, Tilly, Dionne, Alex and Carol each raises her glass.

'To risk!' we say together. But I'm not sure how many of us really mean it.

Chapter Eleven

'Hi, we're in the kitchen!' Tom's voice greets me as I close the front door behind me. I try not to let it happen, but my spirits soar. Damn. They drop almost immediately at the sight of Charlotte.

She is draped across *my* armchair. On the kitchen table is an empty bottle of wine, the remains of supper and several piles of paper.

'How nice to see you, Charlotte,' I say. I know instantly that Tom has not received the telephone message I left for him at the hotel. Perhaps Battling Brenda interceded? Tom offers me his cheek to kiss. He smells of Blue Grass. This is very alarming. Not only is she ordinary, she is old-fashioned. It *must* be love. I ignore the cheek.

One of these days, I'll give Tom a tip. It's a tip a former married lover of Mo's gave to her. For half an hour after spending time with Mo, he'd go and sit in a smoke-filled pub. Fags and beer obliterated all alien feminine aromas.

On the journey home from the workshop I had worried how best finally to confront Tom. I was also worried that I now had a major handicap, playing the part of the aggrieved wife. He would take one look at me and he would *know*. He would know that I had shared a bed not just with one human being but two. He would know and he would be hurt. His hurt would definitely be greater than mine.

In the event, Tom barely looks long enough at me to ascertain that I'm his partner of twenty years, never mind interpret what I may or may not have been doing for the benefit of my health.

I register that Charlotte has taken to wearing strange outfits. They resemble those wraparound pinnies that women used to wear in the fifties. On second thoughts, perhaps it *is* a wraparound pinny.

'Just tidying up, sorting out; almost shipshape now,' she says. 'Had a good day?' she asks me. Charlotte's idea of conversation is mainly to shoot out questions and then provide the answers: this erases the possibility of any dissent.

'We've had a splendidly productive time, haven't we, Tom?' she continues. 'Jewellery going well, Kay?'

She barely pauses for breath, 'I must say if we get the kind of audience we're hoping for on this tour, MUM will be on the up and up.'

'Martin babysitting?' I attempt to break Charlotte's tongue-lock on the conversation.

'No. Angela's au pair is. Very unnerving girl, I must say. This one speaks fluent English, has no apparent signs of nymphomania, alcoholism, bulimia or heroin addiction, she hates the telephone and she's very pleasant with it. Not at all what one expects. But then again, if she's Angela's choice . . .

'And how are the girls?' Charlotte asks. I squeeze in an answer.

'I talked to them last week. Really well, having a wonderful time.'

'Are they?' says Tom absent-mindedly. 'That's nice.'

'Another glass?' he asks Charlotte. She nods her head. 'Could you, darling?' says Tom.

I am still standing in the middle of the room, coat in hand, guilt in my heart, longing to be convicted of the crime of infidelity. Or any crime, come to that, if it brings me a bit of attention.

'Could I what?' I reply mutinously.

'Could you get another bottle out of the fridge, please?' A

muscle in Tom's cheek jumps up and down like a Jack Russell terrier in a cornfield.

It dawns on me. *He doesn't like me. Tom doesn't like me. He couldn't care less what I do.*

I go to the fridge, take out a bottle and place it unopened in front of Tom.

'Really, Kay,' he says. 'Do you have to be so childish?'

'I thought I might go away at the weekend,' I say in reply.

'Good idea,' says Tom, getting up to find the bottle-opener and fresh glasses.

'Do you want to know where I'm going?'

'Not really, love, just as long as you're happy,' Tom says patronizingly. He ruffles his hair; semaphore for, *I am about to tell a lie.*

'You know Charlotte and I are off on tour tomorrow,' he says, keeping his eyes fixed on the cork.

He continues. 'I could try and pop back at the weekend, but I mean, if you're not going to be here, there's not an awful lot of point, is there? I mean I can, for your sake. But on the other hand, if you're going to be off somewhere too—'

This is a typical Tom manoeuvre. He now makes me feel guilty because we could have had a weekend together. Except, of course, he had no intention of spending the weekend with me in the first place. Nice one, Tom.

'I could change the weekend,' I say and I mean it. I smell of retreat.

'So that's agreed then,' Tom announces barely hiding his relief. 'Let's stick with it the way it is, shall we? Wine?'

I shake my head in refusal. I run through the routine of asking Tom how the conference went, who was there, what was discussed. The same questions I have asked for years; questions which he always welcomed in the past if only because it gave him free access to talk about himself. Not now.

'Christ, Kay, is this a cross-examination?' Tom responds irritably.

'OK, all right, why don't you ask me what I've been up to, then, for a change?' I counter. I hear the roar but it's a very long way off now.

'Well,' says Tom evenly. 'What *have* you been up to, dear?'

'Oh, nothing much, really,' I reply. 'You know what it's like when you're away. I come . . . and I go . . . and I come . . .' I smile sweetly.

At least Tom won't ever be able to say that I kept him entirely from the truth.

Charlotte decides to intervene. 'Look at my marvellous cover,' she says showing me her latest paperback. 'I'm really pleased with it. One of our members is an illustrator. Don't you think she's captured the mother's look wonderfully well?'

'Wonderfully,' I respond.

By the time Tom joins me in bed, I have no energy left for a fight. As we lie side by side, the distance between us is the widest it has ever been.

Ding-dong! Ding-dong! Ding-dong! The repeated sound of the doorbell is followed by the clatter of the knocker and Letty's barks.

'Jesus!' says Tom. He rolls off the mattress.

'What on earth are you doing?' I ask. The alarm clock says it is three twenty-seven a.m.

'Where's the bloody axe?' Tom's voice comes from under the bed. 'Who moved the fucking axe?'

Ding-dong! Ding-dong! I pull on Tom's dressing-gown.

'Look, if it's a burglar, he or she is hardly likely to ring the bell first. You don't need the axe.'

Downstairs, as I open the front door, Angela Robinson lurches in. For a moment, I imagine she is about to sink her teeth into my neck.

'Where is he, you cow? Tell me, tell me *now*. You're not going to do this to me. You won't. I won't let you. He isn't yours, he's mine,' Angela screams in what, under normal circumstances, she would term a very down-market way.

'You should be taking HRT, not other people's bloody husbands,' she yells at me. 'Do you hear me?'

'Tell her, Tom, tell her,' Angela shouts at Tom as he descends the stairs looking ridiculous in Kate's red floral dressing-gown. She takes a second look at him.

'You *poor* bastard! You poor *stupid* bastard!' Angela shouts at him, spittle like the crests of waves decorating her mouth. It's difficult to know whether she's referring to his taste in nightwear or a matter more profound. She turns on me again.

'You always look so smug and self-satisfied, no bloody wonder,' she hisses.

I imagine myself as Joan Crawford *circa* nineteen-forty-something in one of those wonderful floaty satin dressing-gowns, orchid in my hair, eyes flashing. I will speak in a low, steely voice, shadows dancing dramatically in the background. In truth, when I open my mouth, I sound like Harry Corbett engaged in a bit of gentle repartee with Sooty.

'Angela, what *is* the matter? I've never seen you so, so, so well . . . so *cross*. Are you cross, Angela?'

'Cross? Cross? You call me *cross*? Of course I'm bloody cross. Who wouldn't be cross with you around like a bitch on heat. I'm not just cross, Kay Woods, I'm incensed.

'I always knew you had no control,' Angela wags her finger in my face. 'But why steal my husband? Why not steal somebody else's? Come to that, what's wrong with the one you've got?'

Angela and I turn to look at Tom. He stands on the bottom stair, axe in hand, hair on end, the hue of the poppies on the dressing-gown exactly matching the veins which criss-cross his eyeballs like fancy wrought iron. I raise one eyebrow quizzically at Angela. Is that a serious question?

Half an hour later, Angela alternates swigs from her second brandy and flinging glares of undiluted hatred at me. We three are in the sitting-room and she has just taken a photograph from her handbag.

'Look at this,' she says to Tom.

'See what she gets up to at home when you're away flogging your guts out.'

Tom gives me a look of surprise as if to say, *this can't be about you, Kay, you're much too conventional and boring*. He looks at the photograph, and silently passes it to me.

The photograph is of Mike and me embracing. Mike has his eyes closed as if in pleasure. I know instantly when it was taken. It was after our chat in the supermarket, when we said goodbye. The angle at which the picture has been shot makes it look as if we could be in a hotel car park, certainly nowhere as mundane as Asda.

'It's Asda,' I say.

'Has to be what?' replies Tom, instantly revealing his extensive knowledge of the supermarket circuit.

'Not *has to*, *Asda*. Asda supermarket car park, that well-known favourite haunt of middle-aged adulteresses who—'

Tom interrupts, 'Kay, how could you *do* this to me?'

A roar like the first blast from a blowtorch rips at my head. It is fortunate Tom holds the axe, since if it was in my hands, I'd use it on whichever of his appendages happened to be nearest.

'How could *I* do this to *you*?' I repeat in disbelief. 'How could I do this to you? Presumably in exactly the same way as you do it to me – with gusto and great enjoyment.'

'Oooooh, my *God*,' Angela wails from the sofa. 'Oh, you heartless, treacherous cow . . .'

I sit by her side. 'Look, Angela, this is the honest truth. I bumped into Mike shopping.'

'Shopping!' Tom and Angela speak as one.

'Yes, shopping. At Asda.'

'I've bloody got it!' Tom suddenly springs up from the sofa.

'This weekend. You're going to spend the weekend with Mike. That's why you didn't say who it was.'

'I did offer,' I counter.

'Aaaah!' bellows Angela again. 'You're going away with my husband. Oh, God, why is this happening to me? How could you? It's not at all what I planned. You cold-hearted, unfeeling bitch.' Angela revs up. 'You really don't give a damn, do you?'

'This is beyond me,' Tom says, performing his I'm-a-little-boy-lost body language.

'You bastard!' It is now my turn to shout at him. 'The one fact of which I am absolutely certain is that it is certainly *not* beyond you. Now, Angela, for God's sake stop crying, and tell me, where is Mike?'

'You should know,' she mutters. She appears slightly more subdued, quieter. But then, as if to prove how incorrectly I read situations, Angela throws her brandy at me.

I am impressed. Angela's performance has successfully begun to make me feel extremely guilty. And I am innocent. Imagine the potential impact if I tried similar pyrotechnics on my husband's paramour who has blood – well, if not blood, then almost certainly at least one of my husband's bodily fluids, on her hands?

It takes another brandy to unravel a very simple story: Mike has disappeared. He did not come through the front door at seven-seventeen p.m. as he usually does, nor indeed at eight-eleven p.m. as he occasionally must.

Angela has phoned all the hospitals and contacted the police. A sergeant told her that it was too soon to panic.

'He also said thousands of people go missing every year, and

Mike may turn out to be one of them.' Angela's sobs saturate the sofa.

'He said, "Everybody's doing it, love."'

Angela's wails increase in volume and then die down again. 'So I told him that I knew Mike was having an affair. He hasn't been going to squash when he says he has, he's even taken half-days off work on the q.t.'

'How do you know?' Tom asks, with sudden concern for his own welfare.

'I hired a detective. It was something my mother always did.'

Tom and I look at Angela, impressed.

Angela explains. 'You know . . . when dad went off the rails a bit. She used to hire a detective and instruct him to make sure my father knew that he was being watched, that way he'd stop doing whatever he was doing and nothing had to be said.

'I thought it might work on Mike, but it's not just that. Mike's been . . . well, somehow peculiar. Contrary. Oh, I don't know . . .' She glares at me again.

'The night before last he even refused to make love. He *knows* we make love on a Wednesday.'

At this recollection of insubordination, Angela dissolves again into floods of tears.

'I'm so sorry,' I put my arms around her shoulders. 'I know exactly how you must feel.'

'Sorry? So you bloody well should be sorry,' says Tom, sticking his face into mine.

I jump to my feet.

'Look here, you supercilious, lying, two-faced, ego-driven Welsh bastard, don't you tell me about who should and shouldn't feel sorry!

'I'm only sorry that it's taken me so long to realize that the only time you've got any sense of where you're going is when you're ferreting up some woman's vagina for pleasure.

'Well, let me tell you. And you, Angela.' I am surprised at my own ferocity, but not entirely displeased.

'Let me tell you both, Mike and I are friends. F-R-I-E-N-D-S. Friends. It *can* happen, you know. Men and women don't *have* to fall into bed together.

'We are *good* friends, as it happens. Although I regret to say that I am not such a good friend that I am the person he turns to when he is in trouble.

'I haven't a clue where Mike is but I do know he must be feeling terrible. He really loves the children . . . And he loves you, Angela. Well, I think he loves you,' I couldn't resist the retaliatory dig.

'Shall I tell you what's really funny about all this?' I don't wait for Angela to reply. 'Mike isn't out for a bit on the side, a quick pump to his ego. I suspect what he really wants is *more* of what he's already got.

'More of his family. More of you. If only you'd stop behaving like a demented air traffic controller who treats life like so many runways round the world.

'I'll bet any money it's not sex that Mike is after away from home, it's less bloody *structure*. The poor man is probably curious to discover who he is when he's not sticking to a timetable.'

Angela stares at me for a fraction of a second, then resumes sobbing. 'I don't know *what* you're on about,' she howls. 'But whatever it is, I know you're lying. You've got my Mike and I want him back.'

'How *could* you do it?' Tom says, his face like thunder. 'How *could* you humiliate me like this?'

I sit down again hard. I almost admire my husband's nerve. Almost.

Chapter Twelve

At seven-fifteen a.m., Tom departs for the railway station. After driving a still vengeful Angela home, he's had only a couple of hours sleep. He is to rendezvous with Charlotte and her entourage. Together, they are bound for a six-city tour of the north, modestly billed as The Man and Motherhood Great Debate. (It was originally called The Great Man and Motherhood Debate but it was decided to switch the position of 'Great' at the last minute, much to Tom's regret.)

The tour will be interrupted by the screening of Tom's documentary on television followed later by Charlotte's series on changing attitudes to motherhood. Their double act will be climaxed, they hope, by the appearance of both their books in the non-fiction bestseller list.

In our house, The Man and Motherhood Great Debate has been renamed The Egg and Chips Tour. This is because Charlotte's performance will of course include insisting that the female capacity to produce eggs means that the first and overriding duty of women is to fulfil their maternal function. While Tom will explain how some men are developing chips on their shoulders because they have been squeezed out of their 'natural' roles as providers, hunters and protectors of their womenfolk. They have reached a point, according to Tom, at which they feel they have no unique use in the modern world. Tarzan has been given his cards.

Tom is, of course, all in favour of equality (or so he tells Kate and Claire). *Of course*, Jane can swing from tree to tree just as well as any Tarzan. But.

But, if we women don't allow men to be top dogs (even if only now and then), our civilization will buckle at the knees at the first invader. My view is that Tarzan, like everyone else, will simply have to retrain, adjust to a different jungle and accept that there's no longer the guarantee of a job for life, even for schoolboy heroes.

I also take exception to Charlotte's prescriptive attitude to women. (How is it that so many of these moral majority females exercise all their own options to the full while telling the rest of us women that 'too much choice' – whatever that might be – is proving a catastrophe for 'the gentler sex'?)

Above all, what bugs me about the Egg and Chips Tour is Charlotte's certainty that it was all so much better for men and women *before*. But before *what*?

Tom departs on the seven-forty-eight train. At eight-fifteen a.m., I put in a wake-up call to Brenda Styles. She answers and I immediately replace the receiver. Just checking.

As she is in London and not with Tom, I feel better. Then I get the shakes. What if she is in London and *with* Tom? I tell myself not to be ridiculous. Charlotte told me the itinerary. As an anchor on reality, I phone the twins.

One of the luxuries of American colleges is a telephone in each room. I am answered by a recorded message. The voice sounds like Marlon Brando. I say I love them, I miss them and I'll try again later. As I put the phone down I remember the time difference. It must be the very early hours of the morning in New Orleans. Are the twins out? Are they safe? Where are they?

I drop them a line.

Dear Kate and Claire,
    Where are you? I've just rung and nobody was there. Of

154

course, you could be sleeping. This thought has just occurred to me, so I'll close now and ring again later. Everything here is fine.

> Dad sends his love,
> Take great care, lots of love,
> Mum

The twins will only have to read the note to know that everything is not fine. A tear-drop smudges the word Mum. I feel terribly alone; no husband, no children and, in spite of my feeble efforts – or perhaps because of them – no certainty. Mike's departure too has shaken me. I allow the feeling to last a fraction of a minute. Then I do a Mo: I think positive.

I have two options in the short term. I can begin working my way through the list of seventeen ways to masturbate – or I can drive out of London, to Olivia's, for the weekend.

I've always avoided homework on a Saturday, so I pack a few clothes, post the card to the twins, put Letty in the car and worry about my daughters for the next sixty-two miles.

I park a couple of miles away from Olivia's farm in Hertfordshire and Letty and I go for a long walk. I mull over how frightened Mike must be feeling now. Or perhaps, although missing the children, he may be relieved? Has he gone for good? If he comes back, part of the punishment is bound to be an even more restricted existence than he had before; one of the penalties of making a failed bid for freedom. But at least he's taken the first step.

Back in the car, I stop at the first telephone box and dial Rosemary's number. She's out, so I leave a message on the machine.

'It's Kay. Sorry I couldn't make swimming yesterday. I'm having second thoughts about the job, if that's OK. I'd like to give it a try. I'll phone Monday. Bye.'

'From now on,' I tell a disinterested Letty as I climb back into the car, 'I'm going to take control of my life.'

'OK, there are three possibilities,' I say to the young man sitting opposite. I know, since he has told me, that his name is Frank and he is Olivia's nephew. He is twenty-four, a graduate in economics and for the past year, he has been learning Japanese and acting as a guide to American tourists in Tokyo. His job earns him several times more than an unemployed economics graduate in the UK might expect to receive.

He looks like the type who once modelled knitting patterns in the fifties: square jaw, blonde short back and sides, clear blue eyes, six foot tall and big hands. He is wearing jeans. Frank is not thick. And he smells wonderfully of mangoes.

He and I, Olivia and several of her friends, including Des, the delightful jockey, have spent an uproarious time around the supper table.

Chrissie, a widow in her thirties who makes *tartes* for other people's dinner parties, left with her two children at midnight. Soon after, Olivia retired to bed. Des is asleep on the sofa and a trio of Olivia's friends – an under-employed actor, a (female) architect and an odd-job man, all of whom she has known since their childhood in Dublin – have retired drunk to bed.

Olivia's two teenage children, when they return from wherever they are, will sleep in the converted barn.

It is four a.m. For the past sixty-five minutes, Frank and I, alone at the kitchen table, have discussed several serious topics – Japanese attitudes to whaling (of which I know next to nothing, but a bottle of wine improves my knowledge of almost anything, including the sea): why golf is a working-class game in Scotland ('Is it?' is my contribution): Dylan Thomas (for over twenty years

I've heard Tom, in his cups, recite large amounts of *Under Milk Wood*) and What Will Frank Do Next With His Life.

Under normal circumstances, I have no reason to assume I am the target of anybody's attention, least of all someone twenty years younger. This evening, however, is different. This evening, *something* has been activated. I don't know how or what it is, but it's definitely *there*. I've twinkled so much in conversation, I've given myself a headache. At four-ten a.m., I act totally out of character.

'So,' I say briskly to Frank. 'We are faced with three possibilities. One, you sleep on the sofa with or without Des. Two, you sleep with me. Three, you sleep in your own bed which I believe also contains the odd-job man and the architect.'

'I'll take two,' Frank says instantly.

My mind goes blank. Which is two? Sleep with Des?

As I mentally run through the options again, my face begins to change colour. That plus my mouth hanging open must make me look as alluring as the average postbox.

'Shall we go?' Frank suggests.

Chapter Thirteen

I have positioned myself almost in the middle of the bed, the covers up to my chin. It's a pity white isn't my colour. Frank is carrying out his ablutions in the bathroom. Over the last ten minutes, I have also sat on the left side of the bed and on the right side. I am finally going to opt for the centre.

Another worry has been how much to take off – or, alternatively, how much to leave on. It's so long since I've done this, I haven't a clue. I put on the nightdress borrowed from Claire – and then remove it. It seems immoral to wear your daughter's nightgown in bed with a man who is not her father.

In the wardrobe, I find Olivia's kimono. I leave the main light on, then switch it off. I put the bedside light on but it throws a spotlight on my face, so I switch that off too. In the middle of my private *son et lumière* show, Frank walks back in.

He wears a towel wrapped around his middle and when I take as good a look as is respectable, my heart sinks. He is too perfect to be possible.

He is without flab, he has a body which is exercised but not to the point of being Stallone-d. He smells wonderfully of a perfume which does resemble mangoes. And he is clean. Oh, my, is he clean.

Frank slides into bed, puts his arm around me and draws me across towards him.

'Are you OK?' he asks. I nod my head positively and vigorously. I am about as relaxed as a taxidermist's prize exhibit.

I feel ridiculous. I can't believe I have done this to myself. But I have to be honest, I am also thrilled. For the first time in my life, I have chosen to take a risk. More significantly, I'm sober enough to know.

Frank strokes my arm and my forehead and my neck, in a gentle, almost fatherly way.

'I have to tell you something,' he says softly. 'I'm very nervous. I've never slept with anyone as old as you before.'

It's not quite the endearment I expected, but what can you do? 'And I've never slept with anyone as young as you before,' I reply.

Frank instantly looks more confident. 'Let's muddle through together then, shall we?' he suggests.

He kisses my neck, my shoulders, and, alarmingly, under my arms. I look into his eyes, expecting the initial B to pop up in one socket, and O in the other. *Body Odour!*

One advantage of sharing a bed with the same partner for a number of years is: no worries. Well, not when it comes to personal freshness. If there's a problem, you can speak out without intimacy collapsing around you like a second-hand deck-chair.

Now I know what Mo goes on about. She says that each time, as a single person, she takes a new partner to bed, a fresh set of anxieties lies in store; about her and about him. Body shape, facial contortions during orgasm, bad breath, farting as you come, excess hair. And it's called pleasure?

I return my attention to Frank who continues enthusiastically to fiddle and stroke. He is young and soft; chamois leather to Tom's tough hide. Gradually, my tension eases. One advantage of age is the knowledge that regrets are best delayed. If I'm here, I'll enjoy it.

After twenty minutes or so, Frank speaks again.

'Can I ask you something?' he says, slightly breathless.

'Of course.'

He supports himself on one elbow and looks into my eyes, deeply serious.

'You wouldn't happen to have a condom on you, would you?' he asks.

I sit bolt upright. 'Certainly not,' I reply, deeply offended. 'What do you think I do? Go around prepared for these kind of encounters? I hope you don't think I do this all the time?'

Frank shrugs. 'Sorry, I'm sorry,' he says. And pulls me back into his arms.

It's my turn to sit up. 'Come to that, why haven't *you* got a condom?'

'I've given it up. I've given up sex. Well, casual sex that is,' Frank adds, slightly sheepishly. He *has* got the smoothest skin.

'I'm *supposed* to have given it up. It was too easy. I felt I was devaluing what should be a spiritual as well as a physical experience. I felt I was treating going to bed like a piece of merchandising. I want it, I'll have it and never mind about the other person or how I might be affecting my own ability to have a sustained relationship with someone.

'More to the point, it was getting too so-so,' he warms to the subject. 'Like the cup of coffee someone offers you and you say yes, even though you don't want it. So, I decided to stop. Or at least cut right back on rations. But . . .' Frank shrugs and smiles wryly. Then he adds, in a rush: 'I've got something else to tell you. I should have told you earlier, I'm sorry.'

'Something else?' I can barely see him for the crowd of anti-social diseases jostling before my eyes, like celebrities at a film première. Is it the gorgeous gonorrhea or the hard-to-resist herpes?

'I hope you don't mind,' Frank pauses. 'But I don't do anal intercourse.'

'Mind? Mind? Why should I mind?' relief adds a slightly hysterical tone to my voice. 'I don't do it myself, actually. Look, I've got a good idea. Why don't we just snuggle down and do something really exotic? Like sleep?'

'No,' says Frank firmly, pulling me back down the bed. 'Fate has played a hand here. I think you've got something . . . something special.'

'I have?' I reply, happy to be fooled that it isn't just an extra two decades.

At seven a.m., I am woken by scratching at the door. Letty has decided to become the moral watchdog of the house. Frank sleeps. I get up, shower and dress. I couldn't bear for him to wake up alongside me – what would I say?

In the event, a fruitless hunt for a condom last night meant that copulation was out. This was on the grounds that Frank said he didn't know where I'd been, and couldn't afford to take the risk.

So he showed me some Japanese massage techniques which, at one point, involved my hands being held behind my back while he did intriguing things with his big toes – and he has surprisingly *big* big toes.

'Look upon this as a rehearsal,' he had said before he fell asleep. 'The performance is tomorrow night.'

That promise has filled me with panic.

In the kitchen I load the dishwasher, stack the empty wine bottles outside in the yard and make a cup of coffee. Then I sit on the garden bench and watch as Letty chases squirrels in the sun in the coppice at the bottom of Olivia's garden. Suddenly, Frank's voice asks, 'More coffee?'

He stands at the kitchen door. Unlike me, daylight suits him.

'That colour looks good on you,' he says. Frank is careful to keep his distance, no assumption of intimacy.

'You're nice in bed,' he adds. I can't remember the last time anybody has said that to me. Well, yes I can, actually. It was Ronnie Stephens, Easter, 1971, and I didn't feel nearly as grateful as I do now.

'Coffee?' Frank asks again.

'No, thank you. Really, it's almost time I went. I've got a lot on and I promised I'd be back, make an early start.'

'Leave? At seven-thirty? On a Sunday?'

It does sound foolish. Frank goes into the kitchen and I follow. He makes more coffee and toast and we both eat silently. I am wordless because if I ask questions about his background, he might think I'm keen. If I make small talk, he might think I'm being flippant. And if I am honest, I'll have to tell him that I can't spend a second night with him.

For a start, everybody in Olivia's house will *know*. Second, it changes the nature of the encounter. Last night was spontaneous, tonight will be *planned*. Third, I'm feeling too unloved to allow myself the risk of liking a man who is half my age. What's more, in spite of intensive efforts on my part to pick up clues that Frank is a prat – instant suntan in his toilet bag; excessive use of the mirror; dark glasses at breakfast – none have been forthcoming. He is dangerously, well, *nice*.

He brushes a strand of hair out of my eyes.

'What you need, Kay, is someone to take care of you,' he says, eerily echoing Mo. Unnerved, I am blunt.

'Look, Frank, what I really don't want or need now is a relationship. I'm . . . involved . . . in London – I mean I couldn't, you know . . . and it wouldn't work because, well . . . and I think you know what I'm trying to say . . .. So, while it was very nice, that is the beginning and end of it. I'm very sorry if this is hurtful, but isn't it best to be frank, Frank?'

162

My cheeks burn. Frank is not impressed. He puts both arms around me and kisses me on the mouth.

'Kay, you are too honest for your own good,' he says.

He sits me down and courteously explains that he has no intention of getting involved. He plans to return to Japan soon. It's simply that another twenty-four hours in my company is a pleasurable way to spend his time. So he says.

'Sometimes the enjoyment is all the richer because both people know that the entire lifetime of the encounter will last only a few hours. Do you understand what I'm saying?

'If both people understand that, then there's no need for game-playing, no need for subterfuge, no need for anxiety. It's pleasure for the body and the soul. Today I can explore your soul and tonight I can admire your body.'

I am miffed. In theory, I'm all in favour of this above-board, no-nonsense approach. In practice, deep down, I want Frank to fall in love with me. Preferably in a big way. I don't know why. Perhaps it's pride. Perhaps then it gives the sex a purpose other than pure pleasure. Pure pleasure makes me nervous.

'Let's take Letty for a stroll and you can decide later what you're going to do,' Frank proposes.

We walk and talk for an hour and by the time we return to Olivia's house, now full of the aroma of frying eggs and bacon, I have decided.

Call me old-fashioned, but first I have to make my position clear to Tom. Just because he behaves like a shit doesn't mean I have to as well.

I *can* be a Casanova along with the next man – but I want my terms of engagement to be consistent, to me at least. No false promises of love; no subterfuge with Tom; no telling myself that I'm in search of a better idea of who I am, only to leap on the first Tom-replacement who happens to come along. And then sliding back into living my life through somebody else's experiences.

'I'm going to leave after breakfast,' I say to Frank. 'I really do have something to sort out but if you feel like it, and you've time before you go back to Tokyo, why don't you come and have a drink?'

'It will be a pleasure,' he says, making a bow, neither wounded nor, annoyingly, that disappointed.

'I mean this as a compliment,' I say. 'You know you're very mature for your age? . . . I hope that doesn't sound too patronizing.'

'It does,' he says, giving me a smile. 'But I haven't finished with you yet.'

I haven't finished with you yet . . . The words run through my head again and again as I drive back to London. And they make me smile.

I arrive at lunch-time. I expect the house to be empty and it is, but there is a note on the table. It's from Tom and, unexpectedly, it has today's date on it. He should be in Sheffield. It reads:

Dear Kay,
   Come round to Charlotte's as soon as you get back.
      Love, Tom.
PS I need to see you to talk. This has got out of hand.

I haven't finished with you yet . . . Is that what Tom is saying too? *I haven't finished with you yet.*

Am I relieved? Or sorry?

Chapter Fourteen

A police car is parked outside Charlotte and Martin's house. I knock on the door and nobody answers. I go round the back and, through the kitchen window, like a publicity shot from a soap opera, I see what looks like a tableau of a family group, each member's face marked with the imprimatur of the soaps: worry.

Charlotte frowns; Tabitha looks bored; a policeman and policewoman converse with Charlotte; Tom leans against the dishwasher and rubs his eyes while Martin looks grim as he walks up and down with Otis in his arms.

I tap on the window. Tom's look of relief when he sees my face touches me. But then again, police unsettle him. He lets me in and gives me a surprisingly enthusiastic embrace.

'What is it? What on earth's happened?' I ask. Tabitha smiles wearily at me as if to say Hello. 'Why are the police here?'

I glance again at Tabitha who now appears vaguely defiant.

'Is it shoplifting? Has Tabitha been shoplifting?'

'Pulleease!' she responds with indignation.

I only suggest it because Kate and Claire briefly went through a stage. They proved alarmingly adept. They justified it by saying they never nicked anything they wanted, only what they didn't want. Hence the cache of delicate leather gloves and boxes of depilatory cream we discovered in their rooms.

'Shoplifting? You must be joking,' Tabitha says scornfully. 'I wouldn't be seen dead doing that. It's so *common*.'

'It's all right, Kay, Tabitha has been terribly brave,' Charlotte's voice resonates with emotion. 'I'm very, very proud of her.'

Tabitha responds by raising her eyes to heaven. 'Look,' she says with all the fierceness that an eleven-year-old can muster, outnumbered by adults six to one. 'I don't know why you lot are making such a fuss. And there was absolutely no need for Charlotte to come back,' she adds, addressing her mother with unconcealed anger. 'We were managing perfectly well on our own, weren't we, Martin? We do normally, so what's the big deal now?'

Charlotte tries to give Tabitha a hug but she pulls away. Martin deposits the baby on the policeman and walks into the hall, indicating that I should follow.

'What exactly has happened?' I ask again.

Martin is whispering a touch theatrically.

'Tabitha and her friend were in the park yesterday evening,' he says. 'They use it as a short cut but they're not supposed to go in there after dark. A man came up to them and exposed himself. He didn't touch them. Luckily, a bloke walking his dog appeared and the fellow ran off.

'Anyway,' Martin continues, resting against the wall and shoving his glasses up on the top of his head, 'Tabitha didn't tell me any of this until seven o'clock this morning. I think she thought the other girl would tell her parents so she'd better do the same.'

'Is she upset?'

'Well, to be honest, she seems more concerned about the fact that she was in the park when she shouldn't have been . . . Anyway, I phoned Charlotte and she spoke to Tabitha.'

'And?'

'Tabitha wouldn't say much except that everyone was making a big deal over nothing. And Charlotte should stay where she was, we could manage. Of course, that was a challenge that Charlotte couldn't refuse. She insisted on coming back – much to my relief, to be honest.

'Well, Charlotte was in too much of a state to drive and you know what it's like on a Sunday with trains. Anyway, the upshot was, Tom offered to drive her back.'

'Did he?' I'm surprised to feel a twinge of pride.

As if on cue, Tom comes out of the kitchen, carrying two mugs of coffee. He seems to sense I may have defrosted slightly. 'I thought you might like a cup,' he says and raises his eyebrows to me, as if to say, 'How's it going?'

'A police artist's here,' Tom says. 'They reckon this bloke might have seriously assaulted another girl. Tabs is doing very well. She's watched this sort of scene so many times on the telly, she's putting heart and soul into the description, even down to the blackheads around his nose.

'All right, mate?' Tom pats Martin on the back and goes back into the kitchen.

'*Is* Tabitha handling it well?' I ask Martin.

'Charlotte and the police think she's handling it *too* well,' he replies gloomily. 'When Charlotte got here . . . I mean, she needed to know how far the man had gone. And I didn't think it was . . . you know . . . appropriate for me to be asking those sorts of questions.' Martin stumbles.

'Apparently, Charlotte asked Tabitha if the man's penis was floppy or straight. Tabitha replied, "Do you mean, did he have a hard-on?"'

I try not to smile. 'Charlotte went absolutely bananas. How did her daughter know such language? What had I been teaching her, all that crap. Tabitha says everyone talks like that at school.

'The police keep asking me pointed questions. I mean I don't mind at all, children *should* be protected and I *am* the stepfather, but it's bloody uncomfortable.'

'Oh, I'm sure they don't think—' I interrupt.

'Oh, yes, they bloody do. But Tom has been brilliant, bloody brilliant,' Martin says.

'He has?'

'Jesus, yes. If he hadn't been here, the police would have stuck me in an ID parade just in case they could clear up a couple of dozen other cases of sexual abuse while they were at it.

'Not that I mind,' Martin adds hastily. 'I'm on the child's side. I love Tabs. And as a man, I take responsibility for, well, you know . . . Except that when they do it in my own home, I can't help but feel, well, it's a bit bloody much.

'Do you think it's all right to feel like that?' he inquires anxiously.

In the early evening, we leave Martin and Charlotte. The tour is to resume tomorrow. Tabitha is booked in with a child psychiatrist so at least the grown-ups will feel better. Martin's anxiety has abated, helped by several cans of draught Guinness.

Tom and I eat in our local Indian restaurant and keep rigidly to conversations which do not involve me or him. So we talk mainly about Kate and Claire and memories of their childhood. It's as if I am in conversation with a stranger.

Over coffee, Tom suddenly says, 'Kay, I want you to know that this is one of the best evenings we've had in a long time. I feel close to you again. Really close.

'I don't want to say anything more than this, but I *am* sorry. I did have a brief affair. You're right, she wasn't – isn't – Russian, it was friendship, a work thing, you know how it is . . . And I felt your interest in me had . . . well, you don't – didn't – seem involved, not like you used to be . . .

'You remember the night that *Birth Blues* went out?' Tom persists.

Birth Blues must have been a year or so ago. It was around the time that Kate had been rushed to hospital with a burst appendix and I'd just got back from Belfast where I'd been working on a long feature for *Tangiers*. I'd spent the previous night at the hospital, alone because Tom 'couldn't get away'.

'You fell asleep watching my film,' Tom says. 'Don't you remember?' he looks so self-pitying. 'You used to be so *interested* in everything I did, Kay.'

What he means is that I used to provide twenty-four-hour groom service. He's right. He still expects the terms I willingly accepted for years. I want them renegotiated – but, apart from Brenda getting the bullet, in what way?

How can I ask of him when I don't yet know what I want myself? And would he, in any case, be prepared to accommodate?

Tom is speaking again: 'Anyway, this woman . . . was around, and it sort of happened.'

I can tell by the way he hunches his shoulders and rubs his cheek, his favourite signs of contrition, that this brief spell in the confessional box is not, for him, without its pleasures. I pick up the little dish of chutney on the table and sniff it.

'Mangoes,' I say.

'What?' Tom asks, annoyed that he has been interrupted mid-flow.

'Mangoes. I love the smell of mangoes. It reminds me of someone . . . You were saying?'

'Well, neither Bren— the other woman, nor I, wanted it to happen.' It's as if Tom believes that if he doesn't use her name, he dilutes the significance of what has occurred.

'It was sort of forced on us. She is involved in a difficult relationship too.' I ignore the 'too'. If I don't ask Tom questions, he doesn't have to lie.

'Anyway, I've told her: it's over,' Tom says.

'Told her yesterday, as a matter of fact. You're smiling, Kay,

169

why are you smiling? I don't see that there's much to smile about. It hasn't been easy for me, you know.'

'I thought you were with Charlotte all day yesterday. Did you call from the train? Or when you got to the hotel?' I ask mechanically. Even the roar has absented itself.

'The train?' Tom says. '. . . Excuse me, could we have more coffee, please?' He seeks the attention of the waiter. 'And another couple of glasses of house white?'

Tom turns back to me and instantly, I *know*. He shrugs his shoulders and starts speaking but what he says is muffled, as if there are half a dozen rolls of cotton wool between him and me. Tom picks up a teaspoon and plays with it.

'What I mean is, I haven't actually told her yet, Kay,' he says, his eyes fixed on the gymnastics he is imposing on the spoon. 'I haven't had a chance. I mean for *your* sake, I want to do this properly, Kay. But I do mean to do it.

'Kay?' He reaches out and squeezes my hand. 'I love you, Kay, honestly I do.'

I look at Tom and, perhaps for the first time, I begin to see him clearly.

The Georgian house off Piccadilly has no name-plate. It is Monday at nine a.m. and Rosemary lets me in with her own key. Each member of Jades, a club for women, has her own key. Inside, the décor and furnishings are as relentlessly uncomfortable as that of many gentlemen's clubs except less shabby. Unimaginatively, success for the clientele of Jades clearly means doing what the boys do.

The restaurant is busy. Rosemary orders coffee, orange juice and croissants. The croissants are a mistake, since every time I eat one in public, I spend the rest of the day removing crumbs, like confectioner's dandruff, from my clothes.

I wear a dark green trouser suit which I bought for Mo's third (and so far, last) engagement party two years ago. It seems to have come back into fashion. I've also chosen one of the more discreet Kitchen Sync brooches; a small circle of clipped silver-painted wire wool, shaped like a nest with a miniature padlock buried in its centre. The joke is that I wear the two small keys to the padlock as earrings, one in each ear.

A quick look around at the assembled ensembles with chains and ID bracelets prominently displayed makes me wonder if I'm not inadvertently transmitting sexual semaphore via my ear lobes.

A woman at the next table wears a black bowler-hat pulled low on her brow. She also has enough facial hair to make the resemblance to Charlie Chaplin too close to call.

Images range from studiously scruffy to an overdose of helmet hairdos, lip-liner and blusher used with the kind of gusto I last saw in a charcoal sketch of a Yorkshire pit.

A beautiful waitress, her arms decorated with enough silver bracelets to conceal the neck of a giraffe, slams the coffee down with the bad-tempered chic usually required of such places.

'Hi, Rosie,' the waitress says. I've never thought of Rosemary as a Rosie but the almost famous often seem to allow waiters and waitresses to assume an intimacy they deny everyone else.

'Fucking horrible morning,' the waitress adds in an upper-class voice. 'Loulou insisted on table seventeen. The best table or else. If you ask me, it's just like all the rest. Then, of course, that Josephine Somebody-or-other . . . You know the actress who writes the clapped-out restaurant column because she's too drunk to stand up straight on stage? Well, she was already sitting at seventeen, so we had merry hell to pay between the two of them.

'It's only breakfast, for God's sake. It's not even as if either of them eats anything.'

Rosemary smiles sympathetically. She wears granny specs, a very short bright red wig and a long, full-skirted grey dress, belted at the waist and with a white Peter Pan collar. Her boots are flat and black with silver spurs. The overall effect is that of a wicked puritan.

'I reckon that old cow Josephine is so crabby because this is her AFD,' the waitress continues, sweeping the croissant crumbs left by the previous occupiers of our table on to my lap.

'AFD?' I ask.

'Alcohol Free Day,' she looks at me condescendingly. 'You can always tell when one of them's on it. What is it we're supposed to drink? Fourteen units a week? More like fourteen-fucking-hundred in this place.

'Glass of champagne?' she asks Rosemary. 'It's on special offer. Three quid a glass.'

An hour later, the deal is struck. I will become *Venus*'s roving correspondent. I will write six pieces on a trial basis at £3,000 a piece plus expenses. This is roughly £2,700 more than I have been receiving from *Tangiers*. The pieces, fiction and non-fiction, are supposed to convey the erotic via human interest. If I'm really pushed and arrive at the lust frontier with nothing to say, I can revert to humour. I do not have to give up my commitment to *Tangiers*.

'I want *trigger phrases*!' Rosemary enthuses. 'Phrases which carry wonderful connotations for the readers, phrases on which they can feed their imagination. I don't want *dirty* writing, that's *passé*, darling. I want *dangerous* writing.'

As she speaks, Rosemary inserts a piece of croissant into her mouth without a single crumb clinging to her lips. This woman is frightening.

I tell Rosemary that I don't believe I'm capable of fulfilling her brief – partly because I'm not altogether clear what 'dangerous writing' *means*. When pressed, it turns out that neither does she.

'It just *sounds* wonderful,' she says, offering a cheek to some-one passing our table. Silently, the young woman grazes it with a kiss and whispers *Ciao* to me as if we've been friends for years. Then she slides away, jewellery clanking like bells on a train of oxen.

My insistence that I am likely to fail is genuine. Rosemary regards this as a coded request for more money.

'OK,' she says, 'Four thousand.'

I stop voicing any more fears lest the money go even higher. Stupidly, I've always preferred to be underpaid. £300 I can live up to – £3,000, I'm not so sure. This, I know, is not grown-up, market-place behaviour.

I hand over to Rosemary the tale (tail?) of the bare bottom which I'd told the workshop a few days ago. She reads it in less time than it takes to pour myself a second cup of coffee.

'Absolutely on the button,' she says. 'Sophisticated writing for women who appreciate intelligent pokes—'

'Blokes?' I repeat.

'No, darling,' Rosemary smiles. 'Pokes. P-O-K-E-S.'

Rosemary suggests that we meet tomorrow evening so that she can take me to an event which is 'the kind of relaxation' quite popular with a certain section of readers of *Venus*.

'Admittedly, not the most avant-garde section. Traditionalists in their tastes, really. But it'll give you a start.'

Then, she says, next week I will be dispatched to New York for a special interview that her assistant is still trying to line up. I usually 'line up' my own interviews, but I decide not to object. Instead, I make a request.

'Could I go a bit later, please?' I ask. 'It's just that my husband has a documentary on the television. And, well, I should be here . . .'

Even as I speak, I'm asking myself, *why* should I be here?

Rosemary smiles. 'Feel free to make your own mistakes,' she says waspishly.

'You know something, Kay,' she adds as she signs for the bill and we prepare to leave. 'I've been doing this a long time. We need a fresh view and my instincts tell me you've got a hidden talent for this kind of thing . . . If, that is, you have the courage to dig it out of yourself.

'Kiss, kiss,' she instructs, pouting her lips in goodbye.

Later, in the taxi, I think back on her words. *'If you have the courage . . .'*

I suspect for Rosemary 'courage' equates with the determination to satisfy her own needs and hang the cost to anyone else.

To me, 'courage' is something to do with trying to fashion a moral code for myself. One that includes treating others as I would wish to be treated. 'Morality' is almost entirely a do-it-yourself exercise anyway these days. We have no Church to voice its disapproval; we have no iron-toothed consensus on what is – or is not – deemed 'Respectable' (with all the hypocrisy that entails); we have no fear of widescale censure should we break the rules.

In that void, it makes it all the more important, perhaps, for us to develop a sense of individual responsibility, a personal morality. I'm beginning to think it's *that* which takes real courage. And I'm not sure I have it.

As I walk into Tom's outer office I can see him through the half-open door, feet up on the desk, reading a manuscript. Pam gives me a kiss on the cheek.

'You look terrific,' she says, a compliment devalued only because it is her standard greeting to everyone, even the gasman.

I walk through into Tom's room. When he looks up, his face is somehow much, much older. He glances at his watch, a nervous reaction, and shouts to the secretary, 'Did you book the minicab? The bastards came fifteen minutes late last time.'

He shuts the connecting door without waiting for an answer. 'Train goes at twelve-fifty,' he says although I haven't asked. Not very long ago, I would have known that anyway. How quickly a crack becomes a chasm.

'Tom, I've got something—'

'Kay, I want you to be honest,' Tom says. We speak simultaneously, Tom wins.

'Kay, when you went away for the weekend, did you stay anywhere near Hitchin?'

'Yes,' I reply, mystified.

Tom's face is a mask of malevolence but hurt is in his eyes, not anger.

'You cunt,' he shouts. 'There I was, grovelling away, apologizing for some stupid little fucking dalliance with someone who doesn't make me feel that everything I do is not quite right, not quite good enough, a sheer bloody failure, and what have you been doing? And for Christ knows how long?

'Screwing yourself silly with the husband of your best friend. Some bloody sisterhood you fucking well belong to!

'Well, I hope that wet-faced creep of an arsehole has got more out of you than I ever managed to.

'He should've fucking called me first. I could've told him. It's not worth the bloody effort, mate. You've got about as much bloody sex appeal as an armadillo.

'I take that back. An armadillo probably has some fucking way of telling you it's come. It certainly doesn't say, "It's all right, why don't you go ahead, I'm not really in the mood tonight."'

I don't attempt to interrupt since experience has taught me that, in full rant, Tom hears only the sound of his own eloquence. Besides, I love the man. Strange as it may seem, it upsets me to see him this way.

'I've just about had enough,' he says, pacing up and down behind his desk.

'You make me feel so bloody guilty, I have to stay away from my own fucking home for days on end. And all the time somebody's been giving you one. Or is it half a bloody dozen?' Tom hasn't finished yet.

'I suppose you're going to tell me that you're in love with the stupid bloody twat? At least I know that a screw is a screw. No bloody confusion about that. But you've got your heart caught up in your fucking knicker-elastic.'

He stands stock-still in front of me and puts both hands on his hips.

'Mike bloody Robinson. I mean if you're going to stick one on me, at least show some bloody taste. He's such a ferret-faced fucking juvenile.'

'I thought Mike was a friend of yours?' I finally respond, albeit mildly. 'Anyway, what's Hitchin got to do with it?'

'Don't come that one with me,' Tom says, sneering. And suddenly changes tack. 'Africa? Has he been to fucking Africa? I hope you've practised safe sex! That's bloody it! We're done for – tests. We'll have to have tests.'

'Glasgow,' I reply.

'What?' says Tom.

'Glasgow. The furthest Mike travels is to Glasgow.'

'Glasgow! That's almost as bad . . . syringes . . . Christ knows what . . . Condoms, I hope you've used condoms! How could you bloody *do* this to us, Kay. How could you humiliate me in front of all my friends, just when it was all beginning to be all right?'

The latter is news to me.

'I haven't used condoms,' I say.

Tom goes white. I suppose his medical background must make him extra sensitive to such issues. I wonder what he murmurs in bed to Brenda?

'I love you darling, but just in passing, any problems with thrush?'

'I haven't used condoms with anybody at any time,' I say with absolute truthfulness. At least Rule Number One, honesty, hasn't fallen at the first hurdle.

'I certainly haven't used any with Mike because I've never been to bed with him. He hasn't asked. I haven't offered. As I keep telling you, I haven't seen him since before the weekend.'

'He drew money from a cash dispenser in Hitchin on Saturday,' Tom says sullenly. 'The police phoned Angela this morning. He doesn't know anyone there, no family, no friends. Bit of a coincidence, isn't it?'

'Life is full of coincidences,' I say airily. 'It's one huge coincidence that the researcher on your film happens to be the Russian woman who now apparently doesn't exist who happens to have a name you can never remember. What is it Betty, Bella, Bethany . . .?'

'Brenda,' the word bursts out of Tom before he can stop himself.

'Which brings me to why I'm here,' I tell Tom.

I know that if I don't lay out some ground for myself now, I'll be sucked back into his manipulations – and I'll never find the courage again.

I explain that I have a new job as *Venus's* roving correspondent. I am returning to full-time work and I shall be away often. Somebody else will have to walk the dog.

Tom is briefly under the misapprehension that *Venus* is a magazine for astrologers. When I succinctly put him in the picture and tell him that I have every intention of writing under my married name, does he congratulate me on my enterprise? Does he tell me how proud he is that I am making a new beginning in my forties? Does he offer to don suitable protection and explore the stranger shores of erotica with me?

He does not.

'Fucking hell!' is what Tom says.

'You must be out of your bloody mind. How could you do this to me? I'll be a laughing-stock. My reputation will be ruined. Christ, you're going to turn us both into a freak show. Every time you write a bloody word, they'll think it's about me.'

'Surely not, darling,' I reply as sweetly as my anger, now raging, will allow. 'My first piece is about penis extensions for the less-endowed man. And both you and I know that can't possibly refer to you, can it?'

Tom is not remotely amused. I upset him further by announcing that I want a temporary separation. I announce that I intend to take lovers (what I don't tell Tom is that I haven't a clue how to go about this and, Frank apart, I can't remember the last time I fancied a man other than my husband). I will tell these potential lovers that I have no intention of becoming involved.

'I see this openness to sexual encounters as a basic means of self-knowledge,' I add and I'm not surprised when Tom snorts in derision.

'Jesus fucking Christ,' he elaborates. 'If you're bloody horny, say so. Don't wrap it up in all this crap.'

His eyes narrow. His ego, temporarily KOd, is up off the canvas again.

'I bloody know what this is all about,' he says triumphantly. He comes around to my side of his desk, sits on the edge and puts his nose an inch from mine.

'You're out for revenge. You've gone shag-nasty. That's what it is. You think that, if he's screwed a bit, then why shouldn't I? How bloody childish can you get? Naughty boy has to be punished. Well, I'll tell you this for nothing. You won't enjoy a minute. You're not built for it.

'You know what revenge does? It fucks you up. It makes you bitter. You want revenge, you bloody have it. See if I care. But don't expect me to be sitting around waiting for you when your little spell of punishment is over.'

'It's not revenge,' I say calmly.

'Of course it bloody is,' Tom insists vehemently.

'It's not about revenge,' I insist. 'It's about redemption. *My* redemption. I've expected far too much of you – of us. Too much that was impossible to deliver.

'That's not your fault, it's mine. I've begun to do what I vowed I'd never do. I live my life vicariously through you and when that isn't satisfying enough, I blame you.

'The only way I have any sense of myself is through your opinions of me, and the twins' opinions. But recently I've begun to see something of what other people bring out in me, and even if I say so myself, it's not *all* bad.

'So this *is* about redemption. I really feel that we're two quarters who can't possibly make up a whole. You're plainly not getting what you want from me and I'm not even clear any more what I want from you.' I shrug.

'If anything, the only person I risk hurting in all this is myself. I have a feeling that deep down, you've probably ceased to care but you haven't got the honesty to admit it – probably for fear of hurting me.' The irony makes me smile.

'It's odd, isn't it, how so many married couples put up with indifference for a very long time and fool themselves into believing it's another form of love?'

I propose to Tom that we pretend all is normal to the twins. In three months' time, if we decide to part permanently, then we'll have to talk to Kate and Claire. On the other hand, if we decide to stay married, we will have to renegotiate the terms.

Tom speaks. 'Well, I'm not moving out of the house, and that's flat. I was right about you all along,' he adds. 'You're no bloody sticker. As soon as there's a bit of trouble, you're up and off.'

'It *is* twenty years,' I protest. I'm beginning to weaken. It's time to leave.

'Oh, and you haven't screwed around?' Tom's voice curls with spite.

'I haven't yet. Not quite,' I reply as evenly as I can. 'But I might.'

I walk out, close the door behind me and lean against it. Christ, what a mess.

I realize that Pam has put down several cassette tapes on her desk and has her hands out as if in supplication. More bad news. The secretary and the researcher keep their heads down.

'Look, Kay,' Pam says, dropping her voice to a whisper. 'I couldn't help but overhear. I'm really sorry. I've been wanting to say this to you for ages and, well, I didn't know how.

'It's me as well,' she says. 'I don't know why, he's such a . . . a . . . an appealing bastard. Look, I don't have to tell you that, do I?' she half smiles.

'It was months back. Just once. Matter of fact, he banged on about you so much, it put me off. We were away filming.'

I smile at Pam. I like her, I really do.

'Filming, you say? Well, you're probably not the first,' I reply wearily.

Pam looks apologetic. 'I'm afraid I'm not,' she says.

Chapter Fifteen

In the five hours since talking to Tom, he has phoned several times. The answering-machine is on, since I suspect that his intention is not to obtain a reprieve but to ensure that he has the last word.

I've filled the hours with non-stop activity. I've swum, produced four brooches for Olivia (my career at *Venus* may be brief so I have no intention of closing down my other cottage industry) and had a fruitless hunt through Tom's bookshelf.

This obsession with finding fresh evidence of his infidelity has almost turned into a hobby. *And how do you fill in your spare time, Ms Woods? Oh, I go potholing in my husband's study in search of love-letters from his mistress. Yes, it is jolly interesting. Another advantage is that you don't have to give it up as you get older.*

It hasn't taken long to discover that it's a sport at which I can't win. If I'm successful and unearth a card or a note or a whole letter, it hurts. When I fail, and find nothing, it still hurts.

I drop my green trouser suit into the dry-cleaners, so it's ready for tomorrow's expedition with Rosemary. If it's an orgy, I want to arrive well-buttoned-up. I'm an observer, not a participant.

The woman in the cleaners' doesn't gas as long as she usually does, so I arrive at the wine bar twenty minutes early. The wine bar is very close to the workshop and I've arranged to meet Mo for a drink.

I find myself eavesdropping on a couple possibly in their fifties.

The woman talks non-stop, the man nods occasionally. She is dressed expensively; her make-up has reached the point at which blusher becomes rouge and foundation becomes face-mask.

A waitress brings a bottle and two glasses and what looks like a dish of mussels in a cream sauce which she places in front of the woman.

The woman talks on fast-forward. 'I have to tell myself all the time, "This isn't fat, it's muscle weight." I need to eat to keep up my energy, Harold. I couldn't possibly sit for three hours in a theatre with nothing inside me, it's not good for me.'

She picks up on the conversation hindered by the arrival of the food.

'So I told her straight, Harold, I said, "What you need is non-interruption therapy. I mean what is it that you can't let anyone speak without putting your opinion here, there and everywhere? What do you think, Harold?'

Harold opens his mouth and his companion rattles on.

'This is delicious, like a taste?'

Harold opens his mouth again and his companion continues. 'I mean, how come she's got so much confidence when twenty people for twenty years have been telling her she needs non-interruption therapy, and still she doesn't change? What kind of a woman is that, Harold?

Harold shuts his mouth and sighs.

'And then when she appeared in those leopard-skin leggings. I mean tight! Nobody wears leopard-skin leggings when they are eight months pregnant. She looked like Humpty Dumpty with a rash.

'We had to fight her to put a shirt on over that stomach. Confident! It's obscene. What do you think Harold?'

Harold waits until the woman's mouth is full of mussels then he seizes his chance.

'What I think,' he says lugubriously, 'is that I'd like to hear her side of the story—'

Then Harold is forced back into his cell of silence.

His comment stabs. Tom hasn't been able to put his side of the story either. Perhaps he's got good reason to behave as he has. Perhaps it's me.

Fortunately, Mo arrives. If anyone can keep me resolute, she can.

'Have you got two cold bottles of champagne, please?' Mo asks the waitress. 'The off-licence has only got warm and I haven't got time to go anywhere else. We'll take it with us, if that's OK?'

'I talked to Dionne this morning,' Mo explains to me. 'She let slip it's her fortieth birthday. So a couple of us are going to bring some drink and lighten up. Enjoy ourselves.'

Mo wears a dark brown trouser suit, lemon round-necked jumper and matching socks, plus pearls and two-tone brogues. Her hair shines, her skin is clear, her nails gleam with colourless nail varnish. Her teeth are white.

If I opted for the same outfit, I'd resemble a very tired dyke in search of a snooker table. One of the unforeseen penalties of growing older is that I am fading.

Mo sits next to me like a tribute to Technicolor. In contrast, I look as if I have been washed several hundred times at too high a temperature.

'Do you know how bloody scarce they are?' Mo suddenly asks. 'Who are?'

'Men. Available men. I take back all I said about Tom. You're very lucky to have him. Hold on to him at all costs.

'I don't think I've ever felt more depressed in my life,' she pauses melodramatically and pulls out a single page of a newspaper.

'Read this. No, let me read it to you, on second thoughts. You're hopeless with figures.'

Mo waves her hand as a thank-you to the waitress who arrives with the champagne, then reads: 'A forty-year-old man who wants a girlfriend between thirty and thirty-four will have a pool of 573,000 available women. A forty-year-old woman trying to find a partner between forty-five and forty-nine will only have 228,000 men to draw on.'

She puts the paper down triumphantly.

'It's still an awful lot,' I say hesitantly, not quite sure how I am supposed to react. 'And you don't *have* to stick to your own age-group.'

'Jesus!' Mo says exasperated. 'It's not the numbers, you idiot. It's the bloody competition. No matter what the men do, they know *there'll always be another one*. There will always be another woman.'

'It's an attitude of mind, Mo,' I say not believing a word of what I say. 'If you had half a million men, you might not find one that's suitable – if in your heart you're ambivalent about the exercise in the first place.

'Perhaps some people are made to live alone and the rest of us torture them into believing that they *must* buy into true romance. I know lots of people who are perfectly happy to be single. They see romance as an unnecessary diversion, not the be-all and end-all of life.'

'Name one,' Mo demands.

And, of course, I can't.

We are five minutes late for the workshop. On one of the tables several bottles of wine and plastic glasses are dumped, plus a bright yellow quiche not unlike a bathroom sponge and sticks of bread and lumps of cheese.

In the centre is a vast chocolate cake, shaped like a hedgehog covered in vast amounts of what look like sticks of chocolate vermicelli.

'It's me,' shouts Dionne across the room, glass in hand. 'It's me!' A drink has obviously been taken.

Mo looks as baffled as I am.

'Taste it, it smells divine,' Dionne instructs, sticking her finger into the thick, gluey icing. I copy. My finger is a fraction of an inch from my mouth when Dionne announces, 'Can't you see? The cake: it's a copy of my mons veneris.'

She doubles up laughing. I hastily wipe my finger on a paper napkin. But Dionne is right, it does smell divine.

Tilly writes on the blackboard. When she finishes, I read, *'The older one grows, the more one likes indecency. Virginia Woolf.'*

'It's not me,' Tilly says, embarrassed. 'Anna told me to put it up.'

Alex smokes a joint with her feet up on a chair. Liz is showing Carol several small Regency figurines.

'Ooh, aren't they lovely,' Carol says, as she examines one, a man and a woman, more closely. 'Oh, my word!' she suddenly adds and puts the figurine down quickly. Liz chuckles.

'Dionne, these are for you,' Liz says with an expansiveness I suspect is based three-quarters on alcohol. I suddenly realize that Liz is close to tears.

'Are you OK?' I ask. Liz is examining the figurine discarded by Carol. It shows a woman, her skirt held high, as a dandy enters her from behind.

'Aren't they lovely?' Liz says. 'I found them in a little shop in Aberystwyth. Present for Phil. We went there last weekend. You know, give ourselves a break. It was supposed to be sex, sex, sex all the way. Or rather, as Phil would prefer to put it, lovemaking, lovemaking, lovemaking.'

'What happened?' I ask, partly because that's what Liz expects.

'We walked, ate, drank and slept like babies. Then I gave Phil

185

this lot. I didn't expect him to be grateful or anything but he said he felt I was putting unbearable pressure on his performance.

'I said, "What performance?" It popped out before I could stop myself. He said he thought me coming here, to the workshop, was a distinct threat to our relationship. And he knew people were supposed to work at relationships but ours has been more effort than the Hundred Years War. He said he'd had enough.'

'So what happened then?' I prompt.

'He said he was sorry,' Liz says glumly.

'Well that's OK, isn't it?'

Liz has tears running down her cheeks.

'No, it isn't. He's right. We each want something different and we each keep pretending what we've got is all right really.'

'Well, a lot of people use that as a basis for a very long and reasonably happy marriage,' I offer, sounding uncomfortably like my mother.

'Yes, Kay dear,' Liz explains, wiping away her tears. 'But Phil and I are *modern*.'

Five minutes later, the reason for the atmosphere of anarchy is apparent. Not only is it Dionne's birthday, but Anna is absent. She had phoned in earlier to say that she had a migraine but that we should consider for discussion the comment of Virginia Woolf.

'Not a lot to say, really, is there?' offers Dionne. 'Except that I agree.'

We decide that this is the official group position and move on. Mo pours more wine, Alex passes round the joint.

'Anybody done their homework?' Tilly asks.

'I did,' Carol replies and shrugs. 'I can't help it. It was the same in school. I always did what I was told to do. Pathetic really.

'Seventeen ways to masturbate and I got to fourteen,' she announces proudly. 'Mind you, I can't deny I cheated.'

'How the hell can you cheat, woman?' Dionne asks.

'Well, you know she said we weren't to use any battery-operated equipment and the like? What Anna didn't think of was the footsie-roller!'

'What a wheeze! A footsie-roller. Oh, God, you didn't . . .? God, what if you'd lost it?' Liz's mouth is full of chocolate cake.

'You'd have ended up in casualty with all those men with vacuum cleaners stuck on the end of their willies,' Alex reports.

Carol looks alarmed.

Tilly calls for quiet and says she has an announcement to make.

'What I want to say is this. I feel very, very, sorry for men.' She is met with silence.

'Admittedly,' she says, 'I've never had a violent experience and I've only had carnal knowledge for a fortnight or so. Well, twelve days actually. But I've been shown nothing but kindness and understanding.'

'Christ,' says Mo, 'How many men have you had in twelve days, sweetheart?'

'Just one. Jacky. He's a pet. And I realize now what difficulties lads face.'

We all look at each other blankly. Then Liz gives a shriek.

'Oh, God, you poor little sod. He's impotent, isn't he? Oh, my poor lamb.'

'Not impotent,' Tilly corrects primly. 'He can't . . . do it, sometimes. Sometimes, he can. I thought it was me at first but he says it's his mother. It's her fault. He's had the problem quite a long time. I mean at least we can fake it, but if they can't do it, well, they can't, can they?'

'OK, girls,' Dionne says, jumping up and heading for the blackboard.

'Our assignment tonight is to redesign the male genitalia. What they need is something compact, easy to carry and above all, reliable. And I mean *reliable*. It has to be pleasing to the eye and, to avoid all complexes, standard in size.'

'Boring!' shouts Alex. 'What's the pleasure in discovery, if they're all the same?'

'Turkey necks,' I offer.

'What, woman? You speak up there at the back!' Dionne instructs in mock seriousness.

'Turkey necks,' I comply. 'Sylvia Plath said that a man's cock reminded her of a turkey's neck.'

Carol squeals with delight.

'That's exactly what my Ken's looks like. A real horror! I keep telling him to cover it up and he thinks it's because I'm shy. It's not that at all. It's just that I can't bear the sight of it.'

'I think they're all quite beautiful,' Mo announces, slightly stoned. 'Quite, quite beautiful. Each very different, but beautiful.'

'OK, here we go,' Dionne announces. She draws what looks like an extended telescope. In a professorial voice, she describes her creation.

'No balls, a retractable penis which is operated by pressure on either nipple, depending on the psychological state of the owner.'

'That won't work,' I say, my pragmatic side refusing to be restrained. 'Every rush hour on the train, bodies pressing against bodies, we'd all be speared by a thousand extending cocks.'

'Some of us are anyway, so what's new?' Alex says drily.

Tilly takes a swig from her glass of wine. 'It's odd, isn't it? I read in a magazine that a woman had some of her fanny removed because it stuck out too far when she wore a swimsuit. She's cutting it off and men are sticking bits on . . . Bloody daft, really. Why can't we all leave well alone? It's not what we've got, it's who it belongs to that counts.'

'God,' Liz says. 'This business of passion can be bloody cold-hearted at times.'

At home, later, I grieve. I grieve because I am unsure whether this will ever be a family house again. And at times, in the past, it has been an extraordinarily happy family house.

I take down the chart from the fridge door and put it in the bin. If all I'm scoring are home goals, what's the point in keeping count?

Chapter Sixteen

The house to which Rosemary takes me is in Guildford. It is a mock Tudor semi. The entire place appears to have been furnished from knick-knacks purchased from the mail-order catalogues which fall out of Sunday newspapers; china Shire horses stand in the grate; a collection of thimbles march across the mantelpiece and characters from Dickens feature on a range of plates which adorn the wall.

On the coffee-table, inlaid with brown tiles, which capture heroes of the Greek myths, sit two large bowls; one of Twiglets, the other of condoms. Neil Diamond provides the background music while a soft-porn movie plays without an audience on the television.

'Feel like a drink?' Rosemary asks as we stand alone in the sitting-room. This popular readers' event seems significant, so far, for its unpopularity. Rosemary wears her Cleopatra wig, an all-in-one rubber catsuit, high-heeled boots and very long artificial nails.

I am only grateful that we didn't travel by public transport.

She pours us each a gin and tonic. 'No ice,' she says. 'Follow me.'

The kitchen is heaving. In the way that human beings do, everyone prefers to be packed into a room the size of four orange-boxes, rather than appear lonely in the sitting-room.

At first, all seems as normal as parties are: a couple of cases of mascara running; a man rocking gently backward and forward, a woman sobbing in the corner saying repeatedly, 'He's a bastard, that's what he is, a bastard. He's a bastard, that's what he is, a bastard. He's a—'

Then I look again. A woman in her fifties sits on the kitchen table, her breasts, huge and mottled with purple veins, hang out of a web of lace which passes for a bra. She wears no top, her skirt is around her waist. Varicose veins are bravely exposed, as are a pair of crotchless pants. She has her head back, oblivious.

A man with a large boil on the back of his neck, his face hidden in her chest, has two fingers up her vagina and is manipulating her with the dexterity he probably usually reserves for his Black and Decker.

Another couple occasionally glance over while chatting about which pub restaurant in Harrow serves the best sirloin steak.

By the double sink, a woman in a toga, which reveals that she has an almost androgynous body, is on her knees, a man's penis in her mouth. The man, in his seventies if not older, holds on to the sink unit for dear life, as if it were a Zimmer frame. Other couples grope and groan or pass the time of day.

'I don't think I'll bother with ice, thanks,' I tell Rosemary. I leave her in the kitchen and retreat to the hall. A man wearing a bright blue satin dressing-gown comes down the stairs. He has dyed black hair, weighs two stone more than he should, but he is handsome. He could be fifty-five, or ten years older, it's difficult to say. He has a swooping swallow tattooed on each hand.

He also has an erection. My stomach sinks to the basement. Convention hasn't equipped me well for such a meeting.

'Pleased to see you,' he says without irony. 'Come here often? Me and the wife come every Tuesday. Change shifts to get here. Funny thing is, she's in the kitchen all the bleeding time at home. And where do you think she is now? In the bleeding kitchen!'

He comes over to me. One hand gently pushes me back against the wall, his knee levers open my legs. The fingers of his other hand skilfully unzip my trousers and lock into my pants. He rubs gently and steadily. It is more pleasant than I wish it to feel, not least because I don't know who the hell he is.

I catch a whiff of the man's breath; the contents of a thousand heated dustbins.

I am wetter. He leers. 'Like that, don't you?' If he'd stayed silent, I might have lingered longer.

'Excuse me,' I say, 'I have to go.'

Upstairs, a couple of indeterminate age and shape vigorously fuck each other on the floor of one bedroom while a trio of men watch disinterestedly, sitting on the bed.

'Give him one, go on,' one man says with about as much enthusiasm as if he was watching a rigged boxing match. 'That's it, go on . . .'

In the second bedroom, a woman in her twenties wearing Gucci loafers is being penetrated doggy-fashion by a man with very greasy hair. Both his hands, wrapped around her waist, are stained orange with nicotine.

'Stay,' he commands me. 'She likes it better if she's got a spectator. Don't you, love?'

'Yes,' the woman says cheerily. 'Do take a perch.'

Her accent is the kind you usually hear from young women who wear pearls and velvet Alice bands and who run their own Montessori nursery schools.

'Anyone for guacamole dip?' says a voice behind me. It's the woman in the toga, her mouth full, this time with a tortilla chip.

'Go on, have some. It's really lovely. Joan makes it herself.'

I decline and go back downstairs, in search of Rosemary. I fail to find her, so I leave. At the garden gate I glance back at the house. It looks *exactly* like the others in the row. So normal. The front door opens and the man in the dressing-gown waves at me.

'See you next week, will we love?' he says cheerily. 'You can rely on a nice crowd here. Lovely to meet you.'

He shuts the door and I am alone in the drizzle. Out of the

'fun'. I'm not offended, I tell myself, I'm more disturbed because it's all so, well, casual. It's also tacky.

A *ménage à trois* may be OK but a *ménage à quarante-neuf* is about forty-six too many. If that's what Rosemary wants me to write about, this may well be my shortest period of employment yet.

An hour later, I'm in the bath when the phone rings. It is Kate and Claire. We chat for over an hour. They are happy and well and cheery. Mo calls later for a progress report on my night out with Rosemary.

'I don't know why, I feel sort of unclean,' I report back, omitting to tell her about the dressing-gown man's facility with his fingers.

'Was it exciting? Come on, it must have been just a teeny bit exciting?' Mo probes.

'Mo, let me make it plain: the house was not exactly huge on heartthrobs.'

'Have you got any Bach's Rescue Remedy?' Mo suggests.

'And what is that?'

'Bach's flower remedies. Try Crab-apple. Put two drops in water.'

'What's in it?' I ask.

'A lot of crab-apples, I presume,' she replies. 'And, of course, a certain amount of brandy. I always take it if a one-night stand goes wrong. It's supposed to treat self-disgust.'

I settle for the brandy.

Early the next morning, I take Letty for a walk and on our return, meet the postman at the front door. He has four letters for me. One is a cheque for £275 from Olivia. Two, I can tell from the handwriting, are from Tom. I put them in the dustbin. The fourth is typewritten.

Inside is a brief letter, dated the day before.

Kay,
    Can you tell the kids I'm all right and missing them please?
I'll see them as soon as I can.
        Love Mike
        PS Hope you're OK.

The postmark is Lytham St Annes. All I know about Lytham St Annes is that it has one of the highest proportions of elderly people in its population. Perhaps Mike has run off with a nonagenarian?

I tell myself not to be flippant. I am relieved to know that he is not dead, suffering from amnesia or bound for the Foreign Legion. Delivering his message, however, is not going to be as easy as he imagines.

Ever the masochist, I phone Angela. 'Who's speaking, please?' she asks in a little-girl-lost voice. When she realizes it's me, her tone turns as hard as Rambo's buttock.

'What do *you* want?' she asks. I can hear someone clanging around in the background.

'It's Kay, Martin,' Angela says, her mouth away from the mouthpiece. She comes back on the line. '*Some* of my friends have been very helpful.

'Martin has just delivered four casseroles he's made for the deep-freeze. So kind of him, don't you think?'

'Angela.' I assess I've got roughly thirty seconds to try and deliver the message. 'Angela, I've heard from Mike. He's fine. He would like you to tell the children he loves them and he'll see them as soon as he can.'

'Fuck off!' she says and puts the phone down.

At the Palms swimming-pool, later in the morning, Rosemary and I have a long chat in the changing-room. I confess I am a closet homebody. The strange delights of sexual excess are, to me, well . . . strange.

'It's about boundaries, isn't it?' Rosemary says, rubbing her crew cut dry. 'I wanted to test you. See how you responded when your own boundaries were stretched. Most people act very defensively when they're challenged. Fear makes them shut down before they've benefited from the experience.

'They shut down and then they condemn. I bet you got on the bus last night telling yourself they were a bunch of ugly perverts. Am I right? Or am I wrong?'

Fortuitously, half of me is hanging upside down with my head in a towel, so I don't have to answer.

'OK, tell me this,' Rosemary says. 'Is hypocrisy better than honesty? Or is honesty better than hypocrisy? Is it better to live with a man who lies and cheats but who pretends to be faithful, or is it better to live with a man who is open and honest and who tells you he has affairs?'

'Is there a third option?' I ask. 'Anyway, I bet most of the women were only there last night because they'd been pushed into it by their husbands or boyfriends or whatever.'

'What bullshit!' says Rosemary. 'Did you meet Joan?'

I shake my head. 'I'm not sure.'

'You can't have missed her. She was on the kitchen table when we arrived.'

'The one with the varicose veins?'

'Yes. Well, Joan is divorced and it's her house. She holds a party there every week. No one's forcing her.'

I step into the shower; one more stereotype down the drain. When I'm half-dressed, Rosemary resumes the conversation.

'Will you try a small experiment?' she asks.

The suspicion recurs that I am more her latest toy than an employee. She sees the look on my face.

'I promise you it won't hurt, it doesn't involve any sexual encounters and you can leave at any time. OK?' she says.

'OK,' I say.

On second thoughts, perhaps you're never too old to be somebody's plaything.

Rosemary presses the bell on a side-door. We are at a massive, seemingly derelict warehouse in the rougher end of Chelsea. A small shutter opens and one eye peers out. We hear a high-pitched scream which might be 'Hieeeehhh!!!'

The door is opened and out bursts the thinnest woman I have ever seen, dressed entirely in rubber; a walking condom. Her hair is a massive concoction of swirls and curls and pitch-black.

'Hieee, Rosemary,' the woman almost sings. 'Long time no see-eee.' She beckons us both in.

'Paula, this is Kay. Kay, Paula. Paula is Belgian. She's made a huge success of her business.'

'Flattery will get you everywhere,' Paula says. Everything Paula says seems so familiar. Did we meet in an earlier life?

We have walked along a corridor painted stark white. We turn left and I stop. A room like an aircraft hangar is lit with dozens and dozens of neon lights. On several different levels, on metal platforms, men and women pack boxes with various pieces of bondage, leather and rubber.

Criss-crossing the room are conveyor belts from which hang dozens of outfits, most of them on armless, headless and legless dummies. The overall effect is of a latex abattoir.

A man in a codpiece, leather chaps, his nipples linked by a

silver chain, a dog-collar round his neck, passes in front of us. His backside is bare.

'Hans,' says Paula. 'Our new house model. Don't forget the talcum powder, Hans,' she bellows.

Rosemary turns to explain to me, 'It makes the rubber go on more smoothly.'

'A beginner?' Paula asks. 'Well, everybody has to start some-where. But you know what they say, Rosemary darling, you can take a horse to water but . . .' Paula shakes her head, turns to me and sighs heavily. 'Still, we can only try. Come with me, my dear.'

'She's a living cliché,' I whisper to Rosemary.

'Don't look a gift-horse in the mouth,' she winks. 'If she likes you, our Paula can be very kind indeed. For a dominatrix.'

Half an hour later, I am dressed in underwear with more holes than a tea-strainer, a rubber catsuit and black thigh-high boots. The look is completed with a latex polo-neck and a large black cowboy hat pulled low on my face. The hat I like.

'Now,' Rosemary says, 'I want you to spend ten minutes walking down the King's Road.'

'You have *got* to be joking,' I reply.

In truth, it's not as bad as I imagined. Actually, it's highly intoxicating. At some point in the last five years, I stopped being looked at – regularly, that is. Like many middle-aged women I was rendered invisible by the signs of age.

Fewer and fewer swift glances in the street; less and less unexpected eye contact with strangers. More need to say in shop queues and market-places, 'Excuse me, I'm next.'

Wear latex and you have no problem. Minute by minute, I grow more confident. I begin to swagger. I look in shop windows so I can see in the glass the way passers-by stop and stare.

I am powerful. I am sexy. I am dangerous.

I probably also look daft, but I don't give a damn.

'Let me suck your cunt dry.' The comment is nasty and vicious and invasive. The man from whom the words come is dressed for the City. He smiles blandly and moves on.

'So how was it?' Rosemary asks. Paula is wrapping the underwear as a gift.

'It was better than I expected until some horrible man practically stuck his tongue in my ear and said something vile. Then I felt ill.'

'Didn't you feel powerful? Didn't you like them looking, wondering? Didn't you feel that some of those men were scared of you?' Rosemary presses. 'It's just another way of letting your *real* self express itself in the clothes you wear now and then. It's liberating.'

'Maybe I'm more comfortable with a lower-key message,' I suggest. 'Perhaps I'm easier in a woolly jumper which says baked beans on toast for tea, not S and M.'

I challenge Rosemary, peeved at constantly being scrutinized. 'Don't you ever get pissed off at being prejudged because of what you wear?'

She smiles. 'What I wear isn't *me*, it's a mask. We all have masks, I just make mine more obvious than some. And we're all prejudged. Sometimes, I'll admit, I do get fed up with the reaction,' she concedes. 'But if I was ignored, I'd hate that even more. That much I do know about myself.'

On the way out, I buy a suede waistcoat for Tabitha. I will give it to her at supper tonight. Martin is cooking and Angela plus children threaten to attend; an assembly of the abandoned. The gift will cheer me up, if nobody else.

I also spot some black-leather slacks on display. They are beautifully cut and very soft. I buy myself a pair.

Rosemary smiles, satisfied.

Half an hour later, we stop for a coffee. I feel confrontational, so when Rosemary comes back to the table with two cappuccinos, I ask her a direct question. 'I know you said you don't believe in love, but how do you know? Have you ever been in love?'

She smiles. 'I was in love once: and I decided never again. The less you risk, the less you hurt.'

'But if you don't risk, don't you also lose out on the chance of happiness?' I suggest.

'Maybe,' Rosemary answers. 'But there's more than one kind of happiness and at least I'll grow old without becoming bitter. My mother was very, very bitter because she kept opening herself up and each time she was let down, the wound went deeper.'

'But why couldn't she turn each relationship into something positive? Even if it did end prematurely?'

'How many times have you tried it?' Rosemary asks sharply. Then she softens. 'I'm content. I really am. I enjoy the business. I enjoy meeting people who are a bit different.

'If life's a drag then I don't see that joining the Wrinkly-on-Sea Amateur Dramatics Society and becoming Rhett Butler every night for a week is any better or worse than living out a sexual fantasy.

'Escapism is the opiate of the masses . . . except that every-body's too embarrassed to admit it.' She lights up a cigarette.

'To be honest, I've had my fill of escapism,' I tell her. 'Ideally, just for a short time, I'd like life to be *exactly* as it appears. Or is that too much to ask?'

'Not too much at all, darling,' Rosemary yawns. 'Just *awfully* boring.'

Chapter Seventeen

A t six-thirty a.m., the most enormous powder-blue Rolls-Royce draws up in our drive.

I've hardly slept. This is partly because of a forty-five minute telephone conversation with Tom, at midnight. The gist of which was that I should view Brenda as a little local difficulty and continue to sail through married life without changing tack.

'Can't you be more, well, more *French* about this?' Tom kept saying.

Next door, Mo sleeps peacefully with Letty full stretch on the bed. Mo has agreed to dog-sit for the next few days. She and Letty have already developed an understanding: the bed belongs to Letty.

The doorbell rings. I collect my case, coat and portable typewriter and let myself out of the house. Rosemary leans against the blue Rolls, the double of Veronica Lake. Blonde hair falls in a wave; cigarette in a holder, red lips, high heels, tailored linen suit with a long, tight skirt, winged sun-glasses pushed on to the top of her head.

On my doorstep is a person I have never seen before. She wears jodhpurs, riding-boots and an officer's jacket. A peaked cap is parked under her left arm. She is slim, devoid of all make-up, medium height and has rich, chestnut hair, wildly curly but clasped back in a band.

'My name is Amy Decision. Spelt D-E-C-Z-Y-S-I-N, ma'am,

but pronounced *Decision*. I am Rosemary's chauffeur and body guard.' She has an American accent.

'Bodyguard?' I plonk my bag down on the gravel path and turn my attention to Rosemary.

'I thought we were going to the Wirral. Why on earth do you need a bodyguard?'

Rosemary smiles and shrugs. 'To save me from myself,' she says. 'And Amy is one of the best.'

'I've bought you a present,' she adds. 'Try it for size.'

She throws me a carrier bag. Inside is a long, light, mackintosh in the style of a trench coat with a wonderful swing to the back. It is in a beautiful shade of pale green.

'Try it,' Rosemary says. I slip it on. It rustles like silk. 'I knew that was your colour,' she says. 'Let's go.'

Amy is a pedantic driver. Never have I observed a person obey each road sign to the letter in quite the same style. Speed limits adhered to, slow-down instructions fulfilled, instructions on No Overtaking result in no overtaking.

The plan is that Rosemary, Amy and I will drive to Manchester where the annual rally of Venus's sex-aids saleswomen, termed VIPs, as in Venus's Important Purveyors, is to be held. VIPs are housewives who hold parties in their homes and homes of friends to sell the products. Parties unofficially known as Venus Fly Traps.

The highest-selling star of the VIPs will be presented with a prize, there are to be ra-ra speeches, a résumé of the company's profits, plans for the coming year and new items on display.

The intention is that I ignore the conference and concentrate on a group of Venus's star sellers who meet for tea each year, prior to the conference, at Alice's house on the Wirral.

Alice, according to Rosemary, earns a quarter of a million a year – and has done for several years.

'Unlike some of the others, she has the support of her husband, Harry. He's a retired lorry-driver, so he gives her a hand with the books and stuff. They've been married thirty-three years.

'Alice says Harry is the nicest, most handsome, the sexiest, the funniest . . . Have I left anything out, Amy?'

'The most generous . . .'

'Oh yes, the most generous man she's ever come across,' Rosemary explains.

'And is he?'

'Judge for yourself. You'll meet him tomorrow.'

At some point on the M1, what feels like several hours later, we are stopped by the police. They want to know why we are cruising at forty-five miles an hour.

'Officer,' says Ms Decision. 'I always err on the side of caution.'

The mystery to me is how she and Rosemary ever got together.

At a motorway café, over breakfast, Amy, unasked, gives a brief synopsis of her life so far (she is twenty-six). In addition to acquiring a number of degrees, she seems very fond of contrary conversions. She is a vegetarian who has converted to meat; a pacifist who has converted to self-defence (she is a black belt); a teetotaller who now drinks – in moderation, of course; a bisexual who has converted to celibacy.

'Total celibacy?' I ask bemused.

'Have you ever met a half-celibate?' Rosemary queries drily.

'It's easier because now my energy flow is always positive never negative,' Amy explains with the kind of earnestness often found in those who are untroubled by a sense of humour. She whispers in a soft little voice which has the effect of making me whisper too. We end up sounding like two novices in a cathedral.

'All those juices I used to waste in the sexual act are now redirected. Today, they nourish my brain cells, replenish my skin, give me so much *oomph* that my active-field zone positively crackles twenty-four hours a day.

'Can't you feel it crackle, Kay?' Amy gazes into my eyes and reaches out for my hand. 'Share your thoughts with me.'

If I am honest, the only crackle I can hear comes from the Rice Krispies that the child at the table next to us is ignoring, busy as he is, listening to Amy's monologue.

'Don't you think I glow, Kay?' Amy asks rhetorically. 'Don't you wish you too could benefit by joining the magnetic aura of those who conserve their bodily fluids?'

The thought makes me queasy. I counter with another question.

'Isn't sleeping with someone you care for quite a positive activity?' I suggest, wary since I suspect one nudge, and Amy may be unstoppable. I am right.

'What can be more spiritual, more empowering than the knowledge of your mutual commitment to abstain? What can be more beautiful than sharing the idea that you don't, instead of you do?'

'How about the other person?' I plod on. 'What about his or her frustration?'

'Frustration? Oh no, Kay. You have it all wrong. I don't believe in preaching, but forgive me, this isn't about frustration, this is about celebration.'

A woman who has come to clear our table stops stacking the plates to listen.

'What I'm talking about here is morals for the millennium; giving up instead of taking. You do understand that, don't you, Kay?'

'Does she do this a lot?' I ask later, as Amy leads us out of the restaurant.

'All the time,' Rosemary replies. 'She's been celibate for nine months and every motorway café in Britain has taken its turn as her pulpit. She almost managed to convince one man to follow her cause. He was in a coach party with his wife on a day tour of Canterbury.

'But then he told Amy he hadn't slept with his wife for five years anyway.'

'And?'

'Amy debarred him. She said he couldn't become a celibate because he hadn't chosen not to have intercourse, it had been forced upon him.'

'Why did he say?'

'He said in that case, shouldn't he give Amy one? Then he'd choose to give up immediately after. He told her it was her moral obligation to perform.

'He was only gently pulling her leg but Amy didn't think it was funny at all. Then again, she rarely thinks anything is funny.

'This year celibacy, next year decadence. That's always been the trouble with morals,' Rosemary says gloomily, 'They're much too prone to fashion.'

Chapter Eighteen

In the hotel lobby in Manchester, where we are booked in for the next couple of nights, a large notice-board occupies centre stage. Decorated with sequinned stars, as if announcing the star turn in a cruise-ship's cabaret, are photographs of two smiling faces. I recognize them both as soon as I cross the welcome mat: Tom and Charlotte.

The noticeboard announces that MUM are holding a televised event that night as part of The Great Tour. Tom is to be a guest speaker on *The Significance of Continuity of Care to the Child.*

Tom is very good on continuity so long as he's not expected to provide it. He wouldn't dream of suggesting that child care is women's work, of course. No, continuity of care is done by that mysterious group in society which Tom calls 'Others'.

'I'd know that rear-end anywhere,' Charlotte's voice booms as I check in at the desk.

'Kay, what are you doing here? *Entre nous*, you and Tom are not having a little soirée, are you? Have you seen him? He's off out somewhere. He and that researcher woman . . . Beryl? Bunty?'

'Brenda?' I suggest, the roar winging its way back into my life.

'That's it, Brenda. I say, Dolly,' Charlotte mercifully diverts her attention to a woman who is twenty-eight going on forty-eight.

Dolly wears a wool skirt, a Puffa jacket, a mauve patterned jumper and her hair is a memorial to dead perms everywhere.

'Charlotte, how wonderful to see you!' Dolly says. 'You were marvellous on that chat show this morning. Absolutely super. Wasn't she terrific?' Dolly looks at me and I smile grimly.

'Tell her, tell her, Dolly, what the woman did in the audience,' Charlotte dictates.

Dolly obeys. 'It was superb! This woman stood up, burst into tears and said she was an architect with three children. What was it, Charlotte? One was on drugs, one was anorexic and I think, did she have one normal, or not?

'Anyway, this woman said that after hearing Charlotte, she recognized it was all her fault. She'd put her career first, she'd put them last. And she was going to join MUM and stay at home.'

'For God's sake,' I react instinctively. Dolly's smile and Charlotte's smirk falter slightly.

'Pardon?' Charlotte says.

'Charlotte, you're a masochist. What on earth is the point of making over-pressed women feel worse?'

I see Amy waving me over to the lifts.

'Why doesn't this architect's husband pull his weight? Or is she a single parent?'

Dolly intercedes with the facts. 'Hubby head of a big business. Commutes to Brussels each week. Wasn't that right, Charlotte? Sounded quite a catch, actually,' Dolly adds, simpering, about as coy as an alligator.

'Aah, so it's OK for him to be away all week, but not her?' I say rhetorically, since I know Charlotte's answer off by heart; her smugness needles me.

'Kay, whatever's the matter with you, today?'

'Look, must be off . . . promised to arrange the flowers for tonight's do,' Dolly says, anxious to avoid a row. 'See you later

Charlotte. And nice to meet you er umm . . . Remember, MUM'S
THE WORD!'

In my room, I phone Mo at work to see if Letty is surviving
without me. All is well, Letty is parked under Mo's desk. I drop a
note to Olivia to thank her for the cheque and promise to deliver
a dozen pairs of earrings within the next fortnight. I also phone
reception and ask for Tom's room-number.

I don't want to call him or visit him, I just want to know his
room-number. I flick through a couple of copies of *Venus* given to
me by Rosemary and I suddenly have an idea.

It's an idea which makes me smile.

The phone in Charlotte's room rings several times before she
picks up the receiver.

'Hi, Charlotte? It's Kay. I've been thinking about our chat.

'You're right. A lot of women *do* want to stay at home. Matter
of fact, I'm visiting a group this afternoon who are ripe to sign
up with MUM, they just need a bit of an inspirational chat from
you.

'Could you squeeze them in? I've got the address . . . That's
very good of you. I'm sure they'll be thrilled to bits to meet you.
Yes, of course I'll be there. I wouldn't miss it for the world.'

The house is large, modern and in a private road on an estate in
which every property is different and the lawns roll free of any
impediment as common as a garden fence.

Several cars are parked in the drive around a cutesy wishing-
well. A plastic leprechaun sits cross-legged on the side of the well.

A piece of timber swings on a wrought-iron frame close to the front door. Burnt in the wood is the word *Alihar*.

'That's not Arabic for *welcome*,' Rosemary explains, 'it's a combination of Alice and Harry.'

We ring the bell twice before we are heard above the din which fills the house, a din soon identified as laughter. A man in his early sixties opens the door. His false teeth gleam, he has the bluest eyes and a decent face.

He wears tan slacks, a yellow cardigan and a check open-neck shirt. On his feet are carpet slippers.

'Rosie, my love,' he says and gives Rosemary a big hug. I'm impressed. It's the first time I've seen anyone touch her.

As he shakes my hand, and smiles hello at Amy, I receive a whiff of Wright's Coal Tar soap and Old Holborn tobacco.

'Kay, I'd like you to meet Harry. I've been trying for years to persuade him to have me as his second wife, but he won't be budged,' Rosemary says.

'Come in, come in,' Harry's false teeth click a welcome as he ushers us through the front door. I catch Rosemary's eye. Is this the man described as the most handsome, most generous, most sexy, etc. etc.? Rosemary smiles at me.

'It's how Alice sees him that counts,' she whispers, accurately reading my thoughts.

The sitting-room is large and cosy, apricot and chintz; lots of family photographs, brass and an open fireplace filled with dried flowers. Several dozen fish swim in a large tank which doubles as a cocktail bar.

On a coffee-table, cakes, sandwiches and biscuits are laid out. On the bar are cups and saucers, a massive bowl of punch and several empty champagne bottles. Nobody appears to be drinking tea.

A woman in her fifties with snowy white, well-cut short hair, slim in lilac slacks and matching jumper and with a wide smile waves from the depths of the sofa. She has three gold earrings in each ear and what looks like half a kilo on her fingers.

'Yoo-hoo, girls,' she calls across the room. 'Helen, will you shift your bum and get these women a drink? The usual, is it, Rosemary? Tea and lemon?' she chuckles.

'And what's yours, sweetheart?' Alice asks me. She has extricated herself from the sofa and come over to give Rosemary a hug.

'I'll have tea too, thanks.' Alice smiles even more broadly.

'What! Do you think Rosemary would really drink tea at my house at four o'clock in the afternoon? Harry!'

Harry comes into the room with a tray bearing four glasses and four more bottles of champagne.

The dozen or so women in the room range in age from their twenties to late sixties. Each is different from the next but what they share in common is a kind of village-green respectability; apart from quite a lot of gold, no one is dressed ostentatiously.

Rosemary explains who I am and why I am here.

'Let me tell you, Kay,' Alice says, 'we pride ourselves on being the M & S of S & M.'

At this the women clap and cheer. 'It's all very tasteful and discreet, isn't it, girls?' Alice says.

'So discreet that if you're going to write anything, I'd like you to be a bit clever with some of the ladies' names, know what I mean, Kay? Harry, do the cabinet for us, love.'

Harry disappears and within seconds a glass cabinet in the corner of the room lights up. Inside are numerous cups, shields and plaques.

'See those? I was in at the beginning and won every trophy going for record sales. Isn't that right, Rosemary? Long before Rosie got involved I was doing it.

'Shall I tell you something?' Alice continues. 'I've noticed a change. A real change. At first it was a bit of a joke, a lark. Have your friends round, couple of drinks, look at the products and laugh yourselves silly.

'Now, it's a bit more serious. They still have a joke but whereas before the first question was, "How much is it?" Now it's "Does it really work?"'

'You know what I tell everybody? I say, "Don't ask me. I know nothing about sex, I'm a happily married woman."' Alice smiles. And I smile back.

'Like that, did you?' Alice says, 'Zsa Zsa Gabor said that. Come with me, love,' she beckons me with her hand.

She walks to the end of the sitting-room and opens the French windows into a large conservatory. On two trestle-tables decorated with the Venus logo is the company's range for next year.

'See those two gold balls, like ping-pong balls?' says a woman who has followed us out. 'They are amazing. Gave my Bill the biggest hard-on in years.'

'Not hard-on, Sharon,' Alice gently corrects, 'arousal. You know what we say, "Words are the difference between taste and waste."'

Sharon retreats back into the sitting-room. A large garden stretches out ahead of us with a small orchard and stream.

'All of this,' Alice indicates with her head towards the outside, 'all of this we bought with Venus money.'

'Doesn't Harry get embarrassed or jealous?' I ask. Alice smiles and shakes her head.

'Never. No reason to. A couple of years back, me and Harry went to New York. Lovely time we had. While I was there, I saw a magazine cover. "See that, Harry?" I said to him, "That's what we've got. Hot monogamy!"' Alice laughs.

'Harry was pleased as punch. We've never had a name for it before. Felt left out for a bit, we did. Like being faithful was what boring old farts did. Now we say we've got hot monogamy.

Sounds good, doesn't it?' Alice pats the seat next to her, so I sit down.

'I wouldn't risk hurting my Harry for the world. He still courts me from morning till night. He says what's in his head and heart can outstrip any old bit of Taiwan plastic,' she chuckles again.

'I don't want to pretend that we haven't had bad times, mind,' she pauses. 'What counts is that you don't let the bad times become a habit. Know what I mean?

'So where *is* this reporter's notebook of yours, then?' She waits while I get it out of my bag.

'I'll tell you why Venus works – at least for the lot in there, shall I? One: it gives some of us a social life. It takes us out of our own homes. It introduces us to other women and if we've lost it, it helps us to find a bit of confidence in ourselves again. Two: there's the money. That makes one helluva difference.'

When the doorbell rings ninety minutes later, we have all drunk several more bottles of champagne. Helen, one of the younger women, a former teacher, is telling us the tale of a customer who used her vibrator to keep an abandoned kitten alive.

'She switched the vibrator on, wrapped it in a doll's blanket and the kitten thought it was her mother purring. Cost the woman a fortune in batteries,' she says. 'But she didn't know where to put her face when the vet arrived.'

Sue is about to begin another anecdote when she is interrupted by Harry. He ushers in Dolly followed by Charlotte.

'Well, hello, Dolly,' I say feeling ridiculous. 'Charlotte, these are the people I was telling you about.'

Charlotte sweeps in wearing a coat and dress in organdie material which makes her look faintly like the Queen Mother.

'I'm delighted to be here,' Charlotte announces, 'I haven't got much time, so if we could rearrange the chairs a little; make sure you're all facing me. Dolly! The bag, please.'

Dolly hands her a bag out of which Charlotte produces the

MUM banner. Red, white and blue, it shows a woman with a babe in arms and two children clutching her skirts. In gold lettering is the motto, *In the Home, In their Heart.*

The banner is draped over the bar, shutting out light to the goldfish. The stars of Venus's sales circuit look on open-mouthed.

'Dolly, the board please!' Charlotte announces, beaming at her captive audience.

Dolly unfolds a mobile notice-board. In felt-tip pen, Charlotte writes the words, *Nature says Nurture.*

'Nurture? Isn't that the name of the cream we sell for fellows who want to double the size of their willies?' Helen asks less-than-innocently.

Dolly stares at her aghast. Charlotte, in crusading mode, is oblivious. Pamphlets are produced, badges given out. Alice looks on, confused.

'Ladies,' Charlotte holds up her hands imperiously. 'Ladies, I am proud of you. So very proud. You are the flower of womanhood. You are the soul of the nation. You know where your duty lies.

'Are you interested in money? No. Are you prepared to take it lying down? No! Are you going to be seduced into the workforce with false promises of independence and cash in your pocket? No. What are we?' Charlotte asks.

'We are full-time mothers and proud of it,' Dolly squeaks out.

'Yes,' Charlotte says to the perplexed faces in front of her. 'We are full-time mothers and proud of it. We know our place is in the home. We know our value lies in what our menfolk and our children think of us.'

'God,' says Sue, 'I sincerely bloody hope not.'

'I want you to sign up. Join the proud army of mothers who are marching across the land—'

'How much?' shouts a woman standing behind the sofa. 'What wages do you pay in this army of yours?'

'What is the unique role women have in life?' Charlotte asks, disinterested as always in engaging in a dialogue.

'Being dumped on,' says a woman with grey hair standing next to me. Applause. Charlotte looks just a mite disconcerted.

'What can match the reward of hearing an infant call out in the early hours of the morning, *Mummy! Mummy!*'

Charlotte really is a dreadful ham.

'Daddy, Daddy?' Sharon suggests. The titters grow. Charlotte is not to be deterred.

'Do you realize how much money this country would save if we encouraged our women to stay at home? For a start, we would wipe out delinquency at a stroke.

'Do you realize how much money we waste on the unnecessary apparatus which enables us to work . . . child-minders, cleaners?'

'Well, I for one wouldn't be without my apparatus,' Sue says firmly. 'It's provided very nicely indeed for me, thank you very much.'

She walks over to Charlotte. Dolly looks nervous.

'How many children have you got then?' Sue demands.

'Four,' Charlotte says looking even more uncomfortable.

'And where are they now? Who's got them now? Come to that, how long have *you* stayed at home? Ten years? Five years?'

'It's not quite like that,' Charlotte says.

'*It's not quite like that* . . .' Sue repeats. 'Well, let me tell you what it IS quite like, Commander MUM. I live with a pig of a man. I stay with him because I also have four children and they think he's the bee's knees – when he's home.

'If I hadn't had this little job, got out of the house, met people like Alice and Harry and Sharon and the others, I would have gone right round the bend. And the kids wouldn't have had a quarter of the basic stuff I've been able to buy.

'So I suggest as politely as possible that you shove your MUM banner right up your maternal instinct and leave us women to make our own choices about how we want to live our lives, OK?'

'Well, really,' says Dolly. 'You can't know what you're saying.'

Charlotte, of course, is not down, only winded.

'Let me stress to you, ladies,' she begins again, only to be shouted down by boos and whistles. Three minutes later, Charlotte concedes defeat.

'Dolly, the bag!' she booms.

Dolly scuttles forward and packs at top speed; put out to find herself cast as a villain when she'd primed herself for the part of Number Two Heroine.

Alice wheels in a tea trolley from the conservatory piled with Venus's future star attractions. They wobble and wiggle like blanc-mange at a children's party. Dolly takes one look and turns ashen.

'Oh, my word!' she says.

'We wouldn't want you to go away empty-handed,' Alice addresses Charlotte. 'So I wonder if you'd accept this as a little token of our . . . respect?'

She hands Charlotte a large box wrapped in gold foil, the Venus logo only just discernible. The parcel looks so distinguished it might hold a coffee-table book on Picasso.

Charlotte rudely pushes away the present and turns on me.

'This is your doing. I've always known there was something odd about you, Kay Woods. All that horrible creepy wiry jewellery you wear.

'Now I see you in your true colours. You're sex-crazed, that's what you are. Any normal woman would have got it out of her system in her twenties. Not you. Oh no, not you.

'You've decided to rev up just when any self-respecting woman has decided it's time to quietly park in one of the lay-bys of life. Angela's told me what you've done to her. You're a disgrace!'

It dawns on me. *Charlotte is jealous*. Totally misinformed but *jealous*. The judgemental, insensitive, ambitious, easily bored

Charlotte believes I am having a better time than she is. *Than she ever did.* Oh, the pleasure.

'What are you, some kind of Pied Piper of pornography?' Charlotte demands, gesturing to the circle around her. 'Dolly, the bag!' she commands again.

'This way, ladies, please,' Harry instructs courteously, hiding a smile as he holds open the sitting-room door for the two women.

About to exit, Charlotte turns and points at me, 'You haven't heard the last of this,' she says. And marches out.

'Here,' says Alice to me, handing over the gift box which Charlotte has rejected.

'Why don't you have it instead? At least I know you'll appreciate it.'

Back at the hotel, I kick off my shoes and pour myself a glass of wine from the mini-bar. Next, I turn my attention to the present given to me by Alice. On the journey back, Rosemary had told me that Alice always has a dozen gifts, ready-wrapped, for first-time Venus guests.

'One size suits all,' Rosemary laughs.

As I unwrap the paper, I expect Sister Sadista's trousseau. I am wrong. Inside is an exquisite framed mock-Victorian sampler.

Carefully embroidered are the words *Woman's Virtue is Man's Greatest Invention, Cornelia Otis Skinner, 1915.*

I can drink to that.

Later, Amy calls up from the lobby to say they are ready to leave for dinner. For the first time in years, I've been without the customary backbone to my routine; Tom's work timetable, his needs, his demands. And, so far, my life has not yet collapsed. Depression has held off. Even a little fun has been had.

On my way out, I touch wood.

Chapter Nineteen

The dinner hosted by Rosemary is held in a private dining-room in a country hotel half an hour from Manchester. A dozen guests and their partners are invited, most of them investors in Venus Inc. or representatives of companies which advertise heavily in the magazine.

Rosemary wears a long silver skirt, a matching halter-neck top and a black wig tied back in a bun. Diamond clusters decorate her ears. Her nails and lips are deep red.

Amy is in black jodhpurs and a cream shirt. Unfortunately my outfit (bought on the advice of Mo) matches that of the waitresses. Black tuxedo, black trousers, white shirt and what I thought were quite snazzy pearl buttons until I saw them on half a dozen women serving us canapés.

'Nobody's noticed,' Amy says. 'Black suits you. You look very good for your age.'

I hate it when someone tells me I look good for my age. It's as if there's a British standard rate of deterioration.

The meal promises to be the usual ritual of too many wine glasses, too much cutlery and endless changes of plates. In the centre of the table is a miniature replica of Venus de Milo carved out of ice, rising out of a flower-bed of edible nasturtiums.

A personal note to each guest has been left on our side-plates – not from Rosemary but from Master Chef Gary Williams.

Master Chef Gary Williams, previously of The Twisted
Bolt (One Michelin Star) in Foxburgh and recently seen on
BBC TV's Super Cook, is pleased to be creating your five-
course meal tonight.

You don't need to be reminded, of course, that Gary's
third book, *A Little Bit of This and a Little Bit of That* is
published by Four Square on 19 June. *Bon appetit!*

We are the first to arrive, followed rapidly by the majority of
the guests. A statuesque woman in maroon sequins with a wonderful head of bright red hair engages me in conversation.

Deirdre Woollam, Rosemary has already told me, began her
working life as a minicab driver. She now runs fleets of luxury
hire-cars and owns a laundrette chain which offers customers a
choice of watching their own dirty linen or somebody else's in the
form of continuous videos. She also supplies ferocious-looking
designer bouquets and flower arrangements for major events.

Deirdre Woollam offers one of her bouquets to Rosemary. It
appears to contain celery stalks and bright red chopsticks in among
the orchids and barbed wire. Take a sniff and risk impalement.

Deirdre is fulsome, physically and verbally. She tells me her
husband, Gerald, is head of geography at a comprehensive on the
Wirral and her daughter, Sally, twenty, who chats to Amy, is
taking a degree in physical education in London.

Gerald seems a relaxed man with an appealing dry wit, who is
in no hurry to make his mark on the evening.

'Sally used to be a bucket lady,' Deirdre confides.

'A bucket lady?' I ask.

'You know, throwing up, bulimic . . . Can't understand it. Her
dad is an absolute gem. Ask anyone. And we've always given her
the best.

'Sport cured her,' Deirdre adds. 'Now she's as obsessive about swimming and running as she used to be about chucking up. Will you look at her hair? Got a lovely girl, Sheryl, who always does mine, but will Sally go to her? Will she hell.

'I can't believe she's one of mine, sometimes,' Deirdre says, but the words are not without pride.

As we take our seats for dinner, Deirdre on my right, I notice that the chair to my left is empty. The place card bears the name Ian Jackson. After the roasted pepper and stilton soup is served, Ian Jackson arrives.

'Ian Jackson, and you are?' He introduces himself with a slight Geordie accent as he takes his seat.

'Kay. Kay Woods.'

The man next to Ian Jackson sticks out a hand.

'Ken Ryan, Import-export. Eastern Europe. And what's your game, lad?'

Ian Jackson waves away the wine waiter. I immediately put down my glass. Pathetic. While Ken Ryan tells Ian Jackson about the expansion opportunities for the sale of caravans in Poland, I inspect Mr Jackson. Rosemary has not seated him next to me by chance.

He is not conventionally good-looking but has what Mo calls Presence. He is perhaps in his late forties. He seems fit, he has black hair flecked with grey, a light tan and a front tooth with a chip in it.

He has large hands and manicured fingernails. After shave is present but very lightly. The smile-lines around his almost turquoise eyes remind me of Tom.

Ian Jackson turns to speak to me but Deirdre Woollam intervenes. She tells us every minicab joke and most of the laundrette ones, too. Eventually, she is distracted by a man across the table who imports Italian office furniture.

'So what brings you to the Wirral?' Ian Jackson asks. It's one of the few questions he poses, instead, as the evening progresses, he gives mostly supportive responses: 'I can imagine how wonder-ful that must have been . . .' and '. . . How terribly difficult for you.'

It creates the illusion that he respects my privacy while offering enough sympathy to encourage me to open up alarmingly: the girls, Mo, Olivia, jewellery, journalism, Letty. Only Tom and our new arrangement do I keep back. Questions directed at him, he deflects.

As we drink coffee, sitting with the other guests in an adjoining room, I try again.

'So how do *you* earn a living?' I ask as Ken Ryan, the import-export man, offers petit fours at the same time as handing out free ball-point pens inscribed with the legend, *Ryan International Trade Emporium: RITE you are!*

Ian Jackson smiles and by way of a reply calls Rosemary over. 'Now tell me,' he asks her. 'How did you two meet?' Rosemary pulls away from his arm.

'Swimming, wasn't it, Kay?' she replies lightly and adds: 'You could say that what first drew us together is a shared affection for getting into deep water . . .'

Ian Jackson's home is an hour's serious drive away from the hotel, plus another twenty minutes navigating a winding country road. We turn a bend and suddenly we are faced with a glass and steel construction which juts out of the hillside. The house is dominated by two vast windows and on one side it has a sun-deck.

Inside, it appears to be the home of a domesticated man but with no photographs and none of the paraphernalia of family living. The sitting-room has a stripped pine floor, lots of rugs and three vast sofas. Indian wall-hangings, and sculptures and pottery which seem to come mostly from South America provide the décor. One wall is lined with books, while another holds a music centre and a large collection of CDs.

Judging from its contents, his taste in music is classical, jazz and blues; in books it's politics, modern fiction and travel. The magazines and newspapers on the coffee-table include *National Geographic*, *Autocar*, the *Financial Times*, the *Collector* and the *Field*. All of which tells me everything and nothing about the man.

Ian Jackson disappears to find brandy. I sit in one of two armchairs positioned at the window. My initial impression is that this man treats his home not as a pit stop but as a refuge. And yet there is something cold about the place . . .

From somewhere deep in the house I hear the ping and clack of a fax machine.

'I won't be a minute,' Ian Jackson says, coming back into the room. He has taken off his black bow-tie and dinner-jacket and undone the top couple of buttons of his shirt.

'What kind of music do you like?' he asks.

I shrug. 'Anything peaceful.'

Bach's cello concerto fills the room. My Katie comes to mind, aged nine, a three-quarter cello held in an arm-lock, practising a simple tune that we nicknamed George in a G-string.

Ian Jackson returns again, this time with a bottle of Chablis and two glasses.

'This is the only alcohol in the house. I've been away. Only got back yesterday, that's why I'm a bit understocked.

'I travel quite a bit in my . . . um . . . ah . . . business,' he continues.

I watch him stretch out, hands linked behind his head. Suddenly, this all seems so . . . *pointless*. I am annoyed with myself that I agreed to come. I'd said I would because Ian Jackson claimed his house was 'just up the road'. He had promised that it had a spectacular view of the bay and he had a couple of books to lend me on Mayan jewellery.

I'd agreed because in this, my new frame of mind, I am open to experience. In the old frame of mind, I would have gone back to my hotel room alone, to sleep. My old frame of mind has a lot to be said for it.

What was once out of bounds has now turned into a public footpath, and life in many ways seems so much more *complicated*.

Ian Jackson reaches forward and takes both my hands in his.

'Kay, I'm too old to beat about the bush. I like you. I'm tired of all the games and the jousting and the acrobats, I want to—'

'Ian,' I try to interrupt. I want to leave. 'Ian, I really think I should—'

'Sssh!' He drops my hands and puts his fingers to my lips. In films, I always view this as a corny move. In reality, it has impact.

'I come to London a lot,' he says. 'Perhaps I could take you out for dinner, a drink? We could take this slowly. I've been married, I've lived alone but now, I'll be honest: I'm lonely,' he says. My heart sinks. *Oh, shit.*

'I was married for five years,' he continues without prompting, suddenly loquacious. 'She left me for an old friend of mine.' Cue for a wry smile. 'It hurt at the time, but you've got to move on, haven't you?'

He rubs his face with his hand, just like Tom does. 'Mind you, I can't pretend it hasn't made me cautious.'

He read the disbelief on my face. 'This – tonight – it's not like me at all. I'm usually very, very careful. Cancer, you know. My birth sign's Cancer. Home-lover, that kind of thing.'

Something stirs. It's certainly not lust. Protectiveness is the word I'm looking for. For all I know about this man, he could be a serial killer, but even if he is he looks so, so . . . defenceless.

If anyone's a threat in this house, it's probably me.

Ian Jackson tells me he deals in antique maps. He occasionally writes travel pieces. He speaks fluent Spanish. He says he and his wife had a child three years after they were married; Josh. Josh died of meningitis at nine months. Ian Jackson was in Ecuador at the time and his ex-wife never forgave his absence.

'I don't think I could risk having a child again. I'd be fearful that I'd let him or her down just when it mattered most.'

'It wasn't your fault,' I find myself reassuring him. 'You couldn't have done anything if you'd been here, could you?'

'I could have helped my wife.' He stares out of the window morosely. Without turning his head, he says, 'Kay, I've never asked anyone this before, but would you spend the night with me, please?'

I have an instinct that deep down, this man is a prat – but how can a decent woman refuse?

The bedroom is a surprise. Ian Jackson had told me earlier that he was an insomniac, yet he appears to have invested hugely in a room in which he allegedly spends so little time. Tartan walls, Victorian oak furniture and a deep-pile olive green carpet. The bed is massive, and on a platform so it looks like an altar.

'This is my toy. It's a folly I inherited from the previous owner,' Ian Jackson says. A panel slides out of the bedside table. He sits on the side of the bed and operates its buttons. One makes the tartan curtains which cover one wall draw back electronically. The second, third and fourth dim various lights. The fifth permits a large television to rise effortlessly from a chest at the foot of the bed. A sixth button produces a CD player and speakers. The seventh induces a minor tremor in the mattress.

'So the earth moves whether you want it to or not,' I say, smiling.

Ian Jackson smiles back. 'The guest bathroom's in there,' he says. 'If you want to borrow pyjamas, there are some in the cupboard. See you in ten minutes.'

He disappears into what I assume is his bathroom. I hear a shower operate.

In the guest bathroom, I briefly wonder whether to leave my

face unmade-up or apply fresh cosmetics. I apply fresh cosmetics. The busier I am, the less chance I'll have to reflect on why in hell I didn't go straight back to my hotel.

Ian Jackson lies on top of the bed. He wears a towelling dressing gown vividly patterned in primary colours. Not at all what I would imagine to be the choice of a man with conservative tastes.

I should have told him before I came upstairs that this encounter is emotional first aid; a one-night stand, nothing more, nothing less.

'Climb aboard,' he gestures with his arm. Please God, he isn't going to be *jolly*. By a rough rule, Mo says, the heartier the lover, the more hopeless.

I slide between the sheets. 'The fun begins,' Ian announces. By which he means I am about to be taken on an electronic tour. Operating his control panel he draws back the curtains to reveal, as he promised, a stunning moonlit view of the bay. Lights are turned off, the bed gently starts to gyrate, music seeps out of the pillows.

Ian Jackson gently takes me in his arms and kisses my forehead and neck. Intimacy with strangers is an odd affair. I can hardly look deep into his eyes when I'm barely accustomed to using his first name. And I can't shut mine for fear of dizziness as the bed rotates.

'Don't be afraid,' he says.

To be honest, of the range of sensations that might have come to mind, fear is not the first. But now, at his suggestion, I *am* alarmed.

'I'm a very good friend of Rosemary's,' Ian murmurs. 'She'd never let any *real* harm come to you.'

I can see the outline of his face in the dark. 'I think I should say I know you're married, Kay,' he continues gently. 'It was obvious, partly because you haven't mentioned men, any man, all night.'

This should be my cue: *I'm not looking for a relationship, it's nice to have fun for one evening but nothing more* etcetera etcetera. But if I do, it will probably have the same impact on the romantic ambience as reading out loud from the menu of an Indian takeaway.

Ethics are admirable, but I'm learning fast: they're easily snookered by poor timing.

So, instead, I try to explain: 'We're having a trial separation. So far, it's been all trial and not much separation but I'm optimistic. I think the theory is that we need to see how well we get on apart. Or rather, I need to see how well I get on apart.'

Ian Jackson unbuttons my pyjama jacket and kisses me lightly from my neck down to my navel. He slides my pyjama bottoms down and continues to kiss. I tense up, he stops.

'With you, I feel as if I've come home,' he says, taking off his dressing-gown. It's too dark to see much. I run my fingers down his back and along the inside of his leg. I kneel and kiss his groin, then his stomach.

I intend to repay in kind if not in commitment.

Much later, Ian Jackson carefully lowers himself on top of me. Familiarity with Tom has bred not so much contempt as acceleration. Sexual intercourse, from the germ of an idea to post-coital pee, takes place in record time. This almost languid delight Ian shows in the way our bodies respond to each other is not only a novelty, it is also highly seductive.

He uses his finger to trace a pattern on my breast, then stops and starts again. I move my hands to caress him and he holds them fast.

'Do nothing, just give yourself to me.'

This, I admit, is a relief. I hate these 'love' manuals which tell you to 'Say What You Want.' It turns the erogenous zone into some sort of manic TV game show. *Down a bit! Up a bit! Left a bit!*

While I'm against barking instructions, I do believe a little encouragement goes a long way. So I sigh and move a little. I move, I groan. Then I *really* groan. Ian Jackson is adept; he has begun to use his fingers, exploring, now moving rhythmically. Perhaps he had piano lessons when he was young.

My only complaint is the way he keeps looking at me, like a mechanic who checks to see if the engine is ticking over nicely.

I shift from that almost hyper-awareness of everything that is happening to that point when, if I let it, sensations transform into colours, circles, lights which swirl and flow together. A time to spin and strain and glide and almost fly.

'You are wonderful,' Ian whispers. '*Really* wonderful.' As I am considerably out of practice, I'm not sure whether this is an automatic punctuation mark in sexual interchange in the 1990s, a necessary Amen as it were, or heartfelt.

Ian opens a drawer in his bedside table and I see what looks like a year's supply of condoms. Again he begins to take control. I feel obliged not to let him make all the effort. This time, I resist. I gently push him on his back, I hold his hands away from our bodies and I ride him. This is hard work. But only fair.

I ride and tighten my muscles. How, I haven't a clue but I can see it has an effect. I relax and tighten again.

'You're a very bad woman,' Ian Jackson whispers with no malice. 'A *very* bad woman.'

I decide it's the nicest thing anyone's said to me in months.

I wake just before seven. The curtains are still drawn back to show a fine haze over the bay. The bed is stationary, the music silenced.

I am alone in the bed but I can hear bath-water running and there is a smell of coffee percolating.

It takes me a few seconds to place myself. Did I get drunk last night? Did I insult anyone? I know I've done something out of the ordinary. Then I remember, and react in two ways. First, I feel rather risqué. Second, bizarrely, I begin to feel hugely homesick.

Ian Jackson emerges from the bathroom. Dressed in faded blue jeans and a dark blue sweater over a red and blue shirt, he still looks all right. Better than all right, actually.

He smiles and strokes my cheek. I suddenly feel embarrassed and tongue-tied.

'Are you OK?' he asks. I nod my head vigorously. 'I've run a bath for you. If you still want to catch your train, we need to leave in an hour or so.

'I didn't think you'd want to go back to the hotel wearing this.' He holds up my tuxedo. 'So I've put a couple of Marisa's – my ex-wife's – things in the bathroom. You can keep them as a souvenir of the time you provided a bit of fun to a man who was in need of it.'

He walks out of the room. I bathe quickly. This is exploitation, I tell myself. I took advantage of him. All that stuff about an open, honest transaction, it's bullshit.

Christ, says another voice. You heard what the man said, *it was fun*. Nothing serious. An *adult* transaction.

I look in the bathroom mirror and remove a small black hair from my chin. If I'd been with Tom, he would have told me about it. Long-term relationships do have some advantages. My foundation has sunk into my pores like silt.

'I've put some coffee by the bed,' Ian shouts through the door. 'What would you like for breakfast?'

'Nothing, thanks,' I shout back. 'Just lots of coffee.'

Folded on a chair I find jeans, a white T-shirt and a navy cardigan. Blue and white socks and white sneakers plus a navy blue belt are also provided. All matching, all meticulously ironed and they all fit. I find this creepy.

The sum of it all is that while my conscience is going through the equivalent of an Outward Bound course, physically I feel surprisingly good.

I hum. Preoccupations, cares, concerns are all submerged by a sudden surge of optimism; a temporary conviction that I am the most attractive, most interesting, most seductive middle-aged woman to get out of bed this weekday morning. Copulation as a quick boost to the ego: I can begin to understand what Tom sees in Brenda; understand, but not condone. After all, he was – and is – married, I am semi-detached.

I'm close to confirming what I always knew. Sexual quick fixes, like Chinese dinners, don't offer long-lasting satisfaction. But as an antidote to loss of confidence; particularly if that loss is induced by a partner's infidelity; as a prophylactic against the belief that life has passed you by; as a means of instant re-evaluation of your physical assets and even as a way of untying some of the knots which have choked off too much of your spirit for too long – they're not bad.

Downstairs, Ian sits in the chair in the window, newspaper on his lap, coffee in hand.

'You look good,' he says and adds wryly, 'thankfully not at all like my ex-wife. More coffee?'

He goes into the kitchen, I sit down in the chair next to his. A box on the table in front of me catches my eye. Instinct makes me reach out.

It is a card index which lists the names of around four dozen women. I pull out a card at random. It reads:

De Vanhoevan: Maureen. Age 49. Divorced. Two children, 22 and

26. *Business Interests: marine insurance. Homes: East Hampton, USA, NY, Berkshire.*

*Likes:*Bal de Versailles; *vegetarian; Pouilly Fumé; 19th-century novels. Birthday 4 July. Son, Josh, died meningitis, 9 months. November 4 1969.*

The card goes on to list addresses, telephone numbers, friends. Then it says:

Ian Watson: Geologist. Widowed. No children. Wife died 1988, cancer. Self-help fish development project, Ecuador. £175,768.

I pick out another card.

Mason-Smith: Julia. Age 40. Unmarried. Wants child. Business interests: private income and divorce lawyer. Homes: flat Fulham, cottage Derbyshire.

Likes: workaholic. Supports children's charities. Potential interests: opera, walking. Our song: Puccini Che Il Bel Sogno di Doretta.

Again there is a list of addresses, telephone numbers, friends, then:

Matthew Jackson: Senior field worker. Specialize children's projects Central America. Divorced. One son, Josh 22, medical student Michigan.

'So what do you think?' Ian Jackson comes back into the room and sounds as normal as if I was inspecting plans for a kitchen extension. He takes the seat next to me.

'You're not in there. Nor will you be,' he continues in the same even tone. 'This encounter is something . . . well, something a little out of the ordinary for me. More of a favour, really. A paid favour, of course. But I can't pretend it hasn't been a pleasure.'

I return the cards to the box.

'Wrong place!' Ian Jackson informs me cheerily.

He restores *De Vanhoevan* to the Ds.

'It's Rosemary, isn't it?' I ask and don't expect to be contradicted.

Ian Jackson smiles, shrugs and replies flatly, 'Of course, my dear. Who else? You know how she is. She likes to have fun with people.'

I am angry now, not just because of the humiliation I've experienced but also because I've been stupid enough to ignore my instincts.

'Last night, when we made love, was that part of the plan?' I can't help asking the obvious question

Ian Jackson smiles condescendingly. 'Yes, of course. But it's usually me who has to take responsibility for the . . . um . . . ah, proceedings. That's the way women of a certain kind seem to need to play it. They want to be wicked but they require a lot of encouragement first in case I think they're *really* wicked. If you follow me.

'You made a refreshing change. And if you are wondering whether I genuinely like you, I do.'

'I'm not,' I say sharply. But of course, I am. I take a sip of coffee to give myself time to think. I can almost, but not quite, see the funny side: I wanted to use him, I can hardly protest when it turns out that he was paid to use me.

'You're amused,' Ian Jackson says. 'That's a surprise. Well, a relief really. I'll be frank, I've never done this before, tell a woman what's actually happened. But that's part of my brief. And to be honest, I prefer it.'

I interrupt. 'The condoms. All those condoms . . . I thought it was a bit odd. This reclusive, cautious man.'

'That was a mistake,' Ian Jackson confesses. 'A slip-up.'

'What are you? A head-hunter?'

'Oh, very funny,' he responds smoothly. 'I'm afraid this isn't a game, Kay. This is my *business*. A very good business, I might add.

'Rosemary wants me to tell you some of the tricks of the trade, but if I do, you'll have to understand that there is no form of identifying me or my – what shall I call them – clients? Not at the risk of finding yourself widely publicized as one of my most long-term . . . clients. I'm sure Kate and Claire wouldn't at all approve if they discovered that you're a sugar-mummy?' He smiles at his own joke.

'You're a con-man.' I appear to be speaking several octaves higher than I usually do.

Ian Jackson replies instantly and without emotion. 'Con-man isn't the word I would use. A Casanova who likes all the credit – cash is even better, of course – might be more accurate. I'm engaged in long-term transactions in which both parties benefit. Of course, a little disappointment at the conclusion of business cannot always be avoided.'

'No money-back guarantee?' I ask sarcastically. Ian Jackson smiles.

'Normally, no. But in this case, I made an exception. If I couldn't bed you, then I promised Rosemary that I'd return the small fee.'

Over the next fifteen minutes or so I try, and fail, to reach Rosemary by phone. I tell him that what happened the night before is another form of prostitution. He should be ashamed of himself. I will report him to the police. I want to return to the hotel. *Now.*

Ian Jackson watches me silently. He makes more coffee and finally he says that if I listen to his mini-lecture, he promises he will drive me back to Manchester. He claims again that Rosemary has insisted I should be given a few 'insights' into his 'craft', so that I can report back to *Venus*'s readers. He adds, coldly, that I am safe in his company. He has a clean bill of health. All that has been hurt is my pride.

Eventually I sit down and I listen. First, Ian Jackson explains that he only ever asks a woman four or five direct questions. If he's chosen the right 'client', that's enough to elicit all the information he needs.

'The rest is a matter of expressing sympathy and out it comes. The whole life-story; all the most vulnerable points.

'I made a couple of notes on you this morning when you were still asleep.' He gestures to an A4 pad at his feet. I reach for it.

Among his scribbles are the words, 'vulnerable on children'.

Ian Jackson explains, 'That's why I pulled out the meningitis story. I wasn't entirely sure last night whether we'd make it to bed. I thought you were in two minds. Am I right? Instinct told me you'd probably go for the vulnerable-man-alone-dead-child line.'

'I see from your cards that Josh is reincarnated regularly,' I remark acidly.

'If I keep the same name for a child it reduces the chances of making a mistake. I also make sure that most of my family emigrated to Australia and my job is always overseas. That solves the problem of long absences and no potential in-laws.'

'Do you promise marriage?'

'Never,' he says firmly. 'I don't promise anything. Not even love. But I choose the women who want to believe that they hear it.'

'Christ, you're calculating. God knows how many women you've left devastated.'

'How they recover is up to them,' he replies coolly. 'We are each responsible for ourselves. Didn't I hear you say something like that last night? If the women have any sense – and quite a few of them do – they appreciate the good times, learn the lessons about their lack of judgement, forget about the money and move on.'

'Don't you feel *any* sense of responsibility?'

'Did you feel responsible for me, last night?'

'Yes I did, as a matter of fact. I felt quite, well, quite protective actually,' I say defensively.

'And so you should. I worked hard enough at it.' It is his turn to be sarcastic. 'Still, I didn't hear you say, "Look, I just want a bit of fun for one night, perhaps two or three, but then that's it, pal?" You were quite prepared to string me along, a poor, emotionally bruised bloke, who more or less told you he wanted to take a risk with you.'

'Well, OK,' I continue to defend myself. 'But I don't do what you do. Women must assume that if they invest time and effort in you, it will change their lives.'

'And money,' Ian Jackson adds solemnly. 'They have to invest money too. Naturally, at first, I spend lavishly on them: weekends away, dinner, gifts . . . then they volunteer to invest in a project that I happen to mention to them. First few months, I make sure that they get a good return. Somehow or other, we end up sharing a credit card. I borrow a bit from their friends, then I disappear.

'I usually net a hundred and thirty to two hundred thousand, sometimes a bit more from each. It's not enough for most of them to go through the humiliation of contacting the police but multiplied three, four times a year it's not a bad living for me.'

'Why do you keep all these women indexed if you never see them again?' I push him further.

'Goodness, haven't you kept cuttings of your best pieces as a writer?' he replies lightly. 'If I didn't have this, what would I have to show for a decade of hard work?'

The journalist in me wins out over the conned woman. 'What if your feelings get involved? What about desire?'

'I told you before. This is business. Desire has no place in it. I choose my subjects carefully,' he replies. 'I keep newspaper cuttings, I subscribe to professional journals. I look for signs that they don't feel cared for, looked after. No matter how successful, how independent the woman, at a certain point in her life she wants to feel looked-after. Don't we all? I provide it – that's the secret of my success.

'I choose older women too. Fifties rather than forties because they fall quicker. They feel they have less time to waste. What was it somebody once said? "Older women are best because they always think they may be doing it for the last time"?'

I wish I was four foot taller and 200 pounds heavier so I could squeeze Ian Jackson's smiling face into the shape, texture and size of a slab of corned beef.

On the journey back, I ask him a straightforward question.

'How much did you diddle out of Rosemary?'

'Eighty, ninety thousand. Not much. It was several years ago, when I was just beginning. She was much too young and too sharp. But I had to start somewhere. Besides, she had money coming out of her ears. And she was certainly needy.'

'Rosemary?' I ask.

'Rosemary,' he repeats.

'What happened?'

'I took the money and did the usual: I disappeared. But she found me. I was in the middle of highly lucrative negotiations with a widow from Chicago.

'Rosemary forced me into making a deal. I agreed to put the money I'd taken from her plus another forty thousand into Venus Incorporated. She agreed to keep quiet.

'To be fair, it's been a good investment. I came up to the Wirral and bought this house on the back of it. Rosemary also occasionally calls in favours. You are a favour,' he adds, looking at me with a bemused expression.

'She probably thought she was helping you. She says you're

not tough enough. You're too open. She wanted me to show you how easy it is to have your feelings traded on. As it is, you've come out of the test pretty well.'

'A compliment from a con-man is flattery at its most devalued,' I reply as crisply as I can. 'Can't you see what you've done to Rosemary?'

Ian Jackson is unmoved; a man inoculated against his own feelings.

'I've taught her the virtue of caution.'

'You sold her a false package. It must take these women years to get over how easily they've been conned.'

'Easily? Certainly not easily,' Ian says swiftly. 'We are talking intelligent women here. As for a false package, what is romance eighty per cent of the time, if it isn't a false package? I enter into a perfectly fair exchange; cash and kind. I'm kind, they give me cash.'

Ian Jackson gives a mock sigh. 'Look, shall I tell you who taught me these tricks? A woman. She was the best there is at this game. She left many a man happier. Poorer but happier.'

'Is that supposed to make it all right, then?' I ask. 'That a woman can do it too?'

'Let me tell you something that might cheer you up,' he says. 'No other client has been in my house. Ever. Girlfriends yes, clients no.'

'And your wife?'

'Never married,' he says cheerfully. 'Nor will I be. Even when I'm not . . . working, my attitude, quite honestly, is fuck and run.

'I must be one of the few middle-aged men who know exactly what they want and don't pretend otherwise. What I don't want is a relationship. I'm happy the way I am. A selfish bastard who likes to be in control.' His tone is mild.

'Besides,' he adds, 'I can't stand it when I'm hurt.'

234

I glance at him as he drives. Cold and in a cocoon. 'Being hurt has its positive side. And I hope you're forced to find that out one day,' I say icily. 'Speaking personally, it's done me a power of good.'

Ian Jackson looks at me sharply.

'You have got to be joking,' he says.

At the hotel, as I check out at reception, I meet Amy Deczysin. She looks embarrassed. She fiddles with the blotter on the desk.

'I have a problem,' she says.

'You've crashed the car?' I suggest helpfully. My train back to London leaves shortly, so I hope Amy is not expecting me to run through a comprehensive list of potential worries.

I try again. 'You're homesick?'

'Almost there,' Amy smiles coyly.

'You're travel-sick? You've developed travel-sickness so you've got to change jobs?'

'God, Kay, are you blind? I'm in love. I'm love-sick.'

'So? Is that a problem?'

'Of course it's a problem. I'm celibate. Sally and I have spent all night discussing it and the situation's unresolved.'

'Sally?'

'You met her at the dinner. Deirdre and Gerald's daughter.'

'She's gay?'

'No. At least not yet,' Amy announces.

'So that's your problem,' I say briskly. 'You've given up doing it and she hasn't begun.' I look at my watch. 'I'm really sorry, Amy, I have to run. Phone me in London, let me know how you get on.'

'Kay,' Amy looks at me shyly. 'I think Sally and me, we were made for each other . . .'

'Who could possibly doubt it?' I say. 'Just count yourself lucky. At least you know exactly where each of you stands.'

On the train, I finally admit to myself a fact I have avoided all morning. I feel used.

Chapter Twenty

At Euston station I cheer myself up by buying a blue silk camisole from the underwear shop on the concourse. I buy camisoles in the same way that I buy earrings, in the belief that I'm the kind of person who wears camisoles and earrings. And, of course, I'm not.

Travelling down on the train, I have run through the previous evening many times over. Mr Jackson, I've concluded, is a bastard. But a very clever bastard. *Meningitis, my butt. Ecuador, my Aunt Fanny.*

I am deflated and depressed, except that I prefer to tell myself that I'm under the weather. It sounds less cataclysmic. It's not that my confidence has been shaken or my judgement questioned. They have. It's more that freedom, as in 'I'm a free woman' at this moment in time, seems a highly exhausting and potentially damaging business.

Then again, the first couple of years of 'security' as in 'I am a happily married woman' weren't that shit-hot either. And twenty years on, I find myself licking a fresh set of marital wounds. So, single or attached, suffering is relative. It certainly appears to be compulsory.

It takes time to adjust, I tell myself. New choices bring with them different rewards, fresh pleasures and unpredictable setbacks. *But why didn't I spot the absence of family photographs? If he dealt in antique maps where were the bloody things? What about the condoms? How could I have been so blind?*

The answer, I fear, is because I wanted to be.

To distract myself, I run over my plan for the day. Write up my encounter with Ian Jackson for *Venus*. Why shouldn't I make £3,000 out of him? God knows what he charged Rosemary. Send the article in along with my resignation, then call on Olivia.

I walk towards the stairs leading to the taxi rank. Suddenly, from the right-hand corner of the station, near the ticket office, I see what looks like a white and grey giant snowball hurtling towards me.

My heart lifts: it's Letty. Behind her, running hard, is Mo, dressed for the office. Behind Mo, running even harder, is Angela. My heart sinks. In Angela's hand is a small blue phial. *Oh, my God.*

Letty reaches me first and bounces up and down with delight like a giant yo-yo on elastic. Mo comes in a close second.

'Quick, quick! Don't stop!' She grabs me by the arm and we hurtle towards the left-hand exit.

Angela gives chase. We gain ground when she is involved in a pedestrian hit-and-run accident. Angela flattens a very large woman who, because she is dressed from head to foot in a black yashmak, briefly looks like an upturned shuttlecock.

Angela, still with the bottle in her hand, extricates herself and picks up speed again.

Outside the bank, I stop. 'Hang on a minute. What *is* going on?' I say to a breathless Mo. 'How come you two are here? Who told you I was on this train?'

'You did,' Mo replies, wheezing heavily. 'You told me yesterday. I decided to pick you up because I've got the morning off. Then, as I drove away from the house, I spotted *her*.'

Mo indicates with her head towards Angela who is bearing down on us grimly.

'Just as a matter of interest, what's she got in her hand?' I ask cautiously.

'I'd say that whatever it is, it isn't apple-blossom bath essence,' Mo replies.

'Tom called you early this morning. He said Angela's been on the phone to him over and over again.' She smiles. 'Tom also wanted to know where you were. Said you hadn't been in the hotel all night. And that he had a right to know where you were.'

'I told him I had a right to know too and I'd find out at the earliest opportunity.' Mo grins again, then realizes that Angela is standing beside her, so she stops.

'Where is he, then?' Angela asks.

'Look, Angela,' I say, watching the bottle all the time. 'I haven't seen Mike. Truly, honestly. I'd tell you if I had.'

'He was on the train with you. If she hadn't taken the bloody parking-space,' Angela glares at Mo, 'I'd have been here early enough to catch you both. You have no idea what contempt I feel for you, Kay Woods. Here,' she suddenly adds. 'Take this.'

Instinctively I dodge. For a split second it feels as if she is about to throw the bottle in my face. Then I realize she has thrust it into my hand.

'It's for Letty. Just because you're a cow doesn't mean the dog has to suffer.'

I look at Mo questioningly. 'Letty's got a seed-corn in her paw,' Mo explains. 'Tom must've told her.'

I'm only half listening. Someone has caught my eye. Mike is standing behind Angela, near the public telephone boxes. He is dressed in casual clothes. He looks thin but otherwise OK. He signals towards me and then to the phone and disappears down the steps to the taxi rank.

'Kay? Kay? Are you listening?' Mo asks. 'What is it, Kay?'

'Nothing, nothing at all. I just thought I'd glimpsed somebody I used to know.'

Twelve hours later, much to my surprise, I find myself in bed with my husband.

The rest of the day had proceeded like this. Rosemary phoned in the afternoon to say that she loved the piece that I had faxed to her. I had written it as if inside the mind of a professional Casanova – not referring to my own case, of course. Only at the end did I say in a postscript that I hoped that somebody one day might break his heart. Preferably in little pieces. With a sledgehammer. Not that I feel any emotion towards Ian Jackson, of course. I just hope, objectively speaking, that he bakes in hell.

I also announced that this was definitely my last article. Rosemary apologized. She said she had meant well. After all, it couldn't have done me that much harm, could it? *Bullshit.*

She insisted that I take the already planned trip to New York and then think again about resigning. We agreed that I will fly tomorrow instead of next week. Rosemary promised there would be no further tricks on the house.

I delivered earrings to Olivia, made from the wire around champagne corks. A silent man called Doug was helping her to hang a selection of Olde England country scenes in beaten copper.

'Aren't they divine?' she'd said. 'Hunted high and low for them – terrifically popular with ex-pats and Saudis. Already sent one lot off to Riyadh.'

'Where did you find them?' I asked, deciding that copper shire-horses, like my jewellery, are an acquired taste.

'Houndsditch Warehouse,' Olivia replied, beaming. 'The same place I found Doug.'

At six, Mo came by for a drink. I did not tell her about Ian Jackson. Mo told me she was spending the night with Chris, an Australian anthropologist.

In the bathroom earlier I'd discovered that she had fixed a notice to the mirror. It read, 'Feed Your Passion; Stoke Your Wild Nature.'

'It comes from all that *Dances with Wolves* stuff,' Mo explained as we sat in the back garden.

'I thought that was a film, with Kevin Costner.'

'Perhaps I've got it wrong . . . anyway, you know what I mean. All that back-to-our-primitive-selves stuff, loping through legends, baring fangs.'

She continued: 'I lay in the bath this morning and thought, Feed your passion; stoke your wild nature, that's *exactly* what I'm going to do.'

'And?' I probed.

'And then I thought, but how? What exactly does it mean? What precisely am I supposed to do?'

'Anna would probably have an answer. Have you heard? Is she better?'

Mo has developed a friendship with Dionne and Liz, so she's better informed about the workshop than me.

'She's fine, but Liz isn't. Phil has left her and, of course, after all those months of freezing him out, she now thinks he's the most fanciable man she's ever come across.'

'How on earth did that happen?' I asked.

'Liz found out he's moved in with the woman who runs the

dry-cleaners'. *And* she's got three kids. And Liz says that Carol told her when she was doing her hair on Saturday that she – Carol, that is – had finally had an orgasm.

'Well, she thinks it was an orgasm. Liz said the way she described it, she wasn't so sure. Anyway, to get back to me feeding my passions,' Mo was unstoppable, 'I decided to do something decisive – so I phoned up Chris.'

'But I thought you said he was impotent?'

'Well, he is, and that really *does* make me wild. Absolutely bloody furious, to be honest. I think he does it on purpose to get attention. But I'm not going to let him know that I mind because if I do, then he'll be getting the attention he wants. See what I mean?' Mo asked rhetorically.

'And besides, he might not be doing it on purpose and then I'd feel terrible because I'd have blamed him for something he can't help. Do you understand?'

I pretended I did. It seemed easier.

At seven-thirty the phone rang. I said hello and there was silence at the other end. Mike? Brenda?

I phoned Martin to see if Mike had contacted him and he said no. But he was standing by 'should Mike need a shoulder to cry on'.

Half an hour later, I heard the key in the door. It was Tom. He had spruced himself up; haircut, new shirt.

He seemed very nervous. He came over to kiss me on the cheek but before I could check myself, I drew back. He shrugged and walked into the kitchen.

He produced from a bag a bottle of champagne, still cold. 'Have you eaten?' he asked. 'You look awfully thin.'

I gritted my teeth and forbade myself to say, 'Who's fault is that, then?'

He dived back into his bag. Smoked salmon emerged followed

by eggs, French bread, tomatoes, fresh basil, salad, a bottle of Chablis, chocolate mousse and ripe Brie.

'That's nice,' I'd said unenthusiastically.

Tom lit candles, set the table in the garden, put Tortelier on the CD player, poured champagne and made what must have been a massive effort not to talk about himself. Since most of my activities over the past couple of weeks do not make for natural discussion-material between husband and wife, conversation was minimal. And very, very careful. Banality at its best.

'British Rail isn't bad now: clean, friendly,' Tom had said.

'Do you think so? My train had more shit in it than the local park,' I had replied, then added lamely in case he thought I was being argumentative, 'But of course, you're right, BR *has* improved.'

A little later Tom had brought up Angela's constant phone calls which he labelled 'neurotic'.

'Aren't you being a bit hard on her?' I suggested. 'After all, she hasn't a clue where Mike is.'

'Have you?' Tom replied, a mite too sharp for our present game. Then he added, 'No, of course you don't. You're probably right, I am a bit tough, a bit too . . . unforgiving.'

At eleven, the phone rang again. Tom picked it up, listened briefly then quickly said, 'Sorry, I think you've got the wrong number.'

I suddenly felt very, very weary.

Half an hour after I'd turned off the light, the bedroom door opened. Tom appeared and slid into bed. He said nothing but pulled me over. I went, but reluctantly.

So here we are.

I suspect that Tom is hesitant to do much lest he reveal techniques and routines learned in Brenda's bed. While I certainly don't intend to share the delights of Ian Jackson, the Wirral Wanderer.

I've decided Tom wants me back because he needs a wife in order to have a mistress. Without me, his relationship with Brenda turns into a very different set of obligations and demands. With me, Brenda remains fun. Something over which he has control.

We do not speak. After what seems like an age of physical effort from all our various parts, I opt for fantasy. I am in a bed shop after hours, strapped to a massive bolster. One by one, naked masked women and men with six-foot feathers come to torment me deliciously to orgasm. I've become a feather luster.

'You're smiling. I can sense you're smiling. What's so funny? If you're going to laugh at me—' Tom protests. For the first time, I reach out to him spontaneously.

'It's not you,' I say.

We climax, me first, in a mild sort of way. As he comes, Tom says, 'I love you, Kay.'

I'm grateful that at least he's got the name right.

A couple of hours later, I wake to go to the loo. Letty has left a trail: a slipper, a sock, a shoe and a used condom. I say 'used': it is the condom Tom wore and discarded into an ashtray at the side of the bed. Letty, on the root, has retrieved and discarded it.

I pick it up gingerly to deposit it in the loo. It is empty, unused, nix. Either that or Tom is the invisible man with invisible semen. I come back and sit on the edge of the bed. What a farce. My husband is totally spent – or he's saving himself for somebody else.

Either way, the only future for us as a couple is in a one-off appearance on Oprah Winfrey. The Man Who Faked an Orgasm with His Wife. And the Wife Who Was Fooled.

I used to think I was perceptive. This has not been my week. A small roar starts in my head. Then, of course, I begin making excuses. Perhaps Tom *has* given Brenda up and the poor man is grieving, as he adjusts? Perhaps I've become too cold?

Perhaps I'll just perform a quick check on his briefcase. Tom is now much cleverer. No credit-card receipts lying indiscriminately around. Still, the evidence isn't difficult to find.

In his leather cigar case is a letter of confirmation. A room booked for two, Elsynge Suite, at a hotel in the Cotswolds. Arriving Tuesday, next week, after Tom's programme is broadcast and the day I was originally going to fly to New York. So I know it's not me he intends to take.

First, I send a fax to the hotel cancelling the room. Then I make a cup of tea. Then I pack. Then I fax the hotel and reinstate the reservation. I am mean, but not that mean. Or perhaps I no longer care who Tom beds, or where.

Finally, I sleep.

Tom wakes up unusually late, just as I'm leaving for the airport. I don't see any point in another post-mortem. Tom is in love – but not with me. Or he is weak. Discussion isn't going to change that, only action. Reluctantly, I've come to realize that that means my action.

'Where are you going?' he asks sleepily, rubbing his eyes like a small boy. How unappealing.

'I told you last night, New York. If you have to travel while I'm gone, Mo will dog-sit. I'll leave a message once I know when I'm coming back. The address of my hotel is stuck to the fridge. I've been thinking, I might stay a bit longer, visit the twins.'

'But what about my film? You'll miss my documentary. You *never* miss my documentaries,' Tom wails after me down the stairs, anxious as always to give me a leaving-present of guilt. Once upon a time, it used to work.

'Don't worry,' I say from the front door. 'If I want to find out how it went, I can always give you a ring in the Elsynge Suite.'

Petty, maybe – but highly satisfying.

Chapter Twenty-One

'Have you got something a little more bluey-black for the eyelashes, please? Not Lancôme. It gives me a rash. And a bit more ochre for the lips, otherwise I come out flat, do you know what I mean?'

I hear the voice from the hall. It is the kind they use in television commercials to flog hot chocolate and Cup-a-Soup; rich and brown.

Stephen Delgado, the man who owns the voice, appears on book-covers, in magazines and on catwalks.

'He is *the* male icon; a masculine Marilyn Monroe,' Rosemary had said before I left London, stuffing a folder full of cuttings into my hands.

'He's probably also a total twat and neurotic but what I'd like to know is how does he feel about himself?

'Is he comfortable being seen as a sex object? Is he gay? How does he treat women? Is he worried about ageing? Really get under his skin. Talking of which, I'm told he's had every kind of cosmetic surgery going.'

Rosemary wants me to report on how the cosmetics industry, in search of bigger markets, is homing in on men and trying to make them aware that there is a body beautiful out there *and they don't have it*. Apparently, Stephen Delgado does.

Make men feel as insecure about their appearance as many

women are, the thinking in the market runs, and they'll buy the same sort of crap at even higher prices.

'But perhaps men won't prove as susceptible? Perhaps their egos are tougher? Perhaps they already hold so many cards they don't need to contemplate rhinoplasty? Stephen Delgado poses a lot of the questions and he can provide some of the answers,' Rosemary had told me.

Even as she was speaking, I could feel my own skin tighten – with boredom. So far, I've looked on wrinkles as God's reward for experience. (Except that I don't believe in God and wrinkles are only a reward if everyone else regards them as such.) I have never had what is termed in women's magazines 'a beauty regime'.

Several half-used tubes of face-pack decorate the bathroom, plus Japanese soap stones, marmalade body wash, hot-oil treatment for hair, cucumber eye-ointment and several loofahs so dried up they resemble clippings of hard skin from a giant's pedicure.

In short, my impulse to buy is strong; my ability to use is much less well-developed.

As for men standing shoulder to shoulder with us women in the queue for liposuction and face-lifts, that isn't quite what I expected the march of progress to be about.

Even flying first class at Venus's expense failed to improve my appetite for the story. Still, by the time I'd landed, I was not so much jet-lagged as just plain lagged, fully insulated by alcohol, food and pampering.

I went to my hotel, showered and slept for ten hours. At eight a.m., I phoned the twins and we had a long chat. Then I went shopping. In Saks I bought a dark brown trouser suit and an amber silk tunic to go with it. Of course, I then had to buy shoes, a bag and a belt to match.

Walking back to the hotel I passed a shop which called itself Pussy Pleasuredom, *For the woman with feelings* . . . Inside, a 100 per cent indifference radiated from behind the counter in the shape of a woman in her early twenties, dressed like a seventies punk.

'Hi,' I said. She'd given me a smile which lasted a fraction of a second.

Most of the so-called environmentally friendly apparatus, underwear, clothing, magazines and videos were imprisoned in foil, wrapped in Cellophane, chained together or padlocked to the shelves. Since Look but Can't Touch was perhaps the problem which assailed most of the relationships of the shop's potential customers, I assumed they didn't object to this kind of hands-off consumerism. Personally, I found it annoying.

Finally, I came across what I was looking for.

'Excuse me,' I'd said politely to the punk, 'Could you help me, please?' She'd tutted as she climbed off the stool and came unwillingly to the rear of the shop.

'Those,' I'd said more boldly than I felt. 'Could I have half a dozen, please?' The woman followed my finger and saw that I was pointing at a display, under perspex, of very large dildos shaped like dolphins.

'One half of a whole dozen?' she'd repeated incredulously. I'd nodded.

'That is *cool*,' she'd said. For the next five minutes as she wrapped each dildo and checked my credit card, she hadn't stopped talking.

She'd visited London, did I know Mary-Ann Slessor who lives in Wimbledon, had I been to the London Dungeon, she had been to Edinburgh for the Festival and that was neat, she saw *Les Misérables* and thought that was the pits, what did I think of American coffee, while I'm here I should go to Le Prince, it's a coffee-shop but it does pretty good tea, did I know you can't get good tea in New York?

'It's not such a bad place though, is it?' she'd suddenly concluded.

'No,' I'd said, drawing breath on her behalf, 'It's not a bad place at all.'

Just as she was about to lay the sixth dolphin-dildo to rest in an 'eco-wise' plain brown bag, she'd had an idea.

'Why don't you buy one of these, then you've got a really neat way to carry all the dildos together? It's a good deal because it's on sale.'

She produced a slim dark-brown leather briefcase. 'See!' she snapped open the case. Inside were indentations.

'It's for vibrators, dildos, personal massagers . . .'

'I'll take it,' I'd replied, in decisive mood.

I'd walked out of the shop, swinging my briefcase, feeling the absolute business.

Back in my hotel room, I changed into my new outfit. And wrote out a gift-tag for each dildo: Mo, Dionne, Anna, Liz . . . each woman in the workshop will be able to hang her gift on the bedroom wall as a memento of the times when we first came together.

Then I went to meet Mr Stephen Delgado.

He lives on the edge of Greenwich Village. The entrance to his apartment block is posh-distressed; dark brown paint; 1940s carpets; pre-World-War-Two elevator – but everything smelling brand-new.

A woman in her very early twenties, dressed in beige sacking turned inside out so that the seams criss-cross her body like tramlines, came to greet me. She had a white face, powdered eyelashes and gold-brown lipstick. I'm sure the style can't be faulted but the overall effect reminded me of The Straw Man in *The Wizard of Oz*.

On the fourth floor, the elevator stopped and she pressed a

combination of numbers into a small panel. The elevator then continued its ascent.

'Mr Delgado has the whole of the top floor. If you don't know the combo, you can't go any further,' she explained. She spoke to me very slowly and articulated each word very care-ful-ly. So I nodded to show that I really did under-stand com-plete-ly. Perhaps she regarded middle-age as a euphemism for senility.

The elevator door opened on to a vast room which, if it hadn't been in New York, might have belonged to a millionaire rancher in the Midwest.

Four sofas were covered in native Indian blankets, there were animal rugs on the floor, a vast fireplace burnt wood which magically gave off no heat, giant cacti guarded the four corners of the room, an oak desk large enough even for John Wayne's quill was positioned against a stone wall on which was hung a massive portrait of a rather irate looking Indian chief. Majestic-looking saddles were strewn around at random, presumably so that any passing cowboys can feel at home.

A bookshelf revealed an eclectic taste: philosophy; Japanese gardens; the New Deal in American politics; seventeenth-century Europe, and thrillers. I pulled out one of the books on seventeenth-century Europe to find only a spine and no contents.

At the far end of the room, giant glass doors were drawn back to reveal a roof-garden and a life-size Palomino horse, tethered, carved out of wood.

As I walked further into the room I realized the voice was coming from above. I looked up and saw a large gallery with a walk-in wardrobe, a massive dressing-table, a large bed covered in several dozen cushions and a jukebox lit up like an old-fashioned cinema organ.

'Mr Delgado,' Ms Straw Man shouted up, 'Ms Woods is here from London, England.'

'I'll be right down,' the chocolate voice purred.

251

'What may I get you? Decaffeinated coffee? Spring water? A tea infusion?' Ms Straw Man offered the latter as if I might need it intravenously.

'Could I have a black coffee, please?' I asked.

She disappeared and was back within a few minutes. 'Mr Delgado would like you to peruse this at your leeesure,' she instructed, and dumped a tooled-leather book on my lap. Like everything else in the room, it was very large.

Ms Straw Man spoke with a forked tongue. Mr Delgado did not come 'right down'.

On the contrary, he is staying where he is for a very long time.

I resort to browsing through the leather book, the life and good times of Stephen Delgado. It is written in a prose style that would make you seriously consider why Mr Delgado hasn't been universally acknowledged as the second Christ.

His birth, to Joe and Marnie Delglowski in Biloxi, was 'the wonder of the neighbourhood'; at college, his football skills were 'universally admired', at The Dining Room where he was a waiter, 'everybody knew that this guy had unique potential'. On and on and on.

Much of the book is taken up with photographs of Stephen Delgado, 'the dimpled Don Juan', in the buff as a baby, as a student, as a contestant in, and winner of, the Mr Beautiful Buttocks 1987 contest, and over the last couple of years, accompanying various women in extraordinary outfits to prem-ières. And then there is Stephen again airbrushed to near-death, selling aftershave, underpants, shirts, shampoo.

Mr Delgado is six foot three, has wavy blonde, apparently uncontrollable hair, blue eyes, regular features, an exercised body, very white teeth, totally spotless skin, full lips and high cheek-bones. 'I'm just a regular guy,' he is quoted as saying.

The book shows Mr Delgado on the cover of endless magazines, some for men, some for women, but all of the respectable consumerist kind which pretend to be a cut above their soft-porn rivals but aren't at all; they just look glossier. Two poses recur: laughing fit to bust and appearing very soulful, almost moody.

All this is interleaved with interviews which variously promise Stephen Delgado 'as you've never seen him before' (pictured in his galley kitchen with a wok in his hand); the 'secret torment' of Stephen Delgado (not finding someone with whom to have babies) and the 'inner fear' of Stephen Delgado (that an acting role won't come up to reveal his miraculous abilities as a Thespian).

This man has real worries. Somehow, it puts famine in the Third World into its proper perspective.

One article in particular catches my eye – a questionnaire.

Distinguishing feature? Dimple on left cheek.

Favourite qualities in a woman? A spirituality that goes beyond the physical being.

What do you like most in others? An ability to look beyond the superficial.

What do you admire most in yourself? Tolerance, humour and a sense of how we must be at one with the universe.

Your favourite moment in time? The time immediately after making love when my partner and I are mutually satisfied and at peace.

I put the book down, feeling nauseous. Judging from the racket coming from upstairs, tolerance, humour and a sense of oneness with the universe are not qualities which are in permanent residence in Delgado.

At noon, Ms Straw Man re-enters with a marble tray. On it are various pieces of raw fish. 'Sashimi?' she askes.

'No, no thank you.'

'Sake?' she asks.

I look at my watch. It's close to sundown in London. 'Yes, please,' I say and add just for the hell of it, 'a double.'

Mr Delgado and his large retinue consisting of make-up artist, stylist, hairdresser and admirers, finally descend the stairs two hours after he first arranged to see me. He is dressed in a white T-shirt, black jeans and black cowboy boots with silver tips and silver spurs. One lump of hair plays peek-a-boo over one eye. He wears a silver ring on his right little finger and a silver ring on his left thumb.

I can smell his aftershave at ten yards. Delgado is so much the stereotype of streetwise nineties male beauty it is almost risible. But still, I can't stop myself looking for longer than is polite.

As he walks, he examines himself in the mirrored glass of a mosaic which hangs to the right of the stairs. It must be all of ninety seconds since he last checked out his appearance.

He holds out a hand. He gives a firm, well-practised I-know-a-confident-grip-is-very-important kind of handshake. He gazes into my eyes, then looks me down and up again.

'Nice to meet you, can I call you Kay? That's a pretty name. Nice to meet you, Kay. You have beautiful eyes, do you know that, Kay?'

'Shall we hang around or call it a day?' asks a man who looks like a fifty-year-old Teddy boy.

'I'll tell you what I want when I want it,' Stephen Delgado replies coldly. And waves the gang away.

The retinue disappears through a doorway which I presume leads to the kitchen. As they do so, a female emerges carrying a couple of cameras.

'The light's OK, so we can do it over by the window. How about near the horse? You're looking good, Stephen, really good. New colour in your hair? It's adorable.'

Delgado introduces the woman who is dressed almost identically to him, in T-shirt and jeans.

'Stevie, this is Miss Kay Woods, Kay, this is Stevie.'

Stevie doesn't bother to look at me as she mumbles, 'Hi'.

'Stevie has to take a couple of pictures for a magazine piece. We'll be five minutes, is that OK?'

Ninety minutes later, the photographer has finished. I am pissed off, since I have been coralled in this apartment for over three hours and I am not paid waiting-time.

'Food?' Delgado says as he finally comes to sit opposite me. Oh, God, not the sashimi again.

'Zoot!' he yells out, 'Get me Danny on the phone. Say we'll meet in twenty at Mon Rêve.'

'Don't you ever say please and thank you?' I ask. Stephen Delgado gives me a sharp look.

'You're right. ZOOT, will you *please* get Danny on the phone. THANK YOU!'

Delgado is clearly accustomed to devouring women for brunch. I am immunized from his charms not just by age and appearance (my age and appearance) but because no matter how blue his eyes, he is clearly an obnoxious prick. I sense that he senses a challenge.

'I like you,' Delgado says, looking deep into my eyes. *Oh, come on.*

'I'll be five minutes,' he promises. 'I'm just going to change.'

'Change?' I respond weakly. 'What's wrong with what you've got on?' He smiles and ruffles my hair as he passes. Damn cheek.

Zoot, the Teddy boy who doubles as a post-modernist butler, re-enters.

'You wan' another drink?' he asks casually. 'Most of us around Mr Delgado tend to drink a lot.'

In Mon Rêve, the women are skeletal; a squad of grasshoppers dressed by Chanel.

The restaurant is tricked out like a monk's cell; dirt-brown walls, iron seats, trestle-tables, straw on the floor; deeply depressing and apparently very popular.

Delgado is greeted like a long-lost relative, much slapping of hands and bear-hugs. 'It's good to see you,' says the fifth waiter as we move to our table.

'Don't you come here very often?' I ask.

'I was in yesterday,' he replies. 'But they like to make me feel wanted. Is that such a bad idea?' He wiggles his eyebrows in a way that he presumably imagines is seductive. I feel another bilious attack coming on.

Mr Delgado's conversation has not so far proved mind-expanding. His three favourite subjects are, I, me, myself.

Is this the hell that reasonably intelligent men put up with in the company of babbling bimbos? How can they do it to themselves?

Delgado orders a Mon Rêve special and, in doing so, proceeds to strip it of most of its ingredients.

'Hold the pumpernickel, no gherkin, hold the mayo, light on the pastrami; any rye crackers? Plenty of those.'

No 'please' or 'thank you' again. This is followed by a long and involved discussion with the wine waiter as to which particular type of mineral water to choose.

'It's the sodium,' Delgado explains. 'My body can't take too much sodium.'

I order a cup of tea and a cottage cheese salad. 'Hold the cottage cheese,' I say deadpan to the waiter.

'That's funny,' Stephen Delgado contributes imaginatively to the conversation again, 'that's really funny.'

All this takes place in front of a reasonably large audience, since many of the women (and most seem to be picking at food with female companions) are openly staring at Delgado, smiling when he looks their way and generally fluttering about like butterflies on speed.

'Does it bother you, all this?' I ask.

'No, ma'am. It's my security. When they stop, I go out of business.'

The arrangement is that I will spend a couple of days with him and interview him as and when I can. He explains that he has agreed to this because Venus Inc. has just invested in the male magazine in which he also has a stake – and he has written a philosophy book which will be published in the UK in a couple of months.

'A philosophy book?' I ask, trying not to sound surprised.

'Yeah, of a kind. It's about thinking yourself into success. It's a step-by-step guide on how to make something of yourself, like I have.

'Look, lady,' Delgado points his finger at my chest, 'I know what you've got going on in your head. You imagine because I'm some sort of sex symbol – I know how I'm seen – I've got no brains. Let me tell you. I have a degree in business studies. I've got intelligence, I've got integrity, but still people look at me as if I'm a piece of meat.' He shrugs. 'So it's their problem. What can I do?'

'Speaking of meat,' says a laconic voice. A tall thin man in his late thirties stands by our table. He wears an expensive suit, a light tan and his hair may or may not be artificially highlighted.

'Danny!' Delgado leaps up and there is more bear-hugging and hand-slapping.

'Danny, I'd like you to meet—' Delgado has clearly forgotten my name.

'Kay Woods,' I say crisply. 'I'm from London. I've come to interview Stephen for a magazine—'

'*Illustrated London News*?' Danny says as he takes his seat and orders a T-bone steak underdone, tomato salad and a spritzer.

'No, it's called *Venus*,' I say evenly.

'As in *Venus in Blue Jeans*? Is it for teeny-boppers?'

'No, it's a magazine for . . .' I see that Delgado is smiling, this time genuinely amused, '. . . more selective tastes.'

The rest of what I say is overtaken by a conversation unravelling behind us which has increased in volume by several decibels.

'. . . How come you're invited to a stranger's wedding?' a malnourished woman in her fifties with her face lifted so many times she looks as if she comes from Shanghai, screams at the deeply lined, overweight man sitting opposite her.

'She's Jeff's secretary,' the man replies wearily.

'ROSA SAYS SHE'S NOT!' the woman yells.

'What does Rosa know?' the man shrugs.

The woman hisses in the man's face. 'You can have affairs. Have I ever said, "Arnie, no more affairs?" You can have affairs but YOU DO NOT GO TO FAMILY WEDDINGS WITH YOUR AFFAIRS. Do you hear me?'

The man shrugs and the two resume eating as if nothing has been said.

'She's right. Family, that's very important,' Danny says, applying lip-salve to his lips. 'One day I would like family. I'd like to find a woman who is my equal.'

As Danny talks, he dissects with dexterity the lump of bleeding meat on his plate.

'Let me show you something, Kelly.'

'Kay,' I correct. 'My name is Kay.'

'Let me show you something.' Danny takes the tip of his knife and saws to reveal a long white streak in the steak, almost like a tapeworm.

'See that? It's the NAV. The Nerve Artery Vein. Very important that, in my work.' He cuts a slice and puts it in his mouth, chewing vigorously.

'Women pay a lot to have me look after that.'

'What do you do for a living, Mr—?' I ask.

Danny wipes a dribble of blood from his chin and reapplies the lip-salve.

'I am proud to say I am a cosmetic surgeon. A very successful cosmetic surgeon. I have an apartment here in New York. I have a house in Sag Harbor where I grow herbs and play tennis. I am a twentieth-century wizard since magically I allow people with realistic expectations to fulfil their desires.'

'Oh, come on,' Delgado says. 'Realistic?'

'I am not responsible for what people want, Stevie boy, I am just responsible for what I can deliver. I deliver what is realistic,' Danny replies equably. He picks up my hands. 'Now, let's take a look at you. What are these?'

'Age spots. And I like them,' I say, smiling but only just.

He studies my face. 'Rhinoplasty, small facial tuck, a little lift of the eyes, bags removed . . . call it twenty thousand dollars, a few weeks' discomfort and what are you, forty-four, forty-five? I could knock ten years off, like that,' he clicks his fingers.

'How about it?' he says. 'We have very appealing terms.'

Danny picks up the steak bone and crunches on it, the juices running down his elegantly manicured fingers.

. 'Nowadays, you know what they say,' he continues. 'Your face counts as much as experience and if your face is . . . well, let's just say, your face is *your* face, then, to be blunt, it's a disadvantage in a competitive arena.

'This is a young woman's world, honey. Am I right, or am I wrong?' he asks Delgado.

'You are right,' Delgado answers.

'The world belongs to those who make the most of it,' I say with as much conviction as I can muster. 'Regardless of age.'

'Come back in a couple of years,' Danny says, picking threads of meat from between his teeth. 'Then you'll be ready to do business. I promise.'

A little later, a limousine drives us to the TV studio where Delgado is due to make a live appearance on a cable afternoon talk show for women – audience seventeen million. On the way, he explains how he met Danny.

'How old would you say I am, Kay?'

I say twenty-five and think thirty.

'Thirty-two. No, I'll be honest. Thirty-four. I look after myself. I work out in the gym for two hours a day. I do cardio-vascular work.'

'What do you mean? You jog?'

'Yeah, I jog. I take no alcohol. I eat clean. I don't do drugs. I don't smoke. I meditate. I avoid stress. I have a dietician and a trichologist, my personal trainer has bought a condominium off my back.'

'It sounds like enormous fun,' I say drily. 'Is all this down to vanity?'

'Vanity? I prefer to call it self-promotion,' he replies. 'I'm a good-looking guy. I'd be stupid not to know it.'

Delgado has removed a small mirror from the breast pocket of his unreconstructed suit and is examining his teeth.

'Green flecks,' he explains. 'No one tells you when you've got lettuce caught between your teeth. You're seen by millions of people and later your dentist calls you up and says, "Hey, whaddya tryin' to do, ruin me?"'

He smiles and continues, 'What I'm saying to you is if I've got something that's not quite right, what's wrong with a little body sculpture? I've got eight point seven per cent body fat, especially around my middle section. See.'

He grabs my hand and pushes a very small tyre of flesh into my hand.

'I want to get that down to seven per cent. See these calves?'

He rolls up his black slacks. 'Feel!' he commands. Gingerly I squeeze his calf. It is like a pumice-stone.

'Implant. One of Danny's best. I can't afford to have skinny legs.'

'What if they slip and slide? Or move sideways?' I ask, genuinely interested. 'Won't your ankles look like coat-hangers?'

'So, I'll get them fixed. I've got an IQ, OK? I can earn as much money with my brain as I can with my butt – but if I use my brain, I'm just one of a hundred million guys.

'If I flash my butt, I'm unique. I am Stephen W. Delgado. I'm somebody. I like that. I like being somebody. And if that means Danny has to sew daisy-chains around my dick, so be it.'

I make a mental note. If I ever travel with Stephen Delgado again, I must remember to bring a sick bag.

'Aaaaaaaagh!' Delgado's war cry fills the studio. 'Aaaaaagh!' screams the row of women in front of me, in answer. Communication at its most sophisticated.

Stephen Delgado is dressed as an Aztec. Or rather, as 1950s Hollywood might imagine an Aztec to look, relying on props from the set of *Ben Hur*.

He wears a helmet, a short tennis skirt, a heavy gold belt and gold sandals with ties which criss-cross up past his implants. From the waist up, he is naked except for a bizarre breast-shield which looks like the radiator grille of a second-hand Riley. He wears bracelets and a lot of artificial tan.

Strapped to his arms and back are a terrifying set of feather 'wings'. Each time he gives his war cry, he spreads these wings, causing multiple panic-attacks amongst the audience.

To keep the collective pulse high, drums pound heavily and consistently. Delgado is above the fray since he stands on top of a mini-pyramid which is raised about thirty feet above the studio audience. In front of him is a mock sacrificial stone. In his hand Delgado holds a rubber dagger.

At the foot of the pyramid is a blurred vision in tangerine. She is blurred because the combination of the studio lights and the colour of her suit and matching shoes seem to give her an aura like an angry halo. This is Margie McDerrick.

Margie's forte is to ask a member of the audience what her fantasy might be and, if it is halfway decent, she then engineers to fulfil it before 'half of America'. Since the intelligence quota of the proceedings appears exceedingly low, I suspect it is the bottom half of America at which Margie aims.

In this fairy story for adults, poor old Delgado has been cast as the Aztec priest who must sacrifice the king's daughter. He has to run down the pyramid, pick up the wannabe sacrifice and then run back up the pyramid with her in his arms.

Margie has already asked Delgado a number of tough and perceptive questions. 'Does he wear Y-fronts or boxer shorts?' 'Neither,' says Delgado. The audience whoop and holler.

'Have you a girlfriend?' 'No, I'm saving myself,' Delgado says. Whoops and hollers again. 'What do you like to do in your free time?' asks Margie, licking her lips.

'Fellatio?' sings out a voice from the row in front of me.

'Cut! Cut!' Margie commands. Delgado looks embarrassed but smiles. The audience is laughing. Margie is apoplectic.

'Ladies,' she shouts. 'This is a family show. A positive-values entertainment. We are not animals!'

Normal service is resumed. The drums roll, Delgado runs easily down the pyramid, balancing his wings. Margie greets him and asks Mary-Lou Wassert to 'Stand up, come on down and dream away!'

Mary-Lou Wassert comes on down – all eighteen stone of her. Delgado smiles gamely.

'Boy, you must have worked hard to get these muscles,' he says cruelly, lifting one of Mary-Lou's arms, the size of half a gammon.

He flicks his hair back, rubs his hands together, bends and raises Mary-Lou a few inches off the floor. She is red with delight.

'Heave!' shout the audience. 'Heave!'

Delgado puts one wobbly foot on the first 'stone' of the pyramid, then a second. Mary-Lou loses her grip and grabs hold of a feathered wing. The two sway splendidly for a matter of seconds and then collapse into the pyramid. Rubber 'stones' from the construction rain down on them and on us.

Some of the audience make a run for it. I see Delgado go down under a dozen women.

'Jesus fucking Christ!' screams Margie, her positive values on sabbatical, 'get these fuckwit she-dogs out of here.'

I sit tight. Judging from the number of feathers in the air, Delgado is being well and truly plucked.

Five security men charge at the mass of bodies – or rather, they try to charge but their batons are immediately requisitioned by the women, who plainly intend to use them as terrible tools of pleasure. Or is it revenge?

I see a large square glass box on the wall an arm's-length away. A notice underneath reads, 'Break in the event of fire'. I pick up a chair and aim at the glass.

It is nine p.m. and I sit sipping hot milk and honey, watching the city from Stephen Delgado's roof-garden. I have a sore throat. This is not because an irate fan has rammed a baton down my gullet but because I have been sitting in an icily air-conditioned private doctor's waiting-room while Stephen Delgado is patched up.

Considering everything he has is at face value – and the face at present has two stitches and several large bruises, mostly around the mouth – he has been surprisingly calm about the whole experience.

I soon discover why. Delgado reckons that each bruise, each stitch will net him half a million dollars since he intends to sue the programme for neglect of personal safety.

Foolishly, in the taxi back from the doctor's, I asked him if he minded the humiliation. What humiliation? he'd responded. 'Three-foot headlines in tomorrow's papers, that's happiness, sweetheart, not humiliation.'

As I pass the sofa where he sleeps, I pull the blanket over him which has dropped to the floor. I feel sorry for Mr Delgado. He's not a nice man. He's demanding, he's insecure, he's unhappy. He doesn't love himself at all. He's about as much company as a Korean translation of the Old Testament.

Thank God I don't fancy him.

Chapter Twenty-Two

My hotel room looks like a funeral home; 150 orchids and a card which reads, '*A face without lines is like a book without words.*' It's a reflective way to start the day.

At the news boutique in the hotel lobby, after a swim, I buy airmail copies of the London papers. Tom's documentary is reviewed. He gets one glowing endorsement in the *Telegraph*:

The Wounded Womb: *perceptive, lucid, powerful, in the old tradition of documentary film-making.*

And a rotten one from the *Guardian*, . . . *Patronizing, pompous, pontificating. For a programme about women's wombs, it had plenty of wombs but lacked any women. Too many male experts and not enough females given space to speak for themselves.*

Back in my room, I pick up the phone and begin dialling my home number. Then I stop. Capitulation to Tom at this point means more than surrender. It means concessions. Tom is a habit. Life without Tom could become a habit too. All I have to do is give myself time. A day at a time. And find new interests.

At eleven a.m. I come out of the elevator and into the lobby. Delgado stands in the middle of the room. He achieves the same impact as a six-foot illuminated light-bulb. He dazzles in a white suit and white T-shirt. He is fully occupied rearranging his hair, examining his reflection in one of the mirrored pillars.

'Can you see it?' Delgado asks without saying hello. 'Can you see it?'

'See what?' I ask frostily.

'Can you see the zit?' Delgado scrutinizes his chin. 'Got any cover-up?'

'Please,' I say. 'The word is *please*. And the answer is no.'

'No, you can't see it?'

'No. No, I don't have any cover-up. Shall we go?'

'Did you like them?' Delgado asks as we leave the hotel. 'I chose orchids because they are stylish, like you. What you did yesterday? That was impressive. You saved my skin,' he touches the stitches. 'Well, most of my skin. I could do you a favour,' he says and smirks.

'Thanks but no thanks,' I reply crisply. *Only another day or so and I need never spend time with Delgado and his ego again; a* ménage à trois *made in hell.*

'"A face without lines is like a book without words" . . . That's beautiful,' Delgado chats on. 'Don't you think that's beautiful? Know where I read them?' he volunteers.

I shake my head.

'I read them in an ad for face-cream. "A face without lines is like a book without words . . . but too many lines and the message is lost." I thought, "That's beautiful. That's poetry."'

Outside the hotel, a woman in her twenties, deeply tanned, painted with cheek blusher, sits in Delgado's open-top limousine. Delgado gets behind the steering-wheel and acts as if she's invisible. She turns and stares at me stonily.

He drives us to the offices of *Sagacity*, 'the monthly magazine for the mature man of any age.' This is the magazine in which Stephen Delgado has invested and Venus Inc. has a share. Delgado also 'writes' a ghosted column, the subject of which he is due to discuss at the magazine's weekly ideas conference.

I've been told by the man in the news boutique that the

magazine is also known as *Sag City*, since it appeals mostly to men with pot bellies who share Delgado's 'philosophy' on self-absorption.

I flick through the magazine as Delgado drives and the unknown woman sulks. I look at one regular feature, 'Me and My Bathroom'. A famous soap-opera actor who shares his house with 'a friend' writes, 'I have an electronic foot-bath, a magnetic manicure set attached to the wall, a soapdish made out of Italian marble, imported from Umbria; I have Calvin Klein towels; toiletries by Christian Dior and bath essence made from a secret Egyptian recipe, that you can only buy in Saks . . .'

Riveting.

The features are the usual mix for the kind of magazines which Mo calls prick polishers: I was a mercenary in Angola; a lunch date with Michele Pfeiffer ('. . . when she ordered fresh asparagus, what could I say?'); the top ten cappuccino-making machines; a profile of a man who's made a billion working a hundred hours a week selling water purifiers to the Gulf States, a fashion spread (clearly for men who don't care who takes the piss out of their tweed knickerbockers and mountain-climber boots in the office), a letters page ('First Class Male') and a regular column about 'feelings' called Sense and Sensitivity, sensibly restricted to half a page out of 200.

At *Sagacity*, you are what you buy.

'Will you call me?' the woman by Delgado's side asks. 'Will you call me, baby?'

'Maybe,' Delgado says, keeping his eyes on the road.

'I won't complain,' the woman wheedles. 'Just say you'll call.'

'If I call, I call,' Delgado says rudely.

When I look up from the magazine, I discover Delgado is watching me in his driver's mirror. What a wally.

Five minutes later, we drive into an underground car park.

'*Ciao,*' Delgado says to the still nameless woman. 'Gino will call a taxi for you.'

The woman is about to open her mouth but Delgado turns his back, heaves himself over the car door (what's wrong with opening it?) and walks away fast.

I scrabble out of the back with less style. I smile sympathetically at the woman and trot after Delgado.

'Just as a matter of interest,' I say to him, slightly breathless. 'Why did you treat her so badly?'

'Why?' Delgado stops and looks at me with a puzzled expression. 'Why? Isn't it obvious? That's what keeps her coming back for more.'

Carl de Angelini's appearance induces guilt. He is repellent. He is so repellent, you feel guilty for being repelled. After all, he is not to blame for his physiognomy. Fortunately for Carl de Angelini, he thinks that he is a pretty cool number.

He sits feet up on the desk in black jeans, pale blue shirt and a black waistcoat embroidered with blue and red roses. A cigarette hangs from his bottom lip. The wet, pink flesh of the bottom lip is not matched by the top lip which is so thin, it almost looks as if Mr de Angelini's maker left this feature out intentionally. *Spot the deliberate mistake.*

De Angelini has a pug nose splayed in a way that is only possible to achieve after years of dedicated nose-picking. Thick, black hair is exquisitely cut but copious amounts of grease do not encourage a person to linger long on the man's locks. Black-rimmed spectacles are pushed on the back of his head and just a smidgen of body odour is detectable beneath a sweet-smelling cologne reminiscent of maple syrup.

Mr de Angelini is editor of *Sagacity*. At the weekly ideas meeting, he is surrounded by half a dozen men of various ages whose faces are mostly battered but pleasant, and three women. All the women wear extremely short skirts, tangled hair and languid expressions belied only by the vigour with which they bite their nails and continually light up fags.

'Carl', when he listens – which doesn't appear to be often – flicks his tongue out. The coat of white fur suggests that a laxative might not go amiss.

'Naa,' he says when someone suggests a piece on the impact of the male shopper in supermarkets – who apparently makes up a third of regular customers.

'Naa, that doesn't blow my shit up.'

As the conference progresses, it appears that very little does – unless, that is, it is Mr de Angelini's idea.

'How about a big piece on the New Penis?' asks one of the women.

'I'm not tradin' my dick in for nobody,' says de Angelini. Everyone laughs dutifully, except me.

The woman persists. 'The New Penis is everywhere – we could do extensions, circumcised sex versus non-circumcised sex, the huge sale in artificial bulges . . . the penis is big,' she says without irony.

The group wait to see if de Angelini gets the unintended pun and when he doesn't, they rapidly wipe the smiles off their faces.

'OK,' the editor eventually says. 'Let's go for it. Maybe we could get a picture of a lot of famous dicks and have a quiz – who does this belong to? Can we get a special offer – a reader's bulge? Slide into your five-oh-ones and watch the women come?'

More uproarious laughter. It's odd to watch the enthusiasm with which these men objectify bits of their own anatomy with the same appetite they once devoted to objectifying the female form.

'I've got an idea,' says a man in his late twenties, baby face, suede boots, shirt with a turned-up collar and belt on a notch that looks painfully tight. 'How about Peacocks and Ugly Ducklings?'

He looks around the room expectantly and sees blank stares.

'You know, handsome men who end up with runts, rubber-faces. Older women with lots of wrinkles. What's in it for either of them, if it ain't money?'

'Beats me,' says de Angelini. 'You'd know about that, though, wouldn't you?' he turns to me. My face colours.

'Would I?' I ask evenly. De Angelini's face flattens into a false smile.

'Well, let's be frank. What you got on Prince Charming here? Ten, twenty years? And the flesh ain't exactly as supple as it once was. Come on, you know what I'm saying, you're among friends. What's the connection? What's the pull in vintage pussy? And don't tell me it's compassion. I've known the Big Man too long for that. He spares no feelings for nobody, 'cept himself.'

'It's business,' Delgado says tersely. 'She's here on business. Didn't you get the fax?'

As he talks to de Angelini, Delgado turns to look at me, and I see pity in his eyes.

'You wouldn't say no, though, would you?' de Angelini prods me. 'Look at my girls here, they wouldn't say no to a piece of Delgado. Would you, girls?'

De Angelini's secretary arrives in the room bearing coffee.

I stand up to leave.

'Hey, don't go,' de Angelini says. 'I was only joking, horsing around. You can take a joke, can't you? Or are you one of these po-faced, PC cunts?'

Some of the staff, the three women included, laugh. As I reach the door, I smile. 'I'm one of those po-faced, PC cunts,' I reply, and walk out.

De Angelini's secretary catches up with me at the lift. 'Excuse me,' she says, 'I just want you to know. You've made my day.'

On the way back to the hotel, I succumb.

I divert to Macy's and spend and spend. In the States, forty-plus is plainly an antisocial disease.

I buy cream which allegedly erases the wrinkles around my eyes, my mouth and my neck. I buy cream to stop my lipstick bleeding. I buy cream that miraculously, overnight, holds back the clock. I buy cream which, in the day, spurts water into my pores so I look damp and moist at all times. I buy capsules for an instant face-lift and essence of oil which, if I place a few drops on my pillow each evening, will stop me frowning in my sleep.

I buy a foundation with air-holes and grains of reflecting mirrors which play games with the light to eliminate the tracks of time.

I emerge from the store considerably poorer and feeling deeply defeated.

An hour later, back in my hotel room, without any enthusiasm at all, I look at the notes I've made on Delgado. Once this is done, I'll find a good hotel perhaps in the Florida Keys where the girls and I can just mess about, swim, sunbathe and chat. Then, I'll get on with the rest of my life.

If I had any secret hope that Tom would come swinging down from the trees in a loincloth looking for me, it has long gone.

The phone rings. 'Excuse me, ma'am, there's a gentleman here to see you. He won't give his name but he says he'll meet you in the bar. Do you want me to tell him you're unavailable?'

'I'll come down,' I tell the man on reception.

'Very good, ma'am. Have a nice day,' he replies automatically. The bar of the hotel is empty and gloomy – oak and olive-green and subdued lighting. Sitting in an alcove looking surprisingly cheerful is Mike Robinson.

Chapter Twenty-Three

In Central Park, Mike and I watch as a woman in a navy blue track suit jogs by. She is maybe two or three years younger than me and her unmade-up face is enhanced by laughter-lines and the clearest blue eyes.

Age has chiselled away at some of the excess flesh on her face, leaving her with slanting cheek-bones that she probably never realized she had in her twenties. Her hair is salt-and-pepper, thick and cut in a chin-length page-boy, now held back in an Alice band.

She has something no younger woman can match – is it experience? Assuredness? A knowledge that life's unpredictability can be survived? Whatever it is, it doesn't come out of a bottle and it draws the eye.

She runs with a baby in a miniature carriage. The baby faces her, the carriage is attached to a harness around the woman's waist. As she jogs steadily, the child sleeps.

She smiles at me as she runs past and I smile back.

'. . . and I haven't been able to get her to talk sensibly since—' Mike is speaking as we walk. He stops because I have stopped.

'I really want you to be all right,' I say spontaneously. 'I really do.'

'You and me both,' he replies drily.

Then he continues: 'I can't see it happening. I've suggested to Angela that we talk about this. We can have a divorce, she can find the sort of man she really wants. She can keep the house, she can

273

have a lump sum from a couple of insurance policies that are about
to come good . . .

'That's funny, well sad really.' Mike pauses, then says, 'Do you
know what one of the insurance policies was for? Before I met
Angela, I promised myself that one day, I'd pull up roots and go
round the world for a year.

'I've kept the policy up because the thought of that freedom
kept me going.'

Mike falls silent. 'And?' I press gently.

'At first, Angela was all in favour. We planned to do it once
the kids were at university. But quite early on I think, I realized it
would never happen . . . Angela started to say that she felt too
settled. Who would look after the goldfish?

'I mean, we have a chance to sail to Fiji and she's preoccupied
with the fucking goldfish!

'Then there was my career to consider . . . then the recession
hit our savings . . . the excuses just went on and on.

'I did try and explain. We'd sit and talk and I'd see Angela's
eyes go blank and her lips tighten . . . she's got a terrific knack of
denying what she doesn't want to be true.

'Do you know something, Kay? I felt trapped. For years and
years, I felt trapped. And when the children arrived, I felt even
more trapped. It was ironic really, I loved them so much. I felt I'd
never be able to leave. And yet because I loved them so much, I
didn't want to spend my whole bloody life working in a job I
hated, living in a way I loathed.

'A couple of months ago, the kids and I were at a funfair on
the common. Angela said we had to be back for supper at a certain
time but we were all enjoying ourselves so I thought, "Fuck it, half
an hour won't make a difference."

'But it did. It certainly did. Talk about "Thou shalt not
disobey." Something flipped in me that night.

'I was like a zombie for the next few weeks and Angela didn't even notice. Or perhaps in her usual fashion she preferred to ignore what was happening. One morning I left for work and never arrived. I took a train to Southsea instead. You've got no idea how relieved I felt. Really relieved . . . It only lasted for a couple of hours, but it was worth it. Just for the sake of those few hours.'

We stop at a coffee-shop in the park, find seats outside and order drinks.

'It must have been tough,' I say after the drinks have arrived.

'It's tougher now.' Mike rubs his eyes. 'I miss the children horribly. I'm frightened Angela's filling them up with some bullshit about how I've abandoned them, but I had to take that risk.

'I've been watching them, you know. The time you saw me at Euston? I'd been parked near the house to catch a glimpse of the kids, see they were all right. I saw Angela leave the night before and drive to your house.'

'My house?' I say.

'Yeah, she's been there quite a bit. I followed because I thought you might have been looking after the children for her. I stayed outside all night and followed her to the station in the morning.'

'So how come you're in New York now?' I ask.

'I've got an old friend here. We met just after university. He takes city people backpacking. He teaches them to track and climb and open their bottles of Chardonnay with their teeth while the tofu toasts over an open camp-fire.

'I've been helping him. I needed time to sort out what I wanted to do. I called you at home to see if you could encourage Angela to meet me. Tom told me you were here and gave me the name of your hotel. He was a bit bloody odd. Sounded as if I should know where you were.'

I smile. 'He thinks we're having an affair. Or rather, he pretends he thinks we're having an affair. Angela's convinced of the fact. Won't have it any other way.'

'That explains why she won't let the kids come near the phone. I misbehaved and now they're going to be part of the punishment.' Mike speaks more in resignation than anger.

'What will you do?'

'I'll fight in the courts. I'm going to rent a flat close to her with space for the kids. I'll find a part-time job with absolutely no prospects whatsoever. Then I'll take time to discover what *I* want from life, not what everybody else thinks I should want.

'How about you?' he suddenly asks.

'How about me?' I reply cautiously.

'Well, is this the start of a brand-new career? How does Tom feel about it? You rushing around the world again?'

Unexpectedly, the tears well up. 'Got a hanky, please?' I ask.

'Oh, Jesus,' he says as he searches through his pockets. 'I'm so sorry. What have I said? Are you OK? What's happened?'

Mike is familiar and from home and I am more intimidated about the future than I have yet allowed myself to acknowledge. So, in the middle of Central Park on a sunny day in spring, I bawl and bawl. And Mike keeps thanking me for helping him with *his* troubles.

Mike's friend Chas is big and bearded and Canadian. He says he has no ties, no grief, only a deep love of anywhere that isn't indoors.

Mike takes me to Chas's apartment in Tribeca and all three of us eat together in the evening in the pizza parlour on the ground floor of Chas's apartment block. It is easy and fun and uncomplicated. The two men discuss the year they spent backpacking together after university; Chas recalls his mainly disastrous attempts at relationships; Mike ponders further and fruitlessly on his marriage to Angela.

It is a conversation which gradually makes less and less sense, sodden as it is in Chianti. Eventually, Mike tells me I should confide in Chas.

'Tell him about Tom and all that. He's got a bloody good head on his shoulders, haven't you, mate?' Chas nods sagely as if to show his head is in good working order.

'But Kay,' Mike adds drunkenly, wagging his finger. 'Make it snappy. Not as long as this afternoon, OK?'

'It's simple really,' I say to Chas, speaking slowly in case anyone should think I've had too much to drink. I pick up the pepper-mill.

'This is Tom. Very important man. Centre of the universe.'

I pick up the salt-cellar. 'This is Brenda. Tom's lover. Who knows for how long?'

I place the salt-cellar and pepper-mill together. 'A lovely couple. But there is a problem.'

I pick up the very small pot of mustard. 'This is me. In the way.' I place the mustard pot between the other two condiments.

'Married almost twenty-one years. Thought I was happy. Twin daughters. Lovely girls, even if I say so myself. Husband bonks someone else. Probably bonked lots of someone elses.

'Ask him about it. He refuses to tell the truth. I realize that it's partly my fault because I've relied on him to live my life for me.'

'I decide I'm going to have a bit of fun too. One way of knowing yourself is to explore the more sensual side of life. Open to adventures. Find confidence in expressing myself sexually, should the need arise.'

'Remember, she's pissed,' Mike instructs Chas, slightly anxiously. 'She's not normally like this.'

'Are you trying to say you've decided to screw around?' Chas asks chummily.

'Absolutely not. No . . . I'm just not going to turn my back on experiences that can open up my horizons. I want it all to happen on the basis of a fair exchange, of course. I know what you want, and you know what I want . . .'

Chas tries again. 'So let me see if I've got this right. You're not screwing around, but you are up for it?'

I pick up the mustard pot and bang it down happily. 'Got it!' I say.

Mike and Chas insist on escorting me back to my hotel. It's early still, around nine. As we enter the lobby, I suddenly remember. At eight-thirty I was supposed to meet Stephen Delgado. He is due to film part of an exercise video for women and I am to observe.

Delgado sits patiently in the lobby, wearing a white track suit. As he rises, you feel he should be carrying a large box of soap powder, he looks so unbelievably clean, so radiant, so healthy. Or maybe it's just that we appear so dishevelled, so disreputable, so desperately drunk.

Delgado offers his hand. 'Hi guys,' he says.

'I'm terribly sorry. I forgot all about our meeting,' I smile brightly at Delgado, trying to look sober. 'But Mike's a dear friend, a very old friend, a very, very dear friend. He suddenly popped up, well, almost out of the blue, you might say.'

For some reason, I think this is exceptionally funny. I join Delgado on the sofa and chuckle to myself. Chas and Mike say their goodbyes and we promise to call each other. Then they leave.

I make a silent promise. I will try hard not to show Delgado how much he gets up my nose.

'Your hair is very shiny,' I say apropos of nothing, since he seems to expect conversation.

'I expect you wash it a lot?' He says nothing but just watches me. Perhaps I'm straining for too high a level of intellectual interchange?

The sofa is vast, as white as his track suit. 'I'm quite surprised I can see you,' I say. The alcohol makes me feel pleasantly sleepy.

'I'm surprised I can see you because you're all white and the sofa is white and really, you're almost totally camouflaged. Do you know what I mean?'

For some reason, I am convinced that this is a very important and extremely interesting point to make.

I come closer to Delgado and say conspiratorially, 'Next time you come here in a white track suit, ask them to change the cover on the sofa. Or, better still, why don't you wear a different coloured track suit? Now, that's a brilliant idea. Don't you think that's a very good idea?'

Delgado orders a large pot of coffee and watches while I drink. I have not a thought in my head, except the absolute certainty that if I don't concentrate very hard, my wrist will droop, my fingers slip and the sofa will no longer be white.

I concentrate and smile. I'm still smiling as Delgado uses his mobile phone to cancel the planned filming of his video.

'OK,' he says when he turns back to me, 'let's go.'

He drives 120 miles with the top of his car down. Most of the time, I sleep. On the occasions when I wake, he says nothing. It's an uncharitable thought, but with his mouth permanently shut and all discussions about his profile, ribcage and the problem he has with his pores curtailed, he could almost be attractive.

At five a.m. I wake properly. Delgado is asleep in the driving-seat, a big blue jumper wrapped around him. He has parked on the edge of a vast expanse of beach badgered by a belligerent surf.

I walk down to the sea. It is cold and exhilarating. I walk about a mile along the beach. I take off my clothes except for my underwear. I tell myself I will dive in on three – and I do. Half an hour later, I am dressed, minus underwear, and on my way back to the car. Delgado is doing press-ups in the sand. I find men who do press-ups in public very embarrassing.

'Hey, you,' he shouts rudely. 'Don't do that, understand me?

'I was worried,' he adds in a more friendly vein. 'I've swum here all my life and even I could get caught by the currents. It's dangerous.'

I say nothing.

'Do you like it here?' he asks, more softly.

The answer is easy. 'I do, I really do. It's stunning. I love the sea anyway,' I reply. 'I grew up with it. My dad always had boats—'

'He did?' Delgado interrupts. 'So did mine.'

'Not a yacht,' I explain. 'A boat, mainsail and gib, nothing fancy.'

'The same as ours,' Delgado smiles.

We sit on that beach for almost two hours talking about boats and different seas and fathers. And he has the good grace not to mention the scene in the office of *Sagacity*. When he gets off the subject of himself, Stephen Delgado is almost a decent human being. An observer might even assume that we are friends.

'I need some fresh clothes, coffee, breakfast, how about you?' Delgado suggests mid-morning. 'We could spend the day here – if you've got the free time?'

'I'm not sure. . .'

'Just take a few hours off,' Delgado presses. 'When you've had enough, we'll drive back.'

'OK,' I agree. 'Unless, of course, you manage to say something interesting. In which case, I'll try to find my notebook.'

He throws his shirt at my head.

The sign says *Welcome to East Hampton*. The place is how I imagine affluent rural Britain might have looked in the fifties.

Large 'Tudor' cottages and salt-box houses stand surrounded by massive lawns and not a fence in sight. The 'village' pond is surrounded by weeping willows. Children ride bikes and play on the sidewalk.

East Hampton has two main streets; every shop is different and yet they all cater to the same trade – the very rich and the very, very rich.

A cornucopia of signs (not least dollar signs) also convey the message to a stranger that even money can't buy freedom: *Do not walk on the grass*; *Do not walk dogs in the park*; *Do not allow children to finger merchandise in this shop*; *Do not chew gum*.

We order coffee in an establishment which calls itself a *Tea Shoppe*. 'Strawberry-flavoured; chocolate swirl; cappuccino with a whipped; espresso; double espresso; decaf; peppermint shake, raspberry cr—'

'Just straight black filter please,' I say.

'Let me take care of this,' Delgado offers. 'Could we have a large pot of black coffee, two scrambled eggs with almonds on toasted pumpernickel and fresh orange juice, twice over, please?'

The waitress smiles straight into his eyes for what seems a lifetime.

'Is there anything else I can do for you?' she purrs at Delgado.

'Yes please,' I intervene. 'Could you tell me where the bathroom is?'

Later, we buy swimsuits and beach towels and jeans and T-shirts and socks and sneakers. A woman tries to sell us a tube of cream for sunless tanning which costs the equivalent of a weekend in Cannes but we refuse and opt for plain old-fashioned Factor 6 oil. Delgado chooses a floppy hat for me and sunglasses and we fight over who will pay the bill.

A gay assistant with mascara-ed eyelashes smiles while we squabble.

'Let your mother give you a treat,' I finally instruct Delgado.

'She's right,' the assistant squeaks.

We return to the almost deserted beach. In the afternoon we buy cold white wine and smoked-salmon sandwiches from a man who parks and sells from the back of his van. I tell Stephen Delgado, because he asks, about the places I visited as a journalist before the children, Egypt, Spain, Syria, Jordan . . .

I'd forgotten how much I'd travelled – or perhaps I'd encouraged myself to forget, in order to make the adjustment to staying at home that much easier.

Delgado, of course, does most of the talking. He is a good mimic. He creates the characters in his life-story; his favourite teacher, his father, his mother who always said that trying to control two girls was more difficult than rearing five boys; he tells me about his friends back home and how many of them are now married; he describes his first agent in New York; and, more cruelly, the kind of women who have bedded and bored him.

The performance makes him amusing but not endearing. So, in the sea, when he suddenly kisses me – using his tongue like a periscope examining my innards – I am furious.

'For God's sake,' I say as I push him away. 'Do me a favour.'

This is not an imaginative remark at the best of times and particularly not now, since Delgado clearly believes that a favour is precisely what he *is* doing me.

'I thought that's what you wanted me to do,' he sulks. 'I thought you were sending out all the signs.'

'Signs? Signs? What signs?'

'All that stuff, intimate stuff, about yourself and your family.'

'Intimate, it's not bloody intimate. It's fact. I could tell the butcher the same stuff but I wouldn't expect him to jump over the counter and give me one.'

'It's a sort of present from me to you,' Delgado says. 'I mean, well, I thought it would be nice for you . . . you know, to get together.'

'I am not in need of charity, thank you very much.' I march out of the sea, sit on the sand and put my head down. Delgado warily positions himself a couple of yards away. My shoulders give the game away.

'You're laughing,' he says accusingly. 'You're not upset at all!'

'Of course I'm laughing. Here you bang on about being a sex object and how people only look at your body and never consider your mind, but that you like it really. Or then again, you say, perhaps you don't like it really. Then what do you do?

'The first time, according to you, someone offers you friend-ship, you give yourself up like some first prize in a game show. Doesn't matter whether you fancy me or I fancy you – you would seriously consider taking me to bed. Well, I for one do not believe in copulation on grounds of compassion. Being pitied, I find, is not the easiest route to an orgasm.'

I'm not angry or insulted or humiliated. On the contrary, I'm confused.

Tom has screwed Brenda because he seeks excitement – or so he says. Brenda screws Tom because she is looking for love. Pam screws Tom because what else do you do when you're drunk at the end of filming? Tom screws Pam because she's Australian and he thinks all that sun makes Australian women randier.

I screw Tom because I love him and then I discover that isn't enough. Ian Jackson screws me as part of a business contract. Delgado screws himself by offering his body as a thank-you note.

Does anybody, anywhere in the world, have an honest fuck any more?

The Settlers Inn is in the centre of East Hampton. It is a sprawling white clapboard single-storey house, polished oak floors, no television in the rooms, an epidemic of chintz and rocking-chairs and copies of *Gourmet Food*.

The receptionist, when we arrive, is vacuum-cleaning the keyboard of the computer behind the desk with what looks like a massive toothbrush.

Delgado speaks: 'We'd like two rooms, two double rooms, please.'

He winks at the receptionist. 'I want the one that has your personal recommendation,' he leers.

Oh, please.

The receptionist's smile is so wide that her mouth, the teeth disciplined by braces, looks like the portcullis at the Tower of London.

At eleven p.m. I am in my bed. We have eaten and talked and laughed a lot. Delgado has signed a dozen autographs but mostly he has been ignored. One advantage of staying in a town with more film stars than parking-spaces is that a minor starlet, whose most regularly featured appearance is his bum, is rendered invisible.

As we say goodnight, I tell him the evening has been surprisingly enjoyable. Considering. He tells me not to be condescending.

At twelve-thirty a.m. there is a knock on my door. It is Delgado. He is dressed and has a brown paper bag in his hand.

'Shopping again?' I ask sarcastically since he had admitted earlier that shopping 'makes me feel I've arrived'.

'I couldn't sleep. I thought you might like a nightcap?'

'No thank you, I have no trouble at all sleeping. I'll see you in the morning.'

'It's hot,' he says, holding up the paper bag. 'Hot chocolate and brandy.'

I let him in. He talks for a further ninety minutes, then tells me

I am the most beautiful woman he has ever met. I put my best efforts into staying awake.

He tells me that he hasn't enjoyed himself so much in years. Age doesn't matter. We can adopt. He now has my fullest attention.

'We can WHAT?'

'We can adopt,' Delgado repeats equably.

'Look,' I say speaking slowly, mainly because I'm tired and sunburnt and have absolutely no desire to take advantage of an addled man.

'You want to go to bed with me because I don't fancy you. It's a challenge. But I don't want to go to bed with you. Now, good night.' I open the bedroom door.

'OK,' Delgado says, 'I'll tell you the truth. I'm curious. You're older, you may know something I don't know.'

I throw a pillow at him and he catches it.

'Look on it as a favour to me,' he continues, I think tongue in cheek. 'I know you're my Good Samaritan.'

'Out,' I say.

At three a.m. Delgado is back for the fourth time. Each knock comes with a different excuse. Do I have an aspirin? Do I have something he can read? Do I want to go for a walk, since he can't sleep?

By the fourth visit, I don't even bother to open the door. From the comfort of my bed, I tell him to go away; he's a spoilt, selfish, self-obsessed, pain in the arse.

'More! More!' he whispers from the other side of the door. 'I love it when you're tough.'

Ten minutes after he has gone again, I sit up in bed. Why not? Am I a female Casanova or what? Presumably, even Delgado can stop talking about himself for a few minutes, once he's on the job. I know already that the man's under-exercised brain offers limited scope for pleasure, but that's no reason why a libidinous, pioneering woman such as myself should turn down his body.

At three-fifteen a.m. I am in his bed. Delgado is tense. It's like being in bed with an iron girder and I am not referring to his erection. That, to describe it in the most generous terms, is going up and down faster than a starter's flag at the races.

I take control. I instruct him to lie on his back by my side and suggest that we practise deep breathing for a while until we can both relax.

'Shouldn't we be *doing* something?' he keeps saying. Finally, his patience collapses. Within three minutes it becomes clear that Delgado is a repertoire man. I am to be given the full works, like it or not.

He twiddles my nipples with the ferocity of a radio ham: he rubs so vigorously in the general area of my vagina that I swear a genie is about to appear. Delgado then attempts to manoeuvre me in all the directions of the compass in a number of grips more appropriate to osteopathy.

Next, he seizes my hand and clamps it on to his erect penis, a move I instantly resist. He begins to flip me over like a pancake, and I finally protest.

'I haven't slept with a woman yet who hasn't come,' Delgado growls.

'How many have had heart attacks at the same time?' I ask lightly. 'Look, do you think as a special favour to me we could do this like normal people do? Do you know how normal people make love?'

He looks perplexed.

'Normal people make love when they are very, very tired. If you could pretend you're very, very tired we might arrive at the same place at the same time – together.'

Delgado shrugs, smiles and slides back down the bed.

Whatever his other imperfections, he proves to be a very

quick learner. And perhaps because I have nothing to lose and I feel not a shred of guilt, I fly far and high. Anna in the workshop, if she knew, would almost certainly elevate me to scholar *cum laude*.

Chapter Twenty-Four

'We will become one of the great love couples in history, Antony and Cleopatra, Bonnie and Clyde . . .'

It is early afternoon and Stephen Delgado is driving us back to New York.

At first, I assume he is joking.

'Delgado and Woods, I don't think so,' I say flippantly. 'It sounds more like a firm of undertakers.'

'Kay,' Delgado says, suddenly serious, 'don't say a word. I know you're going to tell me the age difference is too great. You're going to tell me I should look for someone who's younger, someone who wants children. I know you're going to say all that stuff, but I won't listen. I've made up my mind. I promise I will take care of you, like you've never been taken care of before. Trust me.'

'And no matter what you say or do,' he adds, self-adoration lighting up his face, 'I know what your true feelings are.'

He leans across and kisses me. And parts of my body are not untouched. Who would have foreseen that this man might offer much more than the packaging implied? Indeed, his skill as a lover, once reduced to waltz-time, could keep almost any woman happy. Who needs companionship? Who needs conversation?

'You couldn't have made love to me in the way that you did last night without it being more than just a one-night stand.'

'I couldn't?' I say, bemused.

'This is synchronicity,' Delgado says. 'I came into your life just when you needed me most – and I'm not going to give up now.'

'You came into my life?' I repeat.

'I've never felt this way before, I've never talked to someone so much, so it's got to be love,' Delgado announces emphatically.

'You sure it's not just curiosity? Or even lust?' I suggest prosaically.

'See?' Delgado beams at me. 'See how unselfish you are? See how much you put yourself second? I am going to make you a very happy woman. A woman who is truly loved. You hear what I'm saying? No, don't say another word: I want the world to know, and believe me, the world will be interested.'

I see trouble ahead. Another lesson learned: never fuck anyone as a favour. Even to yourself.

Back in the city, the obvious person to ask for advice is Olivia. We spend an hour on the phone. She says Delgado sounds just like Des, the jockey – a man programmed to talk of love when a polite, 'Thank you for having me' is more appropriate.

'Don't panic,' she says cheerfully. 'Go away with the twins, don't tell him where you're going and have a fabulous time.

'He'll cool down, get a sense of perspective, and given space he'll get over it. I've seen a couple of pictures. Is he as gorgeous as he looks?' she asks.

'It's not his looks—' I begin.

'It must be doing wonders for you, darling,' Olivia interrupts. 'A man ten, fifteen years younger . . . How did you do it?'

It seems unfair to reveal to her the basic truth that it isn't what I do for Delgado which comprises the small, hopefully removable, hook he now has in me, but what he does for me.

Olivia informs me that sales of my jewellery have dropped off.

'Perhaps we need a new selling-point? How about bits of car

engines? Are you good with spark-plugs? Or how about jump-leads? I'm sure you could produce a lovely little necklace out of jump-leads. You've got such a knack with rubbish, Kay.'

Later in the conversation, Olivia asks me if I've heard anything about Angela.

'Like what?'

'Oh, I don't know. Mo mentioned something the other day. She'll probably give you a ring – she's been a bit busy. She spends all her spare time watching blue movies with that anthropologist chap. You know, the one with The Problem? She claims it's part of his therapy.

'By the way,' Olivia adds casually, as we are about to say our goodbyes. 'I'm getting married.'

'You are *what*?'

'I'm getting married. You remember the man I met in the Houndsditch Warehouse? Doug? Well, he's an absolute angel. He hates horses, he likes taking decisions, he's as decent as the day is long, he gets on with the kids, he eats enormous amounts of food, he's a foot taller than me and it's nice to reach up rather than down – and he's wonderful in bed. Otherwise, he's just an average sort of chap.'

'Doug? The silent one?' I try to recall.

'Well, he's not that silent,' Olivia clucks like a mother hen. 'I've got a bit of advice for you.' It wouldn't be Olivia, if she hadn't. 'Watch out. When you find the right fellow, it just sort of happens,' she bullshits happily.

'Terrific. I'll bear that in mind.' Suddenly, I discovered a catch in my throat. 'I'm truly, really, pleased for you, Olivia. Really I am. I'm so pleased, I think I'm going to cry.'

'It's luck,' Olivia replies. 'Just pure good luck. Kay?'

'Yes?'

'Would you give me away? I think it was you who brought me that luck.'

I say yes, of course. My future flashes before me: always the bride's father, never the bride.

Strangely, it doesn't bother me that much.

Delgado phones me obsessively. The more I tell him the truth that I am not interested, the more he is convinced I am masking my real feelings. The difficulty is, I *am* masking my real feelings. If I could have him on stand-by as a bonking-partner for the rest of my life, I would not be a disappointed woman. I recognize, however, that this is not the kind of arrangement one suggests if one is trying to establish standards of decency in one's own life. Delgado is not dumb: he senses my ambivalence but misreads it.

I arrange to meet the girls in Miami. I tell Delgado I have to leave New York for a few days and I'll call when I get back, to confer with him about the article. I don't tell him when I'm leaving or my destination. I leave the name of the Key Biscayne hotel with the New York hotel in case Rosemary attempts to contact me. Otherwise I don't want her to know where I am on holiday. I need a rest from pushing back the boundaries and ravaging robots.

I pack all the anti-ageing creams, oils and essences except one in a carrier bag and ask the maid who comes to clean if she would like to have them. She is eighteen but delighted. I keep the one pot back just in case. I feel saner by the hour.

On the third day of our five-day holiday in Florida, my New York hotel phones me. Could I please do something about the bunches of red roses and leeks which someone called 'D' sends every hour on the hour?

'Leeks, you say?' I ask, wondering at their significance.

'Leeks are very acceptable right now, madam,' says a smarmy voice on the other end. 'Very chic.'

'Well, if they're getting in the way, couldn't you cook them or something?'

'Madam,' says the shocked voice at the other end. 'This is vegetables as *art*.'

I wait until the twins have gone for a swim then I phone Delgado.

'You disappeared,' he wails.

'No, I'm just spending time with my daughters.'

'How are they? Are they well? Are you having a great time?'

This is a smart move on Delgado's part. 'Take the child's hand and you steal the mother's heart,' I once read on a beer-mat in a bar in Copenhagen.

'They're really well,' I say, drawn in in spite of myself. 'They look stunning and we've had lots of laughs.'

'Are they as beautiful as their mother?' Delgado says. I feel sick.

'Much better looking than me. They take after their father,' I answer briskly.

'God, baby, how I'd like to fuck you now,' he whispers. I blush, a full toe-to-hairline blush. The man's capacity to embarrass is unmatched. But the suggestion has its positive side too.

'Look, Stephen, I'm not your baby, nor anybody else's. This is a business call. I've faxed you the piece I've written. Since the situation is more . . . complicated than usual, I feel it's only right that you should know what I've written.

'It's honest, so you might not like it. You can't change anything unless it's a factual error. But you have a right to read it. We can discuss it when I come back.'

I pause for breath. 'Oh, and Stephen? Would you mind not sending bunches of leeks, the hotel is getting rather cross.'

'OK, fine, I'll send them to wherever you are now instead,' he answers equably.

'Look, I'm sorry, you don't understand. This will not work.

Honestly, it won't. It's not our ages. I couldn't care less about that. It's that we're too different. And I don't want to settle down. How can I settle down when I haven't even been properly unsettled yet? Stephen? . . . Are you there?'

'You're a magnificent woman, Kay Woods. I've never met anyone who would sacrifice so much for me. I can hear something in your voice. I'll be waiting for you when you get back,' he continues. 'I'm going to choose my moment and then announce to the media that I'm in love with a beautiful woman . . . When did you say your birthdate was, Kay? They like these little details.'

'I didn't, and why on earth do you have to announce it to anyone? Do not say a word. Do you hear me?'

'Honey,' Delgado says, back in New York glitzspeak again, 'I am a celebrity. I have responsibilities – to my fans, to my management. Besides, the age difference, it's a great spin on the story. I talked to my manager. He says we'll get the front page of the *Daily News* easy.'

'We will not,' I say, my voice fading.

'Sure we will.'

'I need time to sort out my affairs. Publicity now would be, well, it would be very difficult.' I stall for time.

'You got it. Let me know your hotel,' he demands. 'I won't come down, I promise you. I just want to know where you are, that you're OK.'

'You promise you won't appear?' I insist.

He does. So I tell him.

Dealing with Delgado, I've begun to realize that telling the truth has its drawbacks. Namely, when the other person refuses to hear it.

The girls are thinner than when they left London and they talk faster and seem more adult – but they are still my babies. On the beach, we chat about college and home and their father and they don't appear to suspect that anything is wrong.

On the contrary, they say I look 'really well'. 'You were a bit, I don't know, a bit low-key last time we saw you,' Kate says.

'So, have you made friends, boyfriends, that kind of thing?' I ask carefully. Kate and Claire stay silent.

We've always talked openly about sex by which I mean, at various times once the twins entered puberty, I would deliver my monologue.

'Sex is a very precious element in life. Don't waste it. Don't do it with strangers, wait until you've found someone you really care about, someone you love. Take precautions. Never get into dangerous situations. Don't do what you don't want to do no matter how hard someone presses you . . .'

The twins' eyes would glaze over at the third word but I kept on repeating it like a mantra. Perhaps I hoped it would seep into their unconscious and have a subliminal influence.

At seventeen both Kate and Claire went out with a couple of eighteen-year-olds who were friends. After six months, they asked if 'the lads' could stay the night and sleep with them at our house. I said yes, Tom said no.

Kate said, 'We have already, anyway.' And Tom who by then must have been well tucked into the Japanese acupuncturist declared that that way, whoredom lay.

'Claire's seeing a medical student. A wimp,' Kate reports now.

'Mind your own business,' Claire checks her. 'He's nice. OK. He's too nice, really. He keeps crawling around after me and sometimes it puts me right off. Kate's going out with a football player,' she retaliates.

'Does he take cocaine? He must take cocaine – all American sportsmen take cocaine,' I respond, genuinely anxious under the banter.

'God, Mum. What's wrong with you? Of course he doesn't take cocaine. He's so clean-living, he's even got me jogging.'

'And you're both happy and . . . safe?' I question euphemistically. Experience has taught me that the terms on which a mother can enter her daughters' private territory constantly shift. No assumptions can be made.

Claire ignores my queries. Then she takes pity. 'Of *course* we're looking after ourselves. God, Mum don't you ever stop worrying?'

We mess about in the pool and Kate decides we should have a race, swimming the crawl. I let them win. No matter what Charlotte's views are, that's *really* what mothers are for.

As we settle back in the sun, I reflect on how much more *assured* my daughters are, compared to how I was at twenty in the so-called Swinging Sixties.

Kate and Claire seem to know exactly what they are doing and why, and have a much higher expectation of personal happiness. I was looking for Mr Right from fourteen; they both say that their main aim is to avoid him, at least until they're in their thirties and Have Lived A Bit.

Funny really, I saw marriage as a beginning, they seem to view it as a home for those semi-retired from life.

'We talked to Dad on the phone last week,' Claire changes subjects. My scalp tingles.

'You did?' I try to sound unconcerned.

'He said to tell you he misses you and that he's got a surprise planned.'

At reception, when we go to collect our key, the young man behind the desk behaves like Father Christmas. He dazzles us with his smile. 'What a pleasure it is to have you here.' The girls and I exchange looks. Seventy-two hours after our arrival, the welcome seems a mite delayed.

'Follow me,' instructs the young man whose name-tag says Larry Fontaine. He bashes the bell on the desk to call for a replacement and trots off across the lobby with us in pursuit.

We pass our own family room and arrive at a building, mostly concealed behind palm trees, which we've nicknamed the gazebo, since that is what it resembles.

Larry holds up his hand, like John Wayne in charge of a posse.

'Are you ready?' he rubs his hands in anticipation.

We nod.

Larry ushers us through the trees and up the steps of the gazebo. It is a building built mainly of white wood and glass. The veranda runs around the entire edifice and is equipped like an outdoor sitting-room. Vast cane chairs and sofas decorated in pale blue, lime-green and lemon are stuffed with cushions.

A bar is decorated with a massive vase of white flowers. A parrot squawks in alarm. Larry slides back the glass door and we are in a second sitting-room with cream walls, cream rugs, deep pink and pale lavender sofas, wall-hangings, a massive table and chairs. It's like residing in an ice-cream sundae.

Larry escorts us through three bedrooms, each with its own bathroom and sunken bath and shows us – practically puce with delight – the underground pool, the gym and the Jacuzzi.

In the sitting-room, he points to the phone.

'You have special service here in the Leonardo da Vinci *residencia*,' he says, ignoring our efforts not to laugh. 'You pick up the phone and whatever you wish for is here in seconds . . . masseur, food, pedicure. You want to shop? We bring the shop to you.'

Kate rises to the occasion with aplomb. 'Excuse me, but do you have anywhere that plays music?'

Kate has made Larry a happy man. He frogmarches her to the

largest sofa, presses a button and what looks like the dashboard of Concorde appears in view.

Within minutes, we have a film screen descending, stereo system on full blast, the Picasso has slid gently sideways to reveal a library of videos and the parrot is screaming its head off outside.

'Landlubbers ahoy! Landlubbers ahoy!' it obediently squawks. Only when the parrot sees Larry's back departing into the gloom does its personal preference emerge. 'Cunt, cunt, cunt, cunt,' it shrieks, hopping furiously from one leg to the other.

Claire frees it from the stand which has a plaque which reads, *My name is Polly.* Polly falls instantly in love with Claire and flies to her side each time she sits down, peering anxiously into her face.

Kate finds the champagne in a bucket by a basket of roses and leeks in the main bedroom.

She comes back into the sitting-room, reading the accompanying note, *If you're happy, I'm happy. D.*

'God,' she says. 'Who'd have thought Dad had it in him? And I always thought he was a tight-fisted old sod. Well, you live and learn. Champagne, anyone?'

Later that evening as we watch television, Stephen Delgado appears on a chat show. Before he even opens his mouth, both my daughters are making loud vomiting noises.

On the day we are due to check out, Kate and Claire break the news to me. Tom is meeting us at the airport and we are all to fly to an unknown destination, arranged by Tom, for a long weekend. He had asked them not to tell me. It is now too late for me to back out.

I don't want to see Tom because it means that all the emotions he has triggered recently must now come out of temporary cold storage. As a practice-run, my stomach does a flip.

'I'll tell you what *is* odd,' Kate adds. 'I told Dad we'd had a great time and thank you very much for the suite and he said he hadn't a clue what I was talking about. So what do you make of that?'

'Perhaps it's that publisher of yours, what's her name?' Claire teases. 'Wait till we tell Dad that he's got a rival.'

Later, I make a couple of calls. First, I phone Mike in New York. Chas tells me he is working for him on an executive camping trip.

'He's going back to London next month,' Chas reports. 'He says something seems to be mellowing Angela. She let him talk to the kids last time he called and she's agreed to let him take them away for a few days. Mike reckons there's a catch but he's happy. Doing well on the job, too.'

Second, I call Mo to give her an edited version of Delgado. I tell her he is pursuing me because he's not used to rejection. It's the kind of language Mo understands. I tell her that he has spent so long contemplating his own navel, he has a dent mark in his forehead.

I don't tell her that on the basis of one encounter, he is the best lover life is ever likely to serve up to me. Even without this vital piece of information, Mo is impressed.

'I'm going to try being single,' she announces.

'But you are single, Mo,' I remind her.

'No,' she corrects me. 'I'm single and looking for love. You're single and *not* looking. When you're not looking, things happen.'

My third call is to Delgado. I thank him for rearranging our accommodation but I tell him that I insist on paying the bill.

'I can smell your skin, babe,' he says, which is no way to reply. 'You have such smooth skin.'

'I do?' The words pop out before I can stop myself. Then I get back on course. 'About the bill, I—'

'Look, I do ads for the hotel chain. In return, I get thirty days a year use of any of their accommodation. I'm not giving you something, I'm sharing . . . OK? End of subject. Now, when are you back in New York?'

I tell him that I won't be returning to New York.

'According to my daughters, I'm going to an unknown destination, then back to London via Miami. And I really don't want to let this thing go on. Whatever it is. Really I don't. I mean it.'

'Sure, sure,' he says. 'When are you back in London?'

'Next Thursday.'

'That's great. The day after me. I'll see you there. You won't regret this, baby.'

I put the phone down. *Jesus!* I have no doubt Delgado's claims to eternal love will fade within three months. In the meantime, if he reveals me to the world, Tom will laugh himself into the grave, the girls will be horrified and I will be the first woman to suffer a slow death from embarrassment.

Chapter Twenty-Five

The Hotel Henri on the edge of Port au Prince in Haiti is a monstrosity. Fifty suites each with a private pool plus a large main swimming-pool. Marble, wood, crystal, four-poster beds, staff in turquoise uniforms, banquets for breakfast, enough food wasted in garnishes alone to feed a platoon.

The hotel is a monstrosity partly because of the excess – four telephones to each room; two bathrooms to a suite, his and hers; four television sets; two double beds. But also because of the poverty which surrounds it.

I'd read about Haiti but no description matches the reality. The filth, the limbless beggars, the small, sad retinue of lepers who hang around the hotel entrance, hoping for small change flung from car windows.

As we drive through Port au Prince in the late evening, it's as if one muddied street is literally rising and falling in waves. As we draw closer, the reason becomes clearer. The 'waves' are men, women and children huddled together in doorways and gutters, dressed in rags the colour of clay, trying to find shelter for a night's sleep.

'It's quite something, isn't it?' Tom says as the twins, he and I sit around our private pool, having a drink before unpacking.

'Couple of Americans I met recommended it. 'Course, they said it's not too clever to go outside the hotel environment but I think we've got enough to keep us busy here for a few days, hey girls?' Tom says, desperately trying to insure his 'surprise' destination against mass family disapproval.

'I've just done a project on tourism and the Third World,' Kate says flatly. 'You should read it, Dad.'

In our room, as we dress for dinner, Tom and I settle the terms of engagement. This is the first opportunity we've had to speak in private since meeting at Miami airport.

'Look, Kay,' Tom begins. He's got an air about him I haven't seen before; almost desperate, perhaps even scared, as if he's cornered but not by me.

I interrupt. As soon as I saw Tom, I knew something in me had changed. I still had that surge of emotion but for the first time, the traditional mix of affection and familiarity and pleasure is almost obliterated. By what? Contempt? Dislike? Or even, much more damaging, boredom?

I still don't want anyone else to have him but, on the other hand, perhaps this is a small price to pay for not being forced to live with his deceit myself.

'I don't want to sleep with you,' I tell Tom with no small sense of satisfaction. 'And I don't want to discuss anything to do with us or anybody else when we're alone together.

'Let's have a pleasant three days, you can go off to your conference, I'll go back to London and we'll sort something out later when the girls are safely back in college.'

'Kay, I've got to tell you something. I'm trying to get on a different footing, I've got—'

'No, Tom.'

Later, after dinner, as I watch the girls and their father play cards, I reflect on how easy it's been to say No. So why hadn't I done it more often before? Why hadn't I ever taken the initiative and laid out my own terms, instead of falling in with Tom's?

Why?

Perhaps because, deep down, I've always been scared of losing him – and now I honestly don't know if I care.

Early the next morning I slip out of our room and make my way to the main swimming-pool. I'm on my fifth length when I notice a figure, wrapped in a towelling robe, walking through the garden and eventually making itself comfortable on a *chaise longue* at the end of the pool. It's a woman in a large floppy hat. Then I hear her dive in and she surfaces next to me. It is Jenna Oakford.

'I knew it was you,' she says laughing. 'I'd recognize your back anywhere.'

Instinctively, I look around to see if anyone has overheard.

'You're embarrassed,' she says intuitively, laughing again. 'Don't be. I'm not about to throw myself at your husband's feet and demand your hand. Or any other part of your anatomy for that matter . . . Come on, I'll swim with you.'

Over coffee, we laugh even further about the more ridiculous aspects of the party at which we met in London, and sidestep our physical encounter.

Jenna explains that Joe has gone to the other side of the island for a couple of days to record some drummers he's been told about. He's back tomorrow and then they leave to record at home.

'So you're on your own?' I ask.

Jenna nods. 'I don't mind,' she says. 'Well, not much.'

'Spend the day with us,' I offer impulsively. I could kick myself. But it's too late now to withdraw the invitation.

'You can meet Kate and Claire. I'm sure they'll be much more appreciative of what you do than I've managed to be . . . and Tom will be enchanted.'

Kate and Claire *are* impressed. They listen to tapes in Jenna's room and she gives them several CDs. We swim and play water polo, of sorts, and eat and Tom delivers his entire doctor's bag of anecdotes – ones that I hadn't heard in years.

'Does she know?' he says at one point, when Jenna and the girls have gone off to find drinks.

'Does she know what?' I ask evasively.

'Does she know about, you know, Christ, you women tell each other everything in the first five minutes. That's why I find it so bloody unnerving being in the company of some of your friends. I don't mind them knowing,' he adds petulantly. 'I do mind them only knowing your side.'

Poor Tom, he doesn't mind being a shit in private but he does hate it so when it becomes public.

Later, it is just the three of us at dinner. Kate and Claire have made friends with a couple of American girls and have decided to eat in the hotel's pizzeria.

Tom dazzles and flirts and very gradually begins to realize that he is superfluous. We want to be engaged not entertained. And Jenna is only interested in me.

We share a sense of humour. While Tom likes to deliver jokes, Jenna and I swap mutual experiences. Most sentences aren't even completed before we are literally doubled up with amusement.

'I can't see what's so funny,' Tom says more than once.

When we go out on to the terrace for coffee, it feels very natural for me to slip my arm through Jenna's. I know she is going to be a friend and I like that. It's almost as intoxicating as our first and probably only sexual encounter. I also feel, rightly or wrongly, that for now, I am more powerful than Tom.

He trails behind morosely, deprived of his audience.

'I don't know what it is,' he says, staring into his brandy-glass. 'But there's something weird about you two.'

He feels excluded and cruelly, I'm glad.

Two days later, at Miami airport, we go our separate ways: the twins to college, Tom to a conference in St Louis, me to a phone box.

I ring Mo. She tells me she has dumped the anthropologist.

'You know me. Give me a challenge and it turns into an obsession. I was round there day and night trying to, well, help him. It wasn't doing me any good. I've got to look after myself, so I told him for the sake of both our healths, we should call it quits.'

'How did he take it?'

'He was disgustingly cheerful. He said he'd been meaning to tell me anyway that he was due to go off to the Galapagos Islands but I'd been so determined, he hadn't wanted to put me off my stroke. Metaphorically speaking, of course.'

I give her a résumé of the weekend in Haiti but I leave out Jenna.

'Did Tom say anything to you when he saw you?' Mo interrupts.

'About what?'

'Oh, it doesn't matter. I see your boyfriend is on television tonight. By the time you arrive home, your name may be known to millions. The whole workshop's tuning in.'

'Oh, Mo,' I say, genuinely upset. 'You didn't tell them, did you?'

'Course I did. They're all coming over to my place to watch, except Anna of course. Local girl makes good. We're going to wear T-shirts saying, "O-Kay!" I thought "It's Never Too Late" was more appropriate but the others said that it lacked taste. Can't see why, can you?'

The next morning, at six-thirty a.m., Mo is at Heathrow to meet me – a gesture above and beyond the call of duty. She has come, it turns out, motivated partly by self-interest. She wants to be the first to deliver the news.

After we've exchanged kisses and hellos, she hands over a couple of the tabloid newspapers. Inside one, on its showbiz page, Delgado is photographed looking smug. *Dimple Boy is Forty-fied*, reads one headline.

In the second, the story is relegated to the women's page. *'Never mind the dust on the bottle', says spring chick pin-up Stephen Delgado of his mysterious granny lover. 'Taste the quality of the wine.'*

'You've gone bright, bright red,' Mo points out unnecessarily.

'I need to sit down,' I answer.

We make our way to a coffee-bar, order tea and find a couple of seats.

'It's terrifically funny,' Mo pronounces, a shade insensitively. 'You should have heard him on the box last night, he all but mentioned you by name. Liz was pleased as punch. She said she'd never known anyone famous before. And she wants you to bring him to the workshop's farewell party. She promises not to ask anything . . . *bodily*.

'Did I tell you?' Mo adds, 'Phil is back. He said living above the dry-cleaners' was hell. He couldn't stand the fumes. Liz reckons he was driven out by the woman's insatiability. She said he looked as if he'd been' – Mo drops her voice to a theatrical whisper – 'shagged to death. And Liz reckons that's why he's shut up moaning about the lack of sex, at long last.'

'That's nice,' I say absent-mindedly. Mo presses on.

'On the show, Delgado said you were forty-four, you had twin daughters, you make jewellery, you write, you are waiting for a divorce and you sail. Do you sail? I never knew. Come to that, I never knew you were thinking of a divorce either. Does Tom know?'

'What did you think of him?' I ask cautiously, as we walk to the car park.

'I think he's a shit and he should be elbowed at the first opportunity,' she says.

'Not Tom, Delgado.'

'Well, he's a berk of the first order, too,' Mo says bluntly. 'But you knew that anyway. And he's got the most hideous taste in clothes. You should have seen the black silk shirt he had on and the pink jacket. Barry Manilow or what?

'But, my God, he's got a fabulous smile . . . what about the rest of him?' Mo asks slyly. 'Dionne said he looked like the circumcised type. Clean-cut.

'Oh, I almost forgot to tell you. He also said you are the sexiest woman he has ever met. And he would recommend women over forty to any younger man. So what did you do?'

'Do you promise not to tell?' I say conspiratorially, dumping my bags in the boot of Mo's car. 'It's a tip given to me by a Chinese soothsayer I met in Miami.

'I was going to share her wisdom with the workshop when I got the chance,' I continue straight-faced. Mo is entranced.

'Yes, go on,' she urges. 'What did she say?'

'She said, "Men always fall for frigid women because they put on the best show".'

'Kay, how could you? You mean you didn't come at all? You faked it? Wait till I tell Anna!'

'No, I'm kidding,' I confess, smiling. 'All I did was tell Delgado to be normal and that seemed to bring him so much relief, I didn't have to do very much else.'

Mo starts to laugh. 'I'm sorry, Kay,' she apologizes. 'One minute you're stuck in a suburban nightmare, the next minute you're a grey-haired Barbie who's found her Hollywood Ken.'

'I have not found my Ken,' I say tartly. 'I am not totally grey-haired and I don't look remotely like any kind of Barbie. I'm me. The same old me.'

'This wouldn't have happened to the old Kay in a million years,' Mo says, unlocking her car door. 'I'd've thought that was obvious – even to you, my love.'

Mo drops me off outside the house and waves goodbye. If she stays, she says, she'll be late for work. As I turn the key, the door is opened from the inside. That's strange since Tom isn't due back for another two days.

Letty bounds out followed by Angela. A contrite Angela. And she is followed by Martin wearing his 'We-can-get-through-this-trauma-together' look.

'Please, Angela,' I begin, thinking I'm about to receive the gospel according to (absent) Michael yet again.

'I'm sorry. I'm genuinely, frightfully sorry,' Angela gushes. 'I didn't mean it to happen. Martin is here to vouchsafe that I never intended it to happen. But I couldn't have you coming back to an empty house, *knowing*.'

What on earth is the woman talking about? Martin and Angela exchange glances. It must be dawning on them that I haven't a clue.

'Didn't he tell you?' Angela says, as I make an attempt to squeeze past her into my own hall.

'Didn't who tell me what?' I say as patiently as I can, as I head for the kitchen. When I walk into the room, it's like a Knightsbridge florist: bouquets and baskets everywhere.

'They've been arriving since early this morning,' Angela says from the hall. 'I haven't been able to go into the kitchen because of them, it's very annoying. Hay fever, you know.

'Martin?' She calls him and indicates with her hand.

Martin comes into the kitchen, picks up the kettle and gives me a kiss on the cheek and a jumbo hug.

'You'll be fine,' he whispers in my ear. 'Remember, Kay, you're a strong woman. No one can take that away from you.'

The thud of several pairs of feet are heard and what seems like a squat-team of children rush into the kitchen. Angela's offspring in nightclothes. Henry comes up to me and asks, 'Have you seen my dad?'

'Yes I have,' I say, crouching down. 'He misses you a lot. He's coming to see you in a couple of weeks and it's all going to be sorted out. OK?'

'OK,' says Henry solemnly and returns to a fight over the breakfast cereal, poorly refereed by Martin.

'We stayed the night,' Angela says from the door. 'I've been frightened on my own. And Mo couldn't look after Letty, I thought it—'

I put up my hand to stop her string of excuses. 'That's fine, Angela. I'm very grateful.'

'Oh, God,' she begins to wail as the children, indifferent to her histrionics, file past her back upstairs, bowls of cereal in their hands.

'I couldn't bear it if you were kind to me. Please don't be kind. Be angry. Be, be, be . . .'

Perhaps it's jet lag; perhaps it's the heady perfume of the flowers: perhaps it's Angela's face peering from the kitchen door and Martin clucking like a mother hen, but I begin to laugh and, for the life of me, I can't stop.

'She's hysterical,' I hear Angela say. 'Of course, she's hysterical.

She can't be laughing. Not properly. She can't possibly think this is funny,' she asks Martin anxiously.

'Can she?'

In the sitting-room, Martin pours the tea. Angela reveals her news. She has slept with Tom.

'Neither of us wanted it. It just happened. He's been very kind. I was here. He was vulnerable, he said he felt unloved. I felt discarded too. We were two lonely people. I'm sorry.'

'Tom said he felt unloved? Tom said he felt *lonely*?' I ask, trying hard not to smile.

'Yes, poor man. He said you had gone, abandoned him . . . We only did it once.' Angela looks at the floor, swallows hard and looks at me again.

'Well actually, three times. Not consecutively of course. Certainly not. That would make it an affair. And it hasn't been that. It was more sporadic bouts of mutual relief.'

This time, I can't stop the smile.

'Not that kind of relief,' Angela says crossly, her old self briefly resurfacing. '*Emotional* relief. It was more a . . . more a spiritual bonding.'

'Of course, what else,' I say pleasantly. 'A communion with condoms.'

Martin looks at the ceiling.

Angela confesses on, more *mea* than *culpa*. 'I couldn't carry on a subterfuge. I felt you had to know. One feels so much better when one gets something off one's chest, doesn't one?

'Mind you, Tom did say he'd make a clean breast of it when he saw you. So I thought you'd be more . . . prepared.'

'Look, I tried to tell you the night you came here about Mike that I understood how you felt, but you didn't want to listen,' I gently remonstrate. 'You felt discarded by him, you felt like you had no value. It's not surprising you turned to someone else. Although,' I added drily, 'I am slightly surprised it happened to be Tom. What about Brenda?'

'Who's Brenda?' Angela replies, thrown off course.

'Did Tom say he'd make a clean breast to Brenda – and to Pam too?'

I look at Angela, who is now totally confused. The bandage which has wrapped itself around my eyes for over twenty years, handicapping me from ever seeing Tom as he really is, appears to wrap itself around not just Angela's eyes, but her ears and mouth – even as I watch.

'Tom is a very honourable man,' Angela says. 'I've got to know him much better over the last week or so. He's sensitive, he needs someone to direct him, to channel his energies. I'm sure he would have mentioned . . . Brenda, did you say? And Pam, if these were important people in his life . . . don't you?'

Angela suddenly seems to realize that in talking to me, she is also talking to Tom's wife.

'I mean, you'd know that better than me, of course,' she adds hastily.

I wait for the roar. I wait for that all-too-familiar surge of pain and noise. And nothing happens. Instead, there is sweet silence.

'Can you hear anything, Angela?' I ask.

'Like what?'

'Like, well, like . . . a noise?' She shakes her head, baffled. I excuse myself from the room and go back into the kitchen.

'She's upset,' I hear Angela tell Martin, her voice not without some satisfaction.

On the contrary, I have a small task to perform.

I call a dispatch rider, pick the largest bunch of roses from

Delgado's wholesale delivery and write a note which I attach to the flowers.

Dear Brenda,

We have never met but I feel as if I know you. I have an awful lot to thank you for. My very best wishes for the future. These flowers are by way of a goodbye, and to wish you luck.

I have an urge to add *You'll need it*. But I decide that's for her to find out and for me not to worry myself about. I sign my name and sit back.

I am definitely making progress.

I return to the sitting-room and beam at Martin and Angela.

'She's mad,' Angela says to Martin. 'She's unhinged. Oh, God, I've done this to her.'

'Sit down, love,' Martin says to me. 'I brought a couple of Charlotte's Valiums over, just in case.'

'Charlotte takes Valium?' I ask, intrigued.

Martin appears uncomfortable. 'It's a recent thing. She's found the kids a bit, well, a bit overwhelming . . . she's been home more and I think she finds it quite hard work. And MUM is well . . . Frankly, it's all got a bit out of control.

'A whole gang of single-parent fathers have joined up; then the gay foster-parents arrived and a couple of transvestites, too. I told her I was very pleased to see that the maternal instinct was alive and well among my brothers. I told her she ought to change the name to DUM, but you know Charlotte, she didn't think it was funny at all.

'Well, to be frank, I didn't mean it to be funny,' Martin says, anxiety creasing his face like a pleated fan. 'Oh, Jesus,' Martin turns to Angela. 'She's off again.'

I laugh until my stomach aches.

On the editorial floor of Venus Inc., Rosemary is dressed like Katharine Hepburn in *The African Queen*: khaki slacks, shirt, desert boots, sunglasses on the back of her head.

'What do you mean, we can't use your feature?' she says, as we walk towards the art department where the design of the next issue of *Venus* is underway. 'Who says we can't?'

'I say,' I reply firmly.

She stops dead. '*You* say?'

'Yes, I say. I've got a cheque here which should cover the cost of the New York trip, so you won't be out of pocket. Let's go back to the good old days when we were just a couple of passing bathing-suits in a swimming-pool.'

'We can't,' she says abruptly. 'We've planned promos – radio, posters – Delgado is big. This is no toy-boy story. This is the "There's-Life-in-the-Baby-Boomers-Yet" angle.

'This is "The-Sixties-Generation-Are-Alive-And-Kicking." This is what the advertisers love. This is what forty-plus women want to hear.

'We don't care what he feels, we want to know about you. A forty-four-year-old *ordinary* woman – forgive me for being honest, Kay – pulls a good one. Mature years rule.

'Don't you know this is a story of our times? Everyone's been asking what happened to the women of the sixties. The mini-skirts and kohl eyes; the pioneers of the pill and the sexual revolution. Everyone assumed that like your mothers before you, you retreated into furry slippers, soap operas and sex at birthdays and Christmas. But no!

'Libido lives! I'm a decade younger than you and I've never even noticed that your generation has been quietly cooking away – sexually speaking, I mean. And what have you got? A heady brew of experience, aspiration, lack of inhibition and a belief in the right to sexual enjoyment.'

Rosemary pauses mid-tirade. 'As a matter of interest, what have you got? What makes him want *you*? No offence intended, of course.'

I smile. 'A heady brew of experience, aspiration, lack of . . .' I suggest.

'All right, all right,' Rosemary interrupts. 'Anyway this is *the* fairy tale of the year, the decade, the fucking millennium . . . It's good news for older women everywhere. Grey pussy power!

'Kay Woods, once this issue is on the streets, you will be the patron saint of the post-menopausal.'

Rosemary stops and with a flourish gestures to the layout of the magazine. On one side of a double-page spread, branded with the words *World Exclusive*, is a portrait of Delgado looking sultry and a long interview, headed *What He Sees in Her*.

On the other side, it reads, *What She Sees in Him*. The page is blank as is the area left for a photograph, which Rosemary presumably intends to be of me. On the third page, headlined: *And This is How They First Met*, is my original profile. The introduction has been changed, as has almost every other word . . .

I'd written as an opening paragraph, corny, I admit:

Give nature a hand to make more of yourself than she ever
intended. But beware! That experience – for woman or man
– can bring out the beast in any beauty. Meet Stephen
Delgado, millionaire model, the so-called Dimpled Don
Juan. Perfectly formed and, occasionally, perfectly awful.

Rosemary has altered it to:

As soon as I set eyes on him, my pulse quickened and I knew
. . . his golden hair, his laughing eyes, his muscular torso, his
youthful grin . . . my forty-four-year-old heart leapt and it
hasn't landed yet.

Years of trying to comb out the clichés from my copy sent gurgling down the lavatory pan in one go: professional death in a thousand words.

Half an hour later, I am in Rosemary's office. 'I don't see the problem, sweetheart,' she says. 'Let the world know. Who gives a damn? Shack up with him for however long it takes for either one of you to lose interest, then move on. You'll be a better woman for it.'

'I thought you weren't in favour of emotional involvements?' I say coldly.

'This isn't an emotional involvement though, is it?' Rosemary replies brightly, twisting a cigarette into her holder. 'It's a social experiment. Ten-year gap, two totally different worlds. I mean, you don't look even remotely right together . . . it's got everything going against it.' She sucks in air through her teeth in appreciation.

It's time Rosemary learnt that treating everybody else's life as a human laboratory exacts its price.

'This is the deal,' I say, quite pleased at how positive I sound. 'If you go ahead and print that crap with my name or face anywhere near it, I will be forced to reveal the identity of the man who broke *your* heart to each and every tabloid newspaper.

'What's more, I will also reveal how he conned you and several dozen other women and how you set me up, too.'

Thoroughly enjoying the role, I wave my arms in the air, constructing a front page before Rosemary's eyes.

'Can't you see the headlines? *Cold-Hearted Queen of High Tech Sex conned by the Man with the Golden Tongue.*

'Do it,' Rosemary says. 'See if I care.'

This is an unexpected blow but who said blackmail is easy? I rise and walk to the door. I feel disembodied. I open the door and walk down the corridor towards the lift. In every film I've ever seen, this is where a voice shouts, 'Wait', and orchestral music rises to a crescendo.

Instead, Rosemary bellows, 'Go!' and the muzak from the lift plays a mutant version of Elvis Presley's 'Wooden Heart'.

At the first floor, the lift stops. Nothing happens for five minutes or so, then it judders and begins to ascend again. At the third floor, the doors open. Peter, the secretary, stands at the ready. He has a brown envelope in his hands.

'Rosemary said you'd forgotten this.'

'Yes, of course,' I say casually. 'Thank you.'

As soon as the lift doors close, I open the envelope. Inside are the three offending pages, each with a red line through it. *Yes!* As the twins would say.

Also enclosed is a handwritten note from Rosemary.

Dear Kay,

    We will run the Delgado piece as you originally wrote it
and with a nom de plume for your byline. It's a good piece. I
hope we can continue to do business. You've turned out not
at all how I expected – but perhaps that's done me some
good.
        Rosemary

At three in the afternoon the pool is empty except for a small group of schoolchildren. I swim long and hard and by the time I've showered and dressed, for the first time in months, perhaps even years, I know exactly what I want.

I have a nap in an effort to sleep off some of the jet lag and arrive fifteen minutes late at Bonne Bouche. Mo and I are taking Olivia out to dinner to celebrate her decision to marry Doug. Well, to be more precise, to celebrate her decision to marry *anyone*.

Both Mo and I had agreed on the journey back from the airport that Olivia was taking a gamble.

'It's odd really because once upon a time, marriage was looked on as security. Now, it's a risk,' Mo had remarked.

'A high risk with, occasionally, very low returns,' I'd responded.

'Don't get bitter,' Mo had replied, only half in jest. 'It does terrible things to the skin.'

'I'm not bitter,' I'd corrected. 'I just feel that once you're realistic about the odds, you don't feel such a flop when it fails to work out.'

Now, at nine p.m., Mo lets me in through the shop entrance. Olivia wants me to inspect the new Kitchen Sync display.

'Are you all right?' Mo asks, a half-empty champagne glass in her hand.

'Couldn't be better. Why?'

'What about all that stuff with Angela and that—'

'Did you know? Why on earth didn't you tell me?'

'I didn't know for sure. I sort of guessed,' she says, locking the door behind me. 'Angela just seems to have been there a lot of the time over the last couple of weeks.

'In the past, I would have given her and Tom the benefit of the doubt. I would have assumed Angela was having trouble with her ovaries and wanted advice on the cheap. Or they were both involved in something to do with Mike.

'But what with Brenda, now I even tend to look suspiciously on the postwoman calling at your house when he's there alone.'

Mo shrugs, suddenly embarrassed by her obvious show of concern. Spontaneously, I give her a hug and a kiss on the cheek.

'Do you know what you are, Mo Harper?' I say. 'You're an absolute gem.'

Then I feel a bit ridiculous, too.

Fortuitously, I am distracted by the horrific sight of a mass display of Kitchen Sync. Olivia has constructed a giant mousetrap, about five foot long. A fake piece of cheese the size of two boxes of wine, wrapped in hideous yellow velvet, doubles as the display unit for various bits of my jewellery.

A baroque-looking poster reads, *'Jewellery by K. L. Woods, bait to trap the toughest rat'*.

'Olivia's new man has done wonders for her sense of humour,' Mo says drily, as we move through the shop and up the stairs to Olivia's office.

'I always used to find her a bit too pontificating before, didn't you? I mean not every bloody thing in life leaves a lesson to be learned, surely to God? And if she told me another bloody truism about Ed, I think I would have vomited on the spot.

'Aah, Olivia, we were just saying nice things about you and Doug, weren't we, Kay?' Mo adds without missing a beat as Olivia, as radiant as I expected, comes out on to the landing to greet me.

'Kay,' Olivia says, 'You look *fabulous*. What did I tell you? Take the first step and everything else just follows . . .'

Behind Olivia's back, I watch as Mo raises her eyebrows as if to say, 'I told you so'. And we both smile.

At ten the next morning, I finally ring Delgado. I am nervous. I'm not sure why since I know precisely what I'm going to say.

His voice signals delight. He tells me not to come to the hotel because he is besieged by reporters and photographers.

'It's a flat news period,' he says, perceptively by his standards, 'so I'm the best they've got.'

Instead, he gives me the address of a service flat which his manager rents in Kensington. He has arranged for the porter to let me in and will meet me as soon as he can slip away.

'I've got a television spot in Plymouth tonight but I can fly down, so we've got most of the day, babe,' he says.

'We need to talk . . . I'm not sure—' I am determined this time he will get the message. That's why I've decided to deliver it in the flesh.

'See you soon, babe,' he whispers.

Annoyingly, I find the thought quite appetizing.

A consensus of opinion exists. Mo, Rosemary, Olivia, even Liz who, this morning, took the trouble to phone, advocate that I should let my 'relationship' with Delgado run its course, particularly as I appear to have the upper hand.

'You can insist that Delgado keeps it out of the newspapers and it'll strengthen your resolve when it comes to deciding about Tom,' Mo had pronounced, making it sound like an exercise in health improvement.

At eleven a.m., I am outside an unprepossessing Edwardian mansion. The porter lets me in and far from the drab anonymity that many of these short-let flats have, it is surprisingly cosy and lived-in with plenty of knick-knacks, flowers, books, newspapers and magazines. The fridge is full not least with several bottles of booze.

I make myself coffee, sit on the sofa and try to read a newspaper. The words dance annoyingly in front of my eyes. I go and check in the bathroom mirror that I don't have lipstick on my teeth. I redo my hair. I go to the loo three times.

I'm wearing the trouser suit in which I first met Delgado. All of this seems strange behaviour for a woman who is about to tell her would-be paramour that it's all off. Even I can recognize that.

Too bloody scared of the consequences? I look at myself again in the mirror. I am slightly slimmer. I have broken into colour. I have stopped wearing my own jewellery. I feel almost confident. *For now. Touch wood.*

I hear a key in the lock. I walk back into the sitting-room as Delgado rushes into the room, hair flowing, jacket half-off, flowers in hand and happy.

I steel myself. He takes my hand and kisses it. 'Welcome back,' he says. Then he picks me up in his arms and carries me into the bedroom.

'I've got to say—' I begin, then I decide that there are occasions when words are superfluous. This is one of them.

We spend all day in bed. We make love, we eat, we sleep, we talk, we drink champagne, we make love and Delgado continues to maintain a high standard of delivery. So high, I am responsive and grateful and try hard to pleasure him as much as he delights me.

His timing now is intuitive. He brings me almost to climax and holds back again and again, so by the time we do come, there isn't a part of my body which isn't engulfed and lifted. And this time when I hear a roar it begins with a ripple and ends in a sense of total relaxation which I've never experienced before.

At four p.m., when Delgado is due to leave, I break the news.

'Stephen,' I reach for his hand. 'I like you. I really do. You've given me the best time ever. But I don't think we should see one another again, not on a regular basis.

'Perhaps we can become friends. But apart from that, this is all too complicated for me and it's certainly not good for you, however short-lived.'

He stares at me. He's heard it all before, but this time, he believes me. His voice cracks a little when he speaks.

'Shouldn't I decide what's good for me?' he asks tersely.

'Yes, of course, I'm sorry.'

I fall back easily into the habit of apologizing.

I try again. 'Look, I need to find out what it's like to be on my own. I don't want to use you as a crutch. If we stayed together, this would only get stuck at—' I'm about to say *a sexual level*, which is honest but hurtful, so I amend the truth.

'I'm frightened that I would want to keep this at a certain . . . level and that's unfair. Every relationship should have a chance to develop freely, don't you think?'

Delgado is silent. I'd expected tantrums. Rage. Even a tirade along the lines that I was always too bloody long in the tooth but he'd been too decent to say so. I'd certainly expected retaliation for inflicting injury to his ego.

Instead, he leads me to the sofa and sits me down. He strokes my cheek gently. Eventually, he speaks.

'I don't know what you're about, Kay,' he says. 'But you're special. I care for you,' he adds with dignity. 'Because I care for you, I'm going to respect what you say and leave you alone. If you change your mind,' he gives a small smile, 'I'm there.' Then his spirit begins to rise again. 'Unless, of course, somebody else has come along of a certain age who also has a taste for slow-motion sex.'

He kisses me lightly on the cheek and I almost change my mind. But he deserves much better than to be used.

'*Ciao!*' he says at the door, winks and blows me a kiss. Thank God he does. It's a fruitful reminder of how embarrassing he can be when he's horizontal.

Late in the afternoon when my husband is supposed to be in his office, I see him through our sitting-room window, pinned into a corner of the sofa. A woman has his right arm caught in a vicelike grip.

Poor lamb.

It appears Tom has returned from his conference to be greeted by Angela on the doorstep.

Angela does not have affairs. Angela is the kind of woman Tom is so fond of describing, unable or unwilling to disentangle sex from emotion. When she went to bed with my husband, she decided It Meant Something. And since Angela is used to being in charge, up with that Tom will have to put.

I was right in Haiti when I detected panic in Tom's eyes. Bye-bye Brenda, a pause on all the Pams. Angela will brook no rivals, stand no nonsense.

As I let myself in and walk through the hall to the kitchen, Tom's squeak of despair comes out of the sitting-room. 'Kay! Kay! Come in here. Kay, thank God you're home.'

In the kitchen, I make a fuss of Letty and check to see if there are any messages on the answering-machine. Dionne's voice reminds me to come to the workshop's farewell party tomorrow night. I must remember to take the dolphins.

'We've got great expectations of you,' she chuckles, innuendo in every vowel.

'Hello, Kay?' says a man's voice on the second message. 'It's Frank. I'm in London on Friday and I wondered if you fancied a drink?' He leaves his number.

A third message is from Mike in New York. He's coming back to London next week and can he stay while he flat-hunts? I phone him back, pleased to hear that he sounds buoyant.

After a few minutes' general chat, I break the news. 'You're welcome to stay here for as long as you like, Mike,' I say. 'But you might be surprised at the company you'll keep.'

'What do you mean?' he asks.

'Well, I don't know how you'll feel about this, but I think

Angela and Tom are together. Well, to be more accurate, I think Angela is with Tom and Tom's power of choice has been temporarily paralysed.'

'Oh, Kay, what can I say? Are you OK? I'm so sorry.'

'Well, don't be,' I instruct firmly. 'It's good news for you. Angela will want you to have the children more because she'll be so busy sorting Tom's life out. And to be honest, I think it's probably very good news for me . . .'

I retrieve the incriminating 'Brenda' tape from the answering-machine which I've hidden at the back of the cutlery drawer and drop it in the bin.

In the fridge is a bottle of white wine. I open it and place it with three glasses on a tray. It's just possible that if Angela hadn't made her move, I might have given Tom and me one more chance. *Too bloody frightened of the consequences.* And then I would have been lost for ever, sucked down into a marriage that had ceased to do either of us any good.

'Kay! Kay!' the cries of Tom from the sitting-room are growing fainter. He is no longer my responsibility.

I look around the kitchen and, naturally, the tears flow. Big, hot, unstoppable tears. It will take time for the pain to ease. I intend to leave Tom, perhaps even leave the house and claim custody of Letty. Logic tells me I must since I know now what's possible.

I would like to become a person whose life inside the ring of domesticity mirrors what she aims for outside of it; a degree of confidence, a sense of decency, an urge to learn, a taste for fun. *On my own.*

The words have an ominous ring. *On my own.* I pour some wine and raise my glass.

'To risk!' I say out loud, repeating the toast we gave uncertainly at the workshop. This time, I mean it.